E-Learning Groups and Communities

SRHE and Open University Press Imprint

Current titles include:

Catherine Bargh *et al*.: *University Leadership*
Ronald Barnett: *Beyond all Reason*
Ronald Barnett: *Higher Education*
Ronald Barnett: *Realizing the University in an Age of Supercomplexity*
Ronald Barnett and Kelly Coate: *Engaging the Curriculum in Higher Education*
Tony Becher and Paul R. Trowler: *Academic Tribes and Territories (2nd edn)*
John Biggs: *Teaching for Quality Learning at University (2nd edn)*
Richard Blackwell and Paul Blackmore (eds): *Towards Strategic Staff Development in Higher Education*
David Boud *et al*. (eds): *Using Experience for Learning*
David Boud and Nicky Solomon (eds): *Work-based Learning*
Tom Bourner *et al*. (eds): *New Directions in Professional Higher Education*
Anne Brockbank and Ian McGill: *Facilitating Reflective Learning in Higher Education*
Stephen D. Brookfield and Stephen Preskill: *Discussion as a Way of Teaching*
Ann Brooks and Alison Mackinnon (eds): *Gender and the Restructured University*
Sally Brown and Angela Glasner (eds): *Assessment Matters in Higher Education*
Burton R.Clark: *Sustaining Change in Universities*
James Cornford and Neil Pollock: *Putting the University Online*
Vaneeta D'Andrea and David Gosling: *Improving Teaching and Learning in Higher Education*
Sara Delamont, Paul Atkinson and Odette Parry: *Supervising the Doctorate 2/e*
Sara Delamont and Paul Atkinson: *Successful Research Careers*
Gerard Delanty: *Challenging Knowledge*
Chris Duke: *Managing the Learning University*
Heather Eggins (ed): *Globalization and Reform in Higher Education*
Heather Eggins & Ranald Macdonald (eds): *The Scholarship of Academic Development*
Gillian Evans: *Academics and the Real World*
Merle Jacob and Tomas Hellström (eds): *The Future of Knowledge Production in the Academy*
Peter Knight: *Being a Teacher in Higher Education*
Peter Knight and Paul Trowler: *Departmental Leadership in Higher Education*
Peter Knight and Mantz Yorke: *Assessment, Learning and Employability*
Ray Land: *Educational Development*
John Lea *et al*. *Working in Post-Compulsory Education*
Mary Lea and Barry Stierer (eds): *Student Writing in Higher Education*
Dina Lewis and Barbara Allan: *Virtual Learning Communities*
Ian McNay (ed.): *Beyond Mass Higher Education*
Elaine Martin: *Changing Academic Work*
Louise Morley: *Quality and Power in Higher Education*
Lynne Pearce: *How to Examine a Thesis*
Moira Peelo and Terry Wareham (eds): *Failing Students in Higher Education*
Craig Prichard: *Making Managers in Universities and Colleges*
Stephen Rowland: *The Enquiring University Teacher*
Maggi Savin-Baden: *Problem-based Learning in Higher Education*
Maggi Savin-Baden: *Facilitating Problem-based Learning*
Maggi Savin-Baden and Kay Wilkie: *Challenging Research in Problem-based Learning*
David Scott *et al*.: *Professional Doctorates*
Peter Scott: *The Meanings of Mass Higher Education*
Michael L Shattock: *Managing Successful Universities*
Maria Slowey and David Watson: *Higher Education and the Lifecourse*
Colin Symes and John McIntyre (eds): *Working Knowledge*
Richard Taylor, Jean Barr and Tom Steele: *For a Radical Higher Education*
Malcolm Tight: *Researching Higher Education*
Penny Tinkler and Carolyn Jackson: *The Doctoral Examination Process*
Susan Toohey: *Designing Courses for Higher Education*
Melanie Walker (ed.): *Reconstructing Professionalism in University Teaching*
Melanie Walker and Jon Nixon (eds): *Reclaiming Universities from a Runaway World*
Diana Woodward and Karen Ross: *Managing Equal Opportunities in Higher Education*
Mantz Yorke and Bernard Longden: *Retention and Student Success in Higher Education*

E-Learning Groups and Communities

David McConnell

The Society for Research into Higher Education
& Open University Press

Open University Press
McGraw-Hill Education
McGraw-Hill House
Shoppenhangers Road
Maidenhead
Berkshire
England
SL6 2QL

email: enquiries@openup.co.uk
world wide web: www.openup.co.uk

and Two Penn Plaza, New York, NY 10121-2289, USA

First published 2006

A catalogue record of this book is available from the British Library

ISBN-10: 0 335 21280 8 (pb) 0 335 21281 6 (hb)
ISBN-13: 978 0335 21280 4 (pb) 978 0335 21281 1 (hb)

Library of Congress Cataloging-in-Publication Data
CIP data applied for

Typeset by BookEns Ltd, Royston, Herts.
Printed in Poland EU by OZGraf S.A. www.polskabook.pl

Contents

Acknowledgements

I owe a great deal to many people who have, in one way or another, helped me write this book.

My colleagues and co-tutors on the University of Sheffield Masters in E-Learning have contributed through many hours of debate and discussion. My thanks go to Shelagh Avery, Sheena Banks, Nicholas Bowskill, Celia Graebner, Vic Lally, Bob Toynton and Chris Winter. The many students on the course have also contributed to this book by their willingness to discuss their experiences of e-learning. In particular I would like to thank Marielle Patronis, Anthi Iliopoulou and Russell Booth.

Martin Middleton has, as usual, provided constant support and interest in what I do and write.

I wish to acknowledge the support of the Open University in preparing parts of this book.

Some sections of the book are derived from previously published work. Parts of Chapter 1 are from McConnell, D. (2004) Networked Collaborative E-Learning, in Li, E. and Du, T.C. (eds) *Advances in Electronic Business: Vol. I*, Idea Group, Inc. Parts of Chapter 5 are from McConnell, D. (2002) The Experience of Networked Collaborative Assessment, *Studies in Continuing Education*, 24 (1), 73–92. Chapter 6 derives from McConnell, D. (2002) Action Research and Distributed Problem Based Learning in Continuing Professional Education, *Distance Education*, 23 (1), 59–83. Chapter 7 derives from McConnell, D. (2005) Examining the Dynamics of Networked E-learning Groups and Communities, *Studies in Higher Education*, 30 (1), 23–40.

Introduction

This book is about learning, but learning that takes place in virtual spaces where students do not physically meet other students, and where teachers do not physically meet their students. But students and teachers do 'meet': they meet in virtual learning environments (VLEs) through the use of computers linked together through networks such as the Internet. This is called 'e-learning'. The students and teachers often live in different countries, and often come from different cultures.

The book is about how we can design e-learning events and courses that bring these people together and give them a strong sense of belonging, of being a community of like-minded learners.

The book contains ideas about learning and teaching that may challenge some teachers and students. Two themes exist throughout. One is that learning involves students in social processes where they learn in the company of others through collaborative and cooperative learning, and that these best occur in the form of groups and communities of learners. The other is that new learning technologies such as VLEs provide the architecture needed to support groups and communities in cyberspace. These two themes – that of e-learning groups and communities and that of advanced learning technologies – permeate the chapters of the book.

The scope of the book is both local and global. I draw on experiences of students and tutors (my own included) to highlight in some detail what it is like to learn and teach in e-learning groups and communities. This is achieved through a variety of small-scale qualitative research studies aimed at illuminating the experience of e-learning, and which provide in-depth, rich and authentic insights. The book is global in the sense that readers can vicariously 'imagine' themselves in what they read, and from this generalize to their personal or particular contexts and circumstances. The contents of the book offer teachers, students, researchers, managers and others involved in education understandings of student learning in this new environment.

Hundreds of years of teaching in schools, colleges and institutions of higher education have produced teaching practices that are commonly understood. There are similarities in the way teachers across the globe run their classes, and similarities in the kinds of learning they expect from their students. But in the era of e-learning all of this may change. New technologies make it possible to do new things in our classes, and classes of homogeneous groups of students who expect to be 'taught' in traditional ways no longer exist. Indeed, our classes often no longer exist in one physical location. Many teachers in conventional institutions now offer courses at a distance, and run them via the Internet.

E-learning challenges us to reassess our practice and reconstruct the meaning of teaching and learning. We are challenged to see our students in the light of the postmodern self who

- rejects delayed gratification and wants it immediately;
- is not ready to endure distress but develops rather a capacity for fun;
- refuses to do empty routine work but wishes to do something meaningful;
- is not so much interested in materialistic objectives, but rather in the fulfilment of human values;
- is not so much interested in achievement, but in self-realization;
- does not like self-control, but seeks self-expression;
- rejects competition and is interested in a good work climate;
- does not want to become isolated, but is interested in social relations and interactivity. (Wood and Zurcher 1988, in Zammit 2004)

In the field of continuing professional development, which is the main focus of this book, the meaning of this for the practice of e-teaching and e-learning is potentially profound. What might it mean to change what we do in the light of the postmodern self? What might this mean for teaching and learning? If students are not interested in routine but are looking to do something meaningful, how can we design learning that offers them the opportunity to engage in meaningful tasks and learning processes, and that focuses on the examination of 'real' problems and issues that they face in their everyday lives? How can we go about designing learning that meets the postmodern need to fulfil human values? If achievement and self-control are less important, how can we design learning that fosters self-realization and self-expression? If a good work climate is a major requirement, and competition rejected, how can we develop methods of teaching that are built on a sense of students' belonging and that foster cooperation, collaboration and collective learning processes? How can we make it possible for students to feel less isolated, and provide learning environments that support social relations and interactivity?

If we are postmodern teachers working with postmodern students, what will our 'postmodern' teaching look like? What might it mean to teach in this new era of e-learning? These are important questions. I do not intend to provide full and definitive answers to them in this book, but I do take them seriously and hope to suggest some ways in which we might begin to answer them, or at the very least engage with them.

The issues and problems that our students want to find answers to – the ones they face in their everyday lives – are not usually amenable to simple solutions. The problems, questions and issues that occur in society, whether at the personal level or at the professional and institutional level, are often complex and multi-faceted. They cannot usually be solved by individuals working on their own. They require teams or groups to address them. In designing higher education courses, we need to acknowledge this and 'imagine' forms of teaching and learning that can accommodate it. This implies two things:

1 The need to make it possible for students to investigate real and authentic problems and issues that they face in their everyday lives, and
2 The need to make it possible for them to work collaboratively in creative and innovative communities where they can draw on their collective knowledge and resources in addressing these problems.

Values and beliefs

The work of Wood and Zurcher mentioned above highlights a concern for the fulfilment of human values, and implicitly a search for a new identity in the postmodern era. Our values and beliefs are likely to determine how we view the world and how we conduct our lives. This is no less so for the conduct of the professional practice of those of us involved in teaching and learning, a point to which I will return in Chapter 1.

I have been working in the field of open and distance education since the early 1980s, and was one of the first people in the UK to develop computer-mediated communications (see Emms and McConnell 1988; McConnell and Sharples 1983). Since then I have developed a curiosity for understanding how I can use advanced learning technologies in ways that support my educational values and beliefs. These include the value of democratic processes in learning and teaching, and the need both to provide as much freedom to the learner as possible and to structure learning in ways that promote self-management and reflection. I place great value in organizing learning in social groupings where students work together in 'community', where they give attention to each other, their personal and collective needs, and where they participate in collaborative learning processes, including collaborative evaluation and assessment processes. In this book I examine how we can use advanced learning technology to promote these beliefs and values in the educational process.

A great deal of this book is about the postmodern project and the enduring effect of values and beliefs on what we do in our professional practice as teachers. These things come together in the development of new pedagogies for e-learning and teaching. We have to ask the questions: what do we mean by 'learning', what do we mean by 'teaching', and how do the answers to these questions translate into the designs we produce for our e-learning courses? We each have to make choices about these matters, and this book offers a view on one particular way forward.

Community

As we shall see in Chapter 1, there have been many attempts to characterize Internet 'communities' and educational communities, but surprisingly little examination of actual, existing educational communities. We know a fair amount about the theory of establishing communities but very little about how these theories work in practice. We know little of what actually takes place in an online learning community and what members of communities do in those settings. This book is one of the first to provide a detailed analysis of what goes on in e-learning groups and communities. Detailed examples of the dynamics of e-learning communities and groups are provided, showing how members negotiate the nature of their community and develop trusting relations in which meaningful learning can take place.[1] I show how the dynamics of e-learning communities evolve and are controlled by members of the community, and what strategies members use to develop and sustain 'community'. It is important for the development of professional practice that e-teachers and tutors understand the reality of e-learning communities.

Research approaches

My approach to researching e-learning groups and communities is multi-faceted. My main concern has been to provide meaningful and accessible insights into the practice of e-learning based on the analysis of real-life situations. To do this, I have been involved in the following activities:

- observations of e-learning groups and communities, as participant observer and non-participant observer;
- asking questions, of students and tutors;
- interviewing those involved, electronically and face-to-face;
- talking with students and tutors in the e-learning environments themselves about what is happening, and why it is happening;
- examining the life of real and authentic e-learning groups and communities in an attempt to find out how life is lived from the point of view of those involved;
- prolonged immersion in the field.

These activities have allowed me to gain deep insights into the culture of these groups and communities. I have been engaged with events as they happen in the field, and have attempted to bring holistic attention to all the practices as constitutive of a distinct culture. I have studied those enduring practices through which the e-groups and communities have become meaningful and perceptible to participants (Hine 2000: 20).

My approach is holistic: I interact with what is happening online; I use multi-channels for data gathering and understanding and I have long-term engagement with the phenomena being investigated, rather than short-term, more selective approaches favoured by some other researchers.

The verification of ethnographic studies usually depends on the breadth of observations that the researcher carries out (Hine 2000). In my own case I have been an e-tutor on the courses examined for over nine years, and have therefore managed to develop deep understandings of what goes on in them. I have been a participant observer of student learning in those groups and communities where I have been a tutor, and have been a non-participant observer of other e-groups and communities by means of examining transcripts of their work and activities. My sustained and involved presence in these groups and communities has allowed me to verify many observations and come to authentic understandings and conclusions.

Keeping one's distance, or not 'going native', in this kind of research can be important. But so also is being involved and immersing oneself in what is happening in order to gain insights that arise from deep understanding of the practice of e-learning.

It is hoped that the detailed presentation and exploration of issues faced by those working in e-learning groups and communities will provide readers with a rich text from which they can form their own ideas.

Overview of the book

Chapter 1 considers the theoretical and conceptual issues underpinning course designs based on supporting e-learning groups and communities. The focus here is not on theories of instruction, but on principles of learning. The starting points are questions such as 'what kind of learning do we want?', and 'what kind of learning environment or context will help students learn in this intended way?' Course design principles are suggested with this in mind. I show that by adapting to the logic of collaborative e-learning and communities and groups, we have to adopt its language, codes, values, modes of interaction and so on. This, of course, has consequences for the design of e-learning courses, and for our practice as e-teachers and tutors.

Chapter 2 describes the ways in which we can design courses to support e-groups and communities. The focus here is on the ways in which we can use those principles outlined in Chapter 1 to design forms of e-learning that support groups and communities of learners. A model of e-learning is offered for consideration, with a detailed examination of its design.

Chapter 3 moves from the theory and practice of e-learning to an examination of the students' experience of learning in collaborative groups and communities. The chapter covers students' perceptions of such issues as the quality of discussions and group work; group collaborative learning processes; the collaborative processes in the large community; collaborative assessment processes; the contribution of this kind of learning to their personal learning; the role of action research/learning processes, and finally their views on the tutor role in e-learning courses.

Chapter 4 is the first of two chapters on the important topic of assessment. The case for involving students in self-peer-tutor assessment processes is made. Collaborative assessment methods in cooperative and collaborative e-learning are discussed, and examples of the assessment processes are presented. The need to assess participation in the work of e-groups and communities is made, and a model of how to achieve this based on students' and tutors' assessment of four components of collaborative assessment, that is product achievement, communication skill, social relationships and reflective skills, is given. An evaluation of the model is presented.

Chapter 5 continues the focus on collaborative assessment with an in-depth analysis of how students experience participating in their own and each other's assessment. Two main issues are discussed in some detail: the appropriateness of collaborative assessment, and collaborative assessment as a learning process. The importance students attach to learning and assessment processes that take place in a social environment is discussed.

Chapter 6 looks at problem-solving and action research in communities of practice. The questions of how e-learning groups and communities negotiate the focus for their collective learning and how they develop themselves as 'community' are addressed by an examination of the work of three distributed problem-based learning groups. Some implications for practice are discussed.

Chapter 7 asks the questions: what actually happens in an e-learning group? The dynamics of e-learning groups are examined, and the place of identity, control, ontological security and guilt in collaborative e-learning groups is explored. It is shown that collaborative e-learning groups exhibit complex dynamics and diverse learning processes and outcomes.

Chapter 8 concludes the book with a personal review of e-learning over the past ten years or so in which I explore the evolution of one particular model of e-learning that I have helped develop. The relationship between learning technologies and learning groups and communities is discussed.

Note

1. I have changed all names in the book in order to ensure anonymity.

1

Designing for e-groups and communities: theoretical and conceptual issues

Introduction

This book is about learning in virtual, or networked e-learning, groups and communities. Learning in groups and communities suggests forms of learning that are collaborative in nature, where students share their understanding of what is to be learned, cooperate with each other, provide support, and engage in relevant and meaningful processes that help motivate them and that require higher-level cognitive and emotional skills.

When we design e-learning courses based on groups and communities, we have to adopt a different mind-set in relation to our practice of teaching and learning. For many teachers, implementing courses based on collaborative e-learning groups and communities will require some serious reappraisal of existing ideas about the nature of learning and teaching, and indeed the purpose of higher education generally.

In this chapter I want to show that the view of learning that each of us holds, whether it is a tacit view or a well-thought-out and articulated view, determines how we approach the design of any learning and teaching event. The values and beliefs that we hold, and the context in which we work, can define what is important to us and what is not. This has consequences for us when we come to design an e-learning course. In courses based on groups and communities, we have actively and consciously to design for collaborative e-learning to take place. Providing students with access to the technology does not in itself lead to the technology being used effectively or to collaborative learning taking place (Mantovani 1994). Students have to be given a good reason for learning in this way, and we have to provide well-designed and supportive e-learning environments that facilitate effective group and community learning.

I also want to show that a new paradigm of learning – which I call networked collaborative e-learning – is emerging as a new model for designing e-learning events and courses. At the heart of these changes is a belief that e-learning communities (which can take many forms including communities of practice, research communities and learning communities) and identity formation in these new virtual environments are central features that need to be considered in order to make them effective and productive places in which to learn.

A central feature underpinning this view of e-learning is a belief in the benefit to students of participating in collaborative evaluation and assessment processes. The assessment processes and practices of any course often define how students approach their learning, and are therefore central to the design of any course of learning. No less so in collaborative e-learning. When we ask students to learn collaboratively, we must ensure they have every opportunity to be rewarded for doing so. We have to provide opportunities for them to evaluate their learning in supportive, collaborative contexts. The topic of collaborative assessment is so important that I devote two separate chapters to it later in the book. But for the moment, I want to flag here that it is a central component of the overall design process.

A final point that I want to make in this chapter is that in order to run effective networked collaborative e-learning courses, the courses have to be facilitated by teachers and trainers sympathetic to openness in the learning process and who work towards providing an environment supportive of a high degree of self-managed learning, within the context of groups and communities.

Setting the scene

The advent of electronic communications, the Web and the Internet and associated learning technologies have produced a climate in which e-learning is seen as a means towards improving higher education learning and teaching (for example, see Garrison and Anderson 2003; Laurillard 2002; McConnell 2000). There is no one accepted, uniform methodology to explain how a move to e-learning could benefit organizations in both the short and long term (Ash and Bacsich *et al*. 2002). And even though the business models for e-learning are not yet proven (Ryan 2000), many higher education institutions are making plans to globalize their training and development provision (Middlehurst 2000). In this context, most e-learning is being developed in the form of short courses delivered as stand-alone packages. These packages are often designed for individual students working on their own and, as we shall see, are often based on instructional system design principles that do not foster participative learning or critical, analytical thinking.

Learning that involves the analysis of complex problems and issues, and more complex higher-order learning generally, is not amenable to this form of packaged e-learning. Something more dynamic that addresses the complexity of life around us and the complexity of higher-order learning is needed. There is a need for e-learning designs that promote problem-solving approaches to learning, and that foster collaborations between students aimed at helping them develop skill in working together to solve these problems. This chapter therefore addresses the needs of higher education institutions in focusing on complex learning via e-learning systems and processes.

A missing element in the provision of e-learning is a concern with the design of e-learning events and courses. We need a thorough understanding of approaches to design that sustain e-learning in ways that lead to quality learning processes and outcomes. One of the main ideas underpinning networked collaborative e-learning is that the interactions between students are a significant aspect of their meaningful, intentional, planned development (Banks, Lally and McConnell 2003). When students interact with each other, and available resources, they change. For example, such changes may occur in their *abilities, attitudes, beliefs, capabilities, knowledge and understanding, mental models, and skills* (Spector 2000). These changes may reside in the individual, or in the group, or at the organization level. Furthermore, they may be enhanced by the supportive interaction of the individual and the group in which she or he resides. In attempting to plan and then support meaningful, intentional learning we need to understand the context in which it develops best. This idea is underpinned by the early researches of Vygotsky (Vygotsky 1962, 1978) into the importance of experiential settings and social contexts for the development of understanding. Such understanding is clearly important to the management of any professional development e-learning course or event.

A second key idea is that networked e-learning environments can provide a valuable way of supporting such interactions. There are now many software systems, of both Web-based and stand-alone types that can support communication between group members (see Seufert 2000; Bringelson and Carey 2000; and Barajas and Owen 2000 for specific examples and theoretical design considerations). Indeed, it is commonly suggested (Sklar and Pollack 2000) that there has been a general paradigm shift in Internet usage, from a vast reference source or virtual encyclopaedia to a set of virtual communities. In other words, communication between people has become the dominant mode of use. These two key ideas, that of learning in groups and communities, and communicating in networked environments, come together in the notion of networked collaborative e-learning.

In this chapter I write from the perspective of an e-learning practitioner and researcher, and assume that my audience is made up of like-minded people who are interested in implementing e-learning and researching their practice. Although there is still much to be learned in this new and emerging field – cultural differences in approaches to learning and teaching in a global e-learning context being one of them – we can, with a degree of certainty, begin to provide a vision for networked e-learning that works towards inclusion of people from different traditions and cultures and which is based on a pedagogy that supports difference (Hodgson and Reynolds 2005).

Views of learning

To start with, I want to show how our view of learning often determines the way we design e-learning events and courses, and that this has serious consequences for the learning outcomes of those students taking the courses. For example, consider some of the differences between conventional instructional design approaches to the design of learning, and approaches that are based on principles of participatory, collaborative learning. Many teachers and trainers approach e-learning from the viewpoint of instructional system design (ISD) which views learning as a rather passive, linear activity. Learning is seen as a form of 'computation'. Conventional instructional systems design is based on four key concepts or assumptions (You 1993). It is:

Linear: it assumes there is a linear causality where cause and effect are closely related. It also assumes that the whole is little more than a sum of the parts. By reducing the whole into parts, the whole can be understood. Specific learning objectives determine what is to be learned, and each step in the learning process is predetermined and builds on the previous step. Students are required to follow the linear teaching path, and are assessed on their ability to do so. Learning is predictable.

Deterministic: ISD approaches lead to the conclusion that 'determinism is a necessary condition for predictability' (You 1993: 21). Deterministic predictability underpins ISD learning designs, bringing about learning patterns whose direction can be defined in advance and which are therefore difficult to change.

Closed: ISD courses are closed and isolated from their environment. This can lead to a state of inactivity where the learner is obliged to think and act only within the firmly set boundaries that have been imposed by the instructional systems designer.

Negative in their feedback: ISD courses often employ negative feedback mechanisms that are directed at maintaining the learning and teaching functions in a neutral way so as to ensure the predetermined goals are focused on. 'Variance' from outside is minimized and there is little opportunity for the learning design to change in accordance with the learner's views, beliefs or personal learning goals: 'mistakes or errors are thought to be inefficient and ineffective in the light of the predetermined objective, which functions as a reference point for judging the system's operation' (You 1993: 23).

The ISD approach to teaching usually leads to learning designs that do not support critical, interactive learning experiences and do not take account of the complexities and uncertainties of higher order in the learning process. From the ISD point of view, learning is often considered soley in terms of cognitive processes and conceptual structures.

If, however, we design for learning that is nonlinear but interactive and that occurs in social settings such as groups and communities, we engage in a qualitatively different approach to the design process. We are led to ask the question: *What social engagements and processes provide the 'proper' context for learning?* When we look at learning through the lens of convention, we are aware that many teachers see learning solely as the acquisition of propositional knowledge. But what happens to our practice when we view learning as social co-participation and knowledge-building?

From this perspective, learning is a process that takes place in a participation framework, not solely in an individual's mind. Learning is a way of being in the social world, not a way of coming to know it. There is, of course, a link between being in the world (ontology) and knowing about the world (epistemology). Knowing about the world affects how we live in the world, and how we exist in that world likewise affects how we think about it.

Following from this, I want to show that in designing sustained, purposeful e-learning that takes place in groups and communities, it is necessary to adopt a view of learning that requires a participatory design that involves an understanding of social constructionism and knowledge-building; that is based on the development of communities of students; that draws on understandings of situated learning and the character of practice; and that is underpinned by problem-based, exploratory, collaborative and critically reflective learning.

What is networked collaborative e-learning?

Many terms are emerging to describe the use of electronic communications and the Internet in education and training. My preference is for 'networked collaborative e-learning' since it places the emphasis on networking people and resources together; and on collaboration as the major form of social relationship within a learning context. The emphasis is emphatically on 'learning', and not on the technology (McConnell 2000; Banks, Goodyear, Hodgson and McConnell 2003).

Networked collaborative e-learning is therefore the bringing together of students via personal computers linked to the Internet, with a focus on them working as a 'learning community', sharing resources, knowledge, experience and responsibility through reciprocal collaborative learning.

The importance of context

E-learning does not occur out of context. It is embedded in the wider context of any educational, training or development endeavour where values and beliefs about appropriate forms of learning are explicitly and implicitly addressed in the design of the learning event. This has consequences for the work of organizational trainers, teachers and developers, and for students.

The kind of e-learning proposed here supports open, adult learning and professional development where students are able to work in small distributed e-learning groups and negotiate amongst themselves the focus of their work. In this form of e-learning, there are no specific pre-defined learning outcomes. Each group embarks on a learning-journey that requires collaboration but which does not define in detail how they should work together or what the outcomes of their learning should be. In this respect, the groups are following a long tradition of adult learning that supports openness and exploration (Boot and Hodgson 1987; Cunningham 1987; Harris 1987), and that has a history in experiential learning groups (Reynolds 1994; Davis and Denning 2000).

This form of e-learning emphasizes the educational need for students to work in social learning environments which emphasize both the situated nature of learning (Koschmann 1996; Lave and Wenger 1991; Packer and Goicoechea 2000; Salomon and Perkins 1998) and the importance of co-production and co-participation (McConnell 2000). This is linked to the capability of the Internet and the Web to support group work and provide a virtual environment for students to work together, share resources and collaborate. Within this virtual learning community perspective, students have opportunities to have a wide choice over the content and direction of their learning and the management of their own learning. They can also cooperate with others in their learning through processes of negotiation and discussion. Students working in these environments are encouraged to take a critical perspective on their learning and to focus on their own learning and development from a critical, reflective perspective, combined with an understanding of relevant concepts and ideas.

The advantages of collaborative group work

The advantages of collaborative and cooperative learning are well documented (see Johnson and Johnson 1990, 2003; McConnell 2000; Sharan 1990; Slavin *et al.* 1985; Slavin 1995; Thousand *et al.* 1994; Stahl 2002). In their work into the relative impact on achievement of competitive, individualistic and cooperative learning efforts, Johnson and Johnson (1990) looked at 323 studies. Their conclusions indicate that cooperative methods lead to higher achievement than competitive or individualistic ones when measured by a variety of possible indices. They used four indices of achievement:

1 *Mastery and retention of material* Students in cooperative learning environments perform at a higher level than those working in competitive or individualistic environments. When achievement in 'pure' cooperative groups is compared with achievement in groups using a mixture of cooperative, competitive and individualistic learning methods, the results show that the 'pure' methods consistently produce significantly higher achievements.

2 *Quality of reasoning strategies* Individuals working in cooperative groups use focusing strategies more often than those working competitively or individualistically. Learning problems are therefore solved faster. Those involved in cooperative work also use elaboration and meta-cognition strategies (such as showing an awareness, and self-control, of learning) more often than those working in competitive and individualistic situations. Higher-level reasoning is promoted by cooperative learning, and when comparisons are made between students using cooperative, competitive and individualistic learning strategies for tasks requiring higher- or lower-level reasoning strategies to solve them, students in cooperative groups discovered and used more higher-level strategy methods.

3 *Process gains* Process gains such as the production of new ideas and solutions are generated through group interaction. They are not generated when persons are working on their own.

4 *Transference of learning* There is a high degree of group-to-individual transference after working in cooperative groups, that is when individuals have worked in a cooperative environment, their learning is transferred to situations where they have to work on their own.

In general, it seems that at least four factors influence cooperation in e-learning:

1 a willingness by students to participate in this form of learning;
2 an understanding by students, and trainers and teachers, of the benefits of this form of learning;
3 an assessment system that supports and rewards cooperation and collaboration and the active involvement of the student in their own assessment;
4 distribution of power between teacher and student: the student has to see in practice that they have power to control their learning. (Hodgson and McConnell 1992)

Networked collaborative e-learning: a new paradigm?

Conventional e-learning poses some problematic issues in our relationship with students and in the form of learning that is often encouraged. In conventional e-learning, the content of learning material is largely unilaterally decided on by trainers, developers or academic staff. Students have little if any say in the content of the course, and teachers determine the focus of what is to be addressed as learning, and package this into self-study material. As we have seen, the use of behavioural objectives and the reliance on instructional design principles often reduce the complexities of learning to a set of pre-defined outcomes. Knowledge, in this packaged form, is slow to be changed and 'updated' and it can often take several years before changes are made to the material – yet access to 'just-in-time' knowledge is an increasingly important feature of our society today. This conventional form of learning is inherently individualistic: the learning arrangement is largely that between teacher and student. It is usually difficult to establish contact, interaction and discussion between students as a group, and indeed between the teacher and each individual student. Learning rarely takes place in a social context where students and teachers discuss, share and explore in depth issues relating to learning.

Related to the above is the problem of isolation in conventional e-learning programmes. It is my experience that many students rate this as one of the major drawbacks of this form of learning, and it is often a reason for students withdrawing from such programmes. It is also the case that many course-providers running such programmes find the experience isolating.

Assessment in conventional e-learning is usually unilateral, carried out solely by the teacher. This has serious consequences for the form of learning engaged in, and for the students' orientation to learning. With control of assessment firmly in the hands of teachers, students often work instrumentally to seek cues about the best way of passing a course of study, sometimes to the detriment of their learning (Miller and Parlett 1974; Becker *et al.* 1968). The educational technology of conventional e-learning largely supports a form of positivism in relation to knowledge ('positivism is a particular kind of "identity thinking" which tries to grasp and subdue the complexities of reality by imposing definitions and operationalized categories specifically in the interests of control') (Harris 1987). I would agree with Harris in the argument that, despite good intentions, producers of distance learning packages and e-learning packages often engage in 'providing technologically productive knowledge ... a technicization of education' (Harris 1987).

Advanced information and communication technologies offer new opportunities for innovation in the learning process. In comparison with conventional e-learning, the starting point of networked collaborative e-learning is the learning interests and concerns of the students, rather than a concern with presenting to students the knowledge and information held by the teacher, or that deemed to be the knowledge of the field of study.

Collaborative learning can be highly developmental, engaging the student in making sense of their learning and in reconstructing knowledge. It emphasizes critical reflection within a social context where peers and teachers help each other make sense of their learning. The positive effects of social interaction in learning are well documented (for example, see Dillenbourg 1999; Koschmann 1996) and show that the needs of the information society are better met by collaborative learning. Cooperative relationships, shared decision-making, diversity and communication are the shaping characteristics (Gros 2001).

By comparison, traditional forms of learning are concerned more with transmitting largely pre-defined forms of knowledge with little if any connection to personal experience and or critical reflection in the company of other learners.

Networked collaborative e-learning is based on a set of beliefs concerning the purposes of learning; the relationships between the student and teacher, and between each student; and the use of new advanced information and communication technologies. A few observations can be made in relation to this:

Networked collaborative e-learning is based on principles of action learning and action research. The focus of study is largely problem-centred. Students should have as much choice as possible over the direction and content of their learning. They arrive at the focus of their studies through discussion and negotiation with other students and teachers.

It is based on critical reflective learning in a social context. The technology of networked collaborative e-learning supports group and community discussion and the sharing of experience. A social, conversational context is important in the process of learning since it supports the clarification of ideas and concepts through discussion; develops critical thinking; provides opportunities for students to share information and ideas; develops communication skills; provides a context where the students can take control of their own learning; and provides validation of individuals' ideas and ways of thinking, through conversation, multiple perspectives and argument (McConnell 2000). A critical perspective on learning is therefore part of the process of networked collaborative e-learning. The critical perspective derives from reflection on one's own learning; the conversations one has concerning one's own and other students' learning; and the relationship one has with any academic (or public domain) material engaged with in the process of learning.

Collaborative assessment is a necessary component. A critical perspective is also necessary in the assessment process, and in keeping with the purpose of networked collaborative e-learning, assessment should involve the student, their peers and a teacher. This is called triangulated assessment. The need for, and importance of, collaborative assessment are clearly articulated by many learning practitioners and are topics I will come back to later in the book.

It involves a community of students. Students are responsible for managing their own learning and for helping others in theirs. The learning community works through students and teachers collectively managing their learning needs through negotiation and discussion (Pedler 1981)

It supports just-in-time knowledge. Knowledge in networked collaborative e-learning comes from several sources, such as knowledge from other students in the process of discussion; knowledge from being involved in collaborative projects; knowledge from online sources and resources; knowledge from academic papers and books. However, the concept of just-in-time knowledge is central. There are at least two processes under-pinning the development of just-in-time knowledge. The first is 'communication' where the focus is on exchanges and collaborative learning. The objective is to foster knowledge-building through social interaction. This form of learning puts students in contact with each other. The constitution of a learning group is central, and requires a common project on which to work. The focus, however, is still on personal learning. The second process is 'knowledge-building', and the focus here is on collective knowledge-building from exchanges between students and tutors, and students and students. This builds on the concept of communication but requires some specific conditions, such as:

- a shift from 'trivial' conversation to an organized debate that has much to do with a structured collective research approach;
- the expertise of others should be acknowledged without requiring external validation;
- the debates should not be concerned with taken-for-granted patterns of interpretation but should focus on the transformation of behaviours, habits or routines. This requires time and is rarely compatible with day-to-day (on-the-job) practice of students who may be in employment while studying;
- the debate requires an incentive in terms of intellectual commitment. Participation in a collaborative task helps maintain efforts to keep up the level of exchanges in the debate. This task could be an exercise such as writing a joint paper, setting up a professional knowledge resource base or realizing a collective research project. (Saunders *et al.* 1994)

It requires collective responsibility by students and teachers. Students and teachers need to attend to the processes of the community, that is reviewing and modifying the design, procedures and ways of working.

In imagining the design of this kind of e-learning, it is useful to ask what kind of learning context might suit students. Bonamy and Hauglusliane-Charlier (1995) suggest three views of virtual learning:

1   *The virtual classroom as the focus*: here, the control of learning is placed firmly with the teacher or expert. The emphasis is on knowledge

acquisition with little concern for participant interaction or for social negotiation of meaning. There is a 'body' of knowledge to be transmitted, and students are expected to study it, learn it and mirror it back to the teacher in some way, usually by attendance at formal examinations.

2 *The communication process as the focus*: here the control and responsibility for learning resides with each student. In continuing professional development contexts, the student is perceived as an 'expert' in their own way. Knowledge is constructed via social interaction in the online learning environment. The teacher acts as moderator or animator.

3 *Knowledge-building as the focus*: here the attention is on individual and collective knowledge-building. There is reification of knowledge from the collective expertise of the students. The teacher acts as cognitive expert, and helps in the development of an 'evolving knowledge base'. In continuing education contexts, the main application of the knowledge building focus is professional learning and development.

From these three views of virtual learning, three broad models of learning can be suggested, based on a set of characteristics such as the underlying view of knowledge, the processes of learning, the role of the teacher and student and so on. The three models are:

1 the transmission/dissemination model
2 the transmission plus discussion model
3 the learning community model

By reference to such models (see Figure 1.1) we can consciously make choices about the kind of learning we wish to foster in any e-learning context.

When these three e-learning designs are evaluated (McConnell 2000), it can be shown that different designs produce different levels of participation and collaboration, and that collaboration and discussion do not occur on their own – they must be central, sustained aspects of the course. In addition, intended processes and outcomes are not always achieved as planned, and familiarity with the technology does not in itself lead to participation or learning. Frequent participation (daily/weekly) is needed to sustain interest and to ensure the course or learning event is perceived as being 'useful'. Participants in networked e-learning 'use' online material or online resources with relative ease. Finally, different course designs may have an effect on students' motivation to learn.

Learning communities

I have used the term 'community' several times so far without defining what it is. The current interest in Internet-based communities (for example Jones 1995; Rheingold 1993; Smith and Kollock 1999) might in

	MODEL 1 Transmission/ Dissemination	**MODEL 2** Transmission with discussion	**MODEL 3** Learning community
UNDERLYING VIEW OF KNOWLEDGE	Knowledge exists independently of the student. A 'curriculum' is put together by the teacher and is learned by the student. Interpretation can be very limited or not expected.	Knowledge exists independently of the student. A 'curriculum' is put together by the teacher and is learned by the student. Limited room for interpretation and creativity.	Knowledge is constructed collectively. There are multiple 'truths' and interpretations. Learning is problem-based or issue-based.
LEARNING PROCESSES	Student receives material and is expected to learn it on their own. Individualism. Transmission or dissemination.	Student receives material and is expected to learn it. Some discussion occurs, but directed by teacher who poses questions to be answered.	Student poses problems or issues about their practice as a source of learning. Social, collaborative, dialogical learning.
ROLE/VIEW OF STUDENT	Passive receiver of knowledge. All students are viewed as the same – they are given the same learning material.	Students receive knowledge and are asked to show their understanding of it. Students are required to learn the same material.	Active constructor of own learning. Viewed as diverse individuals/expert professionals.
ROLE/VIEW OF TEACHER	Teacher is 'expert', controller and arbiter of knowledge.	Knowledge holder, 'expert', moderator.	Facilitator, student, critical observer, co-expert.
ASSESSMENT	Unilateral by teacher. External criteria used. Exams given.	Unilateral by teacher. External criteria used. Exams plus assignments given.	Collaborative self-peer-teacher assessment used. Both student and teacher criteria applied.
LEARNING OUTCOMES	Graduation. Some personal development.	Personal and professional development.	Creation and sharing of expertise. Personal and professional development.

ICT USED	Web. File transfer.	Web. File transfer. Web/email discussions.	Groupware. Virtual learning environments. Extensive Web discussion forums. Bespoke collaborative learning environments.
METAPHOR	Classroom. Filling an empty jug.	Seminar.	Learning community.

Figure 1.1 Three Models of E-Learning

part be explained by our need to feel we belong to a group of like-minded people – people who share a set of values and beliefs about the world in which we live. There have been many attempts to characterize communities in the educational literature (for example, see Beaty *et al.* 2002; Dirckinck-Holmfeld and Fibiger 2002; Dirckinck-Holmfeld and McConnell *et al.* 2003; Fox 2005; Garrison and Anderson 2003; Harris and Muirhead 2004; Paloff and Pratt 1999; Pedler 1981; Perriton and Reedy 2002; Renninger and Shumar 2002; Hodgson and Reynolds 2005; Smith and Kollock 1999; Wenger 1998). Surprisingly, there has been little research looking at what actually happens in online learning communities: we know very little about how they are formed, how members negotiate shared meanings about the nature of the community, how members work in the community and how the dynamics of learning in communities are controlled and what the affects of this are for those involved. We also know little about the eventual outcomes of learning communities, and how members work together to produce meaningful learning outcomes. These are all important concerns for educators and others running e-learning courses based on community principles. They are issues that will be examined in later chapters of this book.

At least three concepts of community can be mentioned here, each of which may have use in helping us understand the potential of 'community' as a design concept in e-learning contexts.

Learning community A learning community is a cohesive community that embodies a culture of learning. Members are involved in a collective effort of understanding. The learning community attends to issues of climate, needs, resources, planning, action and evaluation. A key feature of the idea is that responsibility for learning is 'shared' among community members. No one individual is responsible for knowing everything; rather, the shared knowledge and skills are distributed among members. Individually, each contributes to the group endeavour, enabling the group to accomplish more than the individual members might separately, with the key gain of deepened understanding of both content and processes by individual members of the group.

Community of practice   Communities of practice are particular kinds of communities where members focus on the development of professional practice. These social networks of like-minded people exhibit three characteristics of community: joint enterprise, mutual engagement and shared repertoire.

Communities of practice are said to have particular effects on the identities of the members:

> Each participant in a community of practice finds a unique place and gains a unique identity, which is both further integrated and further defined in the course of engagement in practice. These identities become interlocked and articulated with one another through mutual engagement, but they do not fuse.
>
> (Wenger 1998: 75–6)

Wenger (Wenger 1998: ch. 6) suggests that we experience identity in practice: it is a lived experience in a specific community such as those in which we work or in which we learn. We develop identity by looking at who we are in relation to the community in which we are practising members. Practically, this occurs through participation in the work of the community.

People in communities of practice share a domain – a field of interest or discipline (Wenger *et al.* 2002) without which they would be just a group of friends. They interact around this domain and show their commitment to it. All of this determines the nature of these kinds of communities.

Knowledge-building community   Several authors propose the idea of knowledge-building as a form of learning, and the knowledge-building community as the context where it can take place (see for example Scardamalia 2003; Scardamalia and Bereiter 2003; and Zhao 2006, for a comprehensive review of the topic). Knowledge-building is: 'a concept that brings together under one umbrella the curiosity-driven inquiry of the young child and the disciplined inquiry and invention of the mature knowledge worker' (Scardamlia 2003).

The knowledge-building community extends the concept of knowledge-building to situations where school students are committed to developing and extending shared understandings. Knowledge-building communities have four characteristics:

1   a focus on knowledge and the advancement of knowledge rather than tasks and projects;
2   a focus on problem-solving rather than performance of routines;
3   dynamic adaptation in which advances made by members of the learning community change the knowledge conditions requiring other members to re-adapt, resulting in continual progress;

4   intellectual collaboration as members pool intellectual resources, making it possible for communities to solve larger problems than can individuals or small groups. (Bowen *et al.* 1992, as quoted in Zhao 2006: 33)

Unquestioning application of the concept of community

In designing for virtual learning communities of whatever kind, we have to be aware that the current trend in talking of learning as 'community' can create a climate in which the idea is applied in unquestioning ways. In the three conceptions described above we can see that there are differences in the meaning of community and in the consequences for those involved in each version. The three concepts are not entirely exclusive: each has characteristics held by the others. But the intent of each may be said to be sufficiently different for us to be able to treat them as having different aims, purposes and eventual outcomes for those involved. For example, the intention of learning communities is to focus activity squarely on the development of a culture of learning; in communities of practice the intention is to place a major focus on identity and identity formation in the context of professional practice; in knowledge-building communities the intention is to place the major emphasis on knowledge-building and problem-solving.

Whatever lies behind the intention of each concept of 'community' will determine to a great extent how we go about designing for learning and teaching, and what eventually counts as learning, when we come to use the different concepts in practice. Each definition of community has embedded in it a set of values and beliefs that govern what is expected of the members of the community. We therefore need to be careful about specifying what kind of community we want and how that relates to the learning goals and purposes we are trying to achieve.

In doing this, we also need to be aware of the unquestioning application of the concept to any educational setting. The idea of community is currently being applied in too many educational contexts with little apparent understanding of what it might, or should, mean. Some of these unquestioning applications can have serious consequences for students and teachers if we are not aware of why we want to introduce 'community' into our practice. There are at least four possible sets of problems in using the concept in unquestioning ways (after Hodgson and Reynolds 2005):

1   *Communities as utopia*: here the idea of community is used in the recreation of community where it is in decline (for example, Rheingold 1993). This rather nostalgic view of community may reflect our need for community where it no longer exists. Here community is being used as the basis for achieving some kind of utopia or ideal.

2   *Consensus-based interpretation of communities*: the members of groups and

communities are susceptible to trying to achieve as much commonality and consensus as possible in the belief that thinking the same leads to acting the same. In this interpretation, difference can be denied in the belief that consensus is the important aim of community. Those who are excluded may be devalued and denied (Hodgson and Reynolds 2005).

3   *Normative effect and rules*: the normative effect of groups and communities leads to the setting of rules that can lead to exclusion of certain kinds of behaviour, beliefs, values and individuals. When boundaries are set, closure may result.

4   *Limited view of community*: we may have particular, but limited, views of what community is or should be. For example, we may assume a particular orientation to our presence in the community by taking on a paternalistic or mothering relationship with others, with a view to 'nurturing' students and so on. Such a view might lead to the development of particular relationships that could work against the spirit of community. Another way in which this may work is when some teachers assume to be self-appointed managers of the members of the community, and in doing so set themselves aside from the community. Finally, the provision of highly individually centred learning materials aimed at use by students on their own and not for use by groups or communities, may give the message to students that they should be working on their own rather than in groups, or as a community.

Whatever view we may have of community will determine the overall design we bring to the learning event, and the forms of learning we overtly or covertly encourage or support.

Communities and networks

Some authors draw attention to the differences between online communities and online social networks (see Castells 2001; Wellman and Gulia 1999). Are online communities the same as online social networks? If not, how do they differ?

Members of social networks display companionship and social support and engage in information exchange. But they show weak ties. They have a sense of belonging in which relationships are intermittent, specialized and varying in strength (Wellman and Gulia 1999). Participants mark a presence without deeper interaction, and interactions are often ephemeral (Castells 2001: 130). On the other hand, members of online communities have a set of shared values and interests (Rheingold 1993) and engage in social organization (Castells 2001: 127). Members' interpersonal ties provide sociability, support, information exchange, a sense of belonging, and social identity (Wellman, as quoted in Castells 2001: 127). They show socially close, strong, intimate ties. Members engage in the sharing of personal experiences and information, and in the development of trust (Wellman and Gulia 1999). Members of online communities are likely to reveal their personal identity, and will draw on emotional energy (Castells 2001: 129–30).

> Strong online ties have many characteristics similar to strong off-line ties. They encourage ... frequent ... companionable contact and are ... voluntary except in work situations. One or two key strokes are all that is necessary to begin replying, facilitating ... reciprocal mutual ... support of the partner's needs. Moreover, the placelessness of email contact facilitates ... long-term contact, without the loss of the ties that so often accompanies geographical mobility.
>
> (Wellman and Gulia 1999: 179)

It would therefore seem that the cornerstone of online community lies in the presence of 'socially close, strong, intimate ties', the development of trust, and shared values and social organization. The *quality* of peoples' relations is an important characteristic in an online community. In designing e-learning courses based on groups and communities we should therefore be aware of the need to incorporate these desired characteristics into the teaching and learning processes. A key question to answer is: how do we design distributed networked e-learning so that it supports those values and beliefs of learning communities we hold to be so central to our practice? Chapters 2 and 3 of this book will address this question.

Designing for learning communities

In designing for Model Three learning (learning communities, see Figure 1.1), some guiding principles are needed, based on an understanding of the nature of learning in professional development contexts.

The nature of learning in professional development contexts

Typically, in any lifelong learning or organizational learning context where complex higher-order learning and problem-solving takes place in groups, a variety of characteristics are exhibited which have to be taken into consideration in the design and implementation of any networked e-learning event. These are:

- The problems and issues being addressed should be defined by the members of the groups themselves, through processes of negotiation and discussion. The problems are usually complex and are often ill defined, which makes fertile ground for the production of mutual understandings and the construction of 'shared resolutions' (Schon 1983).

- The problems and issues often have a personal or a professional focus: they are important to the members of the group, arising from concerns and interests they may have about their own learning needs, to those related to their professional practice or their organization. The outcomes associated with the group work will be of personal benefit to the members, and for those in organizational settings may be of help in their professional practice or to their organizations.

- The problems or issues require negotiation and communication to understand them. Because the issues researched are invariably complex and ill defined, the members of each group have to engage in considerable communication in order to understand them and in order to negotiate changes in their perception of the 'problem' and its resolution as their work progresses. Communication is both task oriented and socially centred. The groups function both as learning communities (Pedler 1981; Snell 1989) in which members have an interest in sharing, supporting and learning collaboratively in a social context; and as communities of practice (Wenger 1998) in which members actively construct understandings of what it means to be professionals in their field of interest.

- Problems of this kind are often best investigated by adopting an action research approach. Members of the groups can be encouraged to view their learning as a form of 'action research' (Carr and Kemmis 1986; Elden and Chisholm 1993; Whitehead 1989; Winter 1989). The action research approach provides them with a model of how to work together, which helps guide them in their collaborations.

- The members of the groups go through a journey of learning: there are no specific pre-defined learning outcomes. Each group embarks on a learning-journey requiring collaboration but which does not define in exact detail how they should work together or what the outcomes of their learning should be.

- The work of the groups involves each member in a high degree of reflexivity. Learning in these groups is highly experiential, and the groups should therefore be encouraged to be reflective and to use this as a source of learning (Boud and Walker 1998; Moon 1999).

A means for achieving these goals is exposure to other students' development within the learning community. Members participate in developing the learning community perspective, which is based on students and teachers taking collective responsibility for the design and evaluation of the event, via constant review and modification of the design, procedures and ways of working. In order to attain this, McConnell (2000) emphasizes the need for a high degree of openness in the educational process, and forms of learning that are largely self-determined. There has to be a real purpose to the cooperative process alongside a supportive e-learning environment (such as a virtual learning environment or group-ware) that supports community learning. These are parts of a whole which, taken together, suggest a philosophy of, and a set of procedures for, the design of e-learning environments.

Challenges in the facilitation of networked e-learning

It will have become clear that in developing Model Three networked e-learning, many practitioners will have to adopt new relationships with learners. They will have to liberate themselves from traditional notions of teaching and instructional design that focus on *teaching*, towards those that focus on the facilitation of *learning*. This will be a major challenge: for practitioners and organizations alike.

A major factor in the effective uptake of e-learning in organizations will therefore be the professional development of trainers, course developers and teachers in this new form of learning provision. Those involved in providing e-learning require assistance in making the paradigm shift from 'conventional' teaching and learning, to teaching and learning in 'virtual', or networked, environments. Networking learning resources, and learners, now makes it possible for us to provide seamless, online learning environments that can be used to support learning in any part of an organization, anywhere in the world.

However, as we have seen, these new opportunities pose significant questions about the design of e-learning, and about the development of understanding and skills required in offering courses in this way. A new paradigm is emerging for thinking about these issues, which is based on our understanding of the nature of knowledge and knowledge construction and which actively employs the unique characteristics of networked e-learning environments.

This is not a simple shift, but a complex cultural change. At the moment, it would seem that the emphasis is often on the technology rather than on how the technology can facilitate learning. Education and training sector personnel are being forced to make decisions about implementation while their knowledge and understanding of the learning potential of the new information and communication technologies is still emerging.

Why do we need professional development?

We are experiencing a paradigm shift in our thinking about learning. This is occurring at various levels. For example, there is a shift from conventional, second-generation distance learning towards virtual distance e-learning. Face-to-face teaching, learning and training is now also incorporating some form of networked e-learning, freeing staff and learners to work at times that personally suit them and to use resources, and methods of working together, that were not possible a few years ago. In the field of distance education and training, 'distance' in learning is no longer the issue that it once was. The paradigm of networked collaborative e-learning shifts the emphasis from geographical separation of learners to the ways in which we can 'network' learners together, whether they happen to be physically co-located or geographically dispersed, in the same country or situated anywhere in the world.

In a recent publication on collaborative e-learning in higher education, the need for staff development was clearly stated:

> There are growing expectations of staff to offer more flexible forms of provision using technology, yet often with little or no training or support available ... To meet these expectations, there is a need for more staff development ... and staff development that caters to different levels of need ... The range of professional development needs is complex and goes well beyond technical skills to include pedagogical and managerial skills/knowledge. For instance, the provision of technology-mediated learning at an operational level indicates various professional development needs that include (Thompson 1997):
>
> • conducting successful group discussions
> • new class management techniques
> • managing online commitments with other responsibilities
> • developing appropriate assessment strategies
> • changing administrative processes
>
> This places considerable responsibility on staff developers to provide appropriate forms of professional development that reflects the diversity of needs and different forms of possible provision. Indeed, the staff developers may also share the same professional development needs themselves ... and there is therefore a need for 'training the trainer' initiatives to address this problem ...
>
> (Banks, Lally and McConnell 2003: 30)

Learning how to work with the technology and take advantage of networked e-learning are the key issues to be addressed. Any teacher or trainer will have to develop skill and understanding of three important components of e-learning practice:

1 *Initiating activity* – in initiating activity, the teacher/trainer:
   • sets up discussion and work groups in the virtual learning environment
   • invites participation
   • welcomes participants

- helps set an agenda in consultation with participants
- suggests a design for the environment
- provides initial scaffolding for learning to take place

2 *Fostering group self-management* – fostering group self-management requires that the teacher/trainer:
- develops and maintains a supportive emotional learning climate
- encourages the community to examine (by reflection) its own social processes
- encourages members to talk, share and debate with each other
- encourages the setting up of protocols for using the medium (for example, how often people might expect to be online; how they will communicate effectively)
- shares responsibility for running and managing the group
- creates a sense of ownership among participants
- helps the community achieve its goals

3 *Maintaining activity* – the teacher/trainer maintains activity by:
- netweaving – finding patterns and making connections in the work and communications of the community, and reflecting this back to the community
- helping learners learn through discussion and social interaction
- ensuring there is a real meeting of minds and not just unassociated communications
- helping learners transfer existing learning metaphors to e-learning contexts
- showing 'how' you communicate is as important as 'what' you communicate, for example, by personalizing what you say. Thus face-to-face talk is highly personalized, asynchronous and synchronous textual communications are less personalized, and the written word is least personalized.

In working in networked collaborative e-learning contexts, teachers and trainers (and learners too) have to be given time to develop new skills on which they can draw in order to ensure they work together as harmoniously as possible.

The facilitation of Model Three networked e-learning is probably the biggest challenge that practitioners and organizations promoting e-learning are likely to face in the coming years. Although the production of e-learning material is by no means a simple achievement, it is probably, by comparison, a less complex process than the development of know-how about effective learning processes and skills required by e-learning facilitators. This is where our energy and time should be devoted in order to ensure e-learning becomes a quality experience, and one that supports equality in learning (EQUEL 2004).

Conclusion

The current interest in e-learning in many higher education organizations is understandable: new information and communication technologies offer the potential of enhancing learning and teaching opportunities and of broadening the scope and availability of learning resources. They also promise to make training and learning more affordable and effective. However, e-learning practice is often still very traditional with a focus on packaging resources as stand-alone learning material. This can have benefits in those situations where well-defined skills and information have to be passed on to students, but as a method for knowledge development and sharing it has serious limitations.

Networked collaborative e-learning groups and communities – where there is a premium on sharing of resources, knowledge, experience and responsibility through reciprocal collaborative learning – offer an alternative method which has the prospect of helping students work closely on shared problems and issues relating to their professional practice. I have argued in this chapter for this form of e-learning as I think it offers a true alternative to traditional forms of e-learning. Students can collaborate on real-life problems and can share understandings and develop new insights into their practice that would otherwise not always be possible. Networked collaborative e-learning requires a change in our view of learning and a change in our view of our role as teacher or trainer. We have to view students as able, self-managing people who can make decisions about their learning and who can learn in virtual social settings where the emphasis is on negotiation, collaboration, knowledge-sharing, problem-solving and self-assessment. As practitioners in this new field, we have to view our role as being that of resource person, facilitator, critical observer and co-expert. We have to be able to create learning designs that support new forms of learning and that sustain and develop students in virtual learning contexts. This is quite a challenge but it is well within our grasp, and it is to this challenge that I now turn.

2

Design principles: a model

Introduction

This chapter is about understanding the bridge between theory and practice and how we can use theory about learning communities and group work to design e-learning courses, and to inform and shape our practice. In later chapters I will examine how these designs, and the practice that is embedded in them, work in reality and what the outcomes and implications are for those students and tutors who are involved.

Designing e-learning courses that support groups and communities is not a simple shift aimed at incorporating group works into a traditional, teacher-led course that has a predefined syllabus, aims and objectives. We have seen in Chapter 1 that the purpose of courses designed to support groups and communities is to help students negotiate the focus of their learning, to 'imagine' problems and their solutions, to work with their tutor in developing a 'syllabus' that is directly related to their needs and interests, and to work collaboratively and cooperatively as a community of learners in doing all of this. The learning outcomes of courses of this kind emerge from community negotiations where the members of the community, students and tutors alike collectively review, assess and evaluate their learning (and teaching). This form of learning is perhaps like a community of researchers where power relations are more democratically shared and where there is a determination to build new insights, ideas and knowledge and become skilled in researching and in developing critical thinking.

Designing for networked e-learning groups and communities

I want to start by discussing my work and that of colleagues in running distributed networked e-learning events and courses, all of which are underpinned by a pedagogy aimed at developing and sustaining virtual learning communities. In designing e-learning courses that are based on the group and community learning principles discussed in the previous chapter, we need to consider the overall purpose and structure of any course in relation to the learning processes we are aiming to foster. The collaborative and cooperative learning purposes with which we wish to shape the course have to be considered. In doing this we are acknowledging the prime place of negotiation and process in the course, as opposed to the more traditional focus on 'content'.

Since 1996, we have been running a part-time Masters in E-Learning designed to support learning in e-groups and communities. The course started as part of a project aimed at supporting local further and higher education teachers in South Yorkshire in the north of England. The area is economically deprived since the demise of the coal mining industry, and the teachers involved in the project wanted to learn how to use new information and communication technologies to help meet the challenge of widening the participation of adult learners in further and higher education. At that time the course was run using email as the main communication medium, and consisted of five online modules, with some face-to-face meetings where we spent time developing the community and negotiating course methods and content with the students. We soon progressed to using Lotus Notes, which we found to be an easy and efficient method of running the course.

The course evolved and was made available nationally in its 'blended' learning format, and we began to recruit internationally, with students from continental Europe and South Africa, as well as the UK, participating. The student body increased over the years and we began to receive requests to take the course from people in Australia and the Near and Far East. However, many of these potential students did not want to travel to the UK for the face-to-face meetings. We wanted to widen the scope of our market, but could only do that by redesigning the course to make it completely virtual, with no face-to-face meetings. At that time many of our students told us that face-to-face meetings were a very important part in making the long online elements of the course a success (although some also said that it would be possible to run the course without them). We tended to agree with them, but at the same time felt a need to take a risk and design the course to allow a wider range of students from many more countries the opportunity to participate. After considerable discussion and some argument, the course team agreed to redesign the course, and it has been running since the year 2000 as a completely virtual e-learning course. The question of whether online courses need face-to-face components is an important one to which I will return later.

Over the life of the course, the various iterations and evaluations have led to several periods of redesign, during which we have paid attention to developing our practice as e-educators and tutors. This has involved us in carrying out research into our practice, sometimes individually, sometimes collectively. The development of the Internet and virtual learning environments has also had an impact on our practice, as has the rise in interest by researchers into teaching and learning online.

The Masters is now offered entirely via the Internet using WebCT, a Web-based virtual learning environment. WebCT supports asynchronous and synchronous communications and has a wide variety of tools that can be used to support distributed learning. The course is taken by a wide variety of professional people who want to develop their understanding of new forms of e-learning. The Masters is a global programme, with students from the UK, Eire, mainland Europe, South Africa, Hong Kong, Singapore, Japan and Australia and Canada. Current participants include:

- professional trainers and developers, self-employed or in public and private sector organizations;
- teachers and lecturers in secondary, further, higher and open education;
- adult continuing educators;
- people working in libraries and resource centres;
- open and distance learning educators and developers.

In the design of this distributed networked e-learning course, we aim to help course participants appreciate and understand the ways in which they can use the Internet and the Web in their professional practice, and how they can design and evaluate learning events that focus on group and community work, and which are based on sound principles of active, problem-based learning. We emphasize the implementation of innovatory online practice by creating a supportive and creative research learning community where participants feel free to experiment and 'learn by doing', while constantly holding a critical perspective on their practice and the theory underpinning it. The course design emphasizes the educational need for learners to work in social learning environments that emphasize both the situated nature of learning (Koschmann 1996; Lave and Wenger 1991; Packer and Goicoechea 2000; Salomon and Perkins 1998) and the importance of co-production and co-participation.

This is linked to the capability of the Internet and the Web to support group work and provide a virtual environment for learners to work together, share resources and collaborate. Within this virtual learning community perspective, participants have opportunities to:

- have a wide choice over the content and direction of their learning;
- manage their own learning, and cooperate with others in theirs through processes of negotiation and discussion;
- take a critical perspective on learning and academic issues with strong relationships to their professional practice;
- focus on their own learning and development from a critical, reflective perspective, combined with an understanding of relevant academic ideas and concepts.

With an emphasis on the development of a learning community in which students and tutors work together to negotiate much of the learning content, we also have to pay attention to how that community reflects on its purposes and evaluates itself and its work. One aspect of this is the assessment of students' work. In formal educational settings where students are studying for credit, we have to provide some kind of assessment. This raises questions about the use of traditional forms of assessment in these contexts. There are two questions to consider here. First of all, can we ask students to work collaboratively and cooperatively and then assess them and their work in traditional ways? Second, can we run e-learning courses as learning communities, with the implication that tutors as well as students are members of that community, and allow the tutor unilaterally to assess the students? Some may say that the answer to the first question could be 'yes', though I would argue (as I do later in Chapter 3) that if we do assess students by traditional methods, they are likely as a consequence not to collaborate in their work very effectively or with any real engagement. Competition will emerge. The answer to the second question has to be 'no', although for some it may be a qualified 'no'. If we as tutors are sincere about being part of the learning community, we cannot adopt a relationship with respect to assessment that completely privileges us above students. If we do, the power that we strive to share with students in the community will be seen to be meaningless.

I will discuss these important issues in Chapters 4 and 5 of this book, as they are central to the whole concept of designing for e-learning groups and communities. For the moment, I want to make the point that any e-learning course that purports to be based on learning-community ideas of the kind outlined in the previous chapter requires tutors to share the power of making judgements about students' learning with the students. There has to be some kind of collaborative self-peer-tutor assessment process.

A holistic design

In the various designs of the Masters course, we have rethought our pedagogy so as to embed the technology in the course and make it a central element, and not just 'bolt' it on to an already existing design. We want to synchronize all the elements of course design and produce what I call a 'holistic' approach to the design of e-learning courses. This requires matching our educational values and beliefs about learning to what the technology affords so that we can provide an experience for the whole community – students and tutors alike – that has the following characteristics:

- a group and community perspective on learning and teaching processes
- synchronous and asynchronous communications
- shared workspaces, and document sharing/production

- collaborative and cooperative shared knowledge production
- collaborative self-peer-tutor assessment processes
- collaborative evaluation of the experience of learning and teaching
- redesigns of the course that are based on the evaluation of student and tutor experiences.

We know from experience that forming an e-learning community is more than providing a design, and is more than the sum of a set of activities aimed at promoting ties. Any design we put into action has to provide useful information, companionship, different levels of support and more than anything perhaps a strong sense of connection that help those involved develop a sense of identity. The process starts before the students come on the course, when we provide them with background information explaining the purpose of the course, the kinds of student participation envisaged, and a brief statement about the 'role' of the tutor that we come back to for fuller discussion once the course has started (see Box 2.1). We provide this information so that students can start to consider the nature of the course and how they might relate to the learning and teaching processes. As we shall see later, once they start the course, there is a collective focus throughout on shared understandings of these issues.

Box 2.1   Background Information Sent to Students

Masters in Education in E-Learning

Background to the MEd
Our aim on the MEd is to offer you a series of loose but supportive course activities to help you think through the issues that **you** define as being important for your learning. Getting the balance between your interests and professional concerns, and our sense of 'mapping out the territory' and helping you weave your way through it, is not an easy or simple task and is not one that is likely to be conflict free. But it is worth striving for, and we hope that we can collectively work at maintaining a good balance, constantly reviewing as a learning community where we are and what we are doing and why we are doing it.

Like all other Masters programmes at the university, course work has to be assessed. On this programme, which is concerned with your professional development as well as your academic development, we recognize the need to involve you in these assessment processes – partly in recognition of your own ability and need to have a say in determining the 'value' placed on your learning, but also to recognize and emphasize the learning potential of the assessment process, for you as a participant and for us as course tutors. We do this through processes of collaborative self-peer-tutor assessment, which we will discuss in more detail later in the Workshop 1 online period.

We use the term 'workshop' deliberately (rather than the more conventional term of 'module') to indicate an active, exploratory, action research approach to learning. This underpins all the work on the MEd.

For this first workshop, we have tried to develop a range of course work and assessment processes which, we hope, will reflect different learning purposes and offer a variety of experiences for us all to engage in.

Online participation

You are required to participate as fully as you can in the online discussions, in the learning sets and in the general discussions. We cannot be prescriptive about the exact meaning of 'fully participate' – we can discuss our different meanings of this when we are online – but the online activities and discussions in a sense 'replace' the usual course requirement of attending face-to-face meetings in a 'normal' part-time Masters programme, and are therefore central to your own learning and to that of the learning community. It is in these online discussions and group activities that we can gain a sense of the usefulness of computer-mediated communications in the learning process, validate each other's learning and professional development and sustain the development of the learning community. We therefore expect you to log on to the course website at least 3–4 times every week.

In Phase 4 of the workshop, you will be asked to review your online participation and to engage in discussion with your learning set members' and tutor about the 'level' and quality of participation.

The role of the tutor

In a course design that tries to be collaborative, open to change in the light of experience and which supports you in managing your own learning and that of your peers, the role of the tutor is inevitably qualitatively different from the traditional one that you will be used to. Tutors on the MEd in E-Learning have the main role of helping you determine what you want to focus on in each workshop: it is a facilitative role. In addition, tutors help each learning set group negotiate their work in collaborative and cooperative ways. We do not 'teach' or lecture in the conventional way. We believe that professional people such as yourself have considerable knowledge and skill to bring to your learning. We 'map out' the territory of collaborative e-learning for each workshop, but then work closely with you in determining how you can use that 'map' to investigate your own ideas and practice in an active, action research way. This approach to tutoring and learning will be explored with you in some detail in Workshop 1 and throughout the course.

In addition it is important to offer students the opportunity actively to prepare themselves for working in a collaborative learning community. This can be done in a variety of ways. One activity we have found most useful is to ask them to write a personal professional story (Box 2.2). Writing something about themselves helps students reflect on their professional development and prepares them for using reflection as a source of learning on the course. It offers them the opportunity to stand back and take stock of their career, and to consider what have been the key influences on their career so far, what have been the highs and lows of their career, why they are embarking on a two-year programme of study and what they hope to achieve in doing that, and so on. These autobiographies will become important documents to draw on in Workshop 1 and throughout the course, and students will be asked to share some of what they have written with other course participants.

Box 2.2 Example of Pre-course/Workshop Activity

MEd in E-Learning 2003

Pre-course activity
Writing a personal professional story
As part of the development of our learning community we would like you to write a 'Personal Professional Story' in readiness for the first workshop. The purpose of this exercise is twofold:

- To help you to reflect on your personal professional development so far;
- To serve as a basis for sharing your reflections on your professional development experiences with other members of our learning community.

To this end, we would like you to prepare a short piece of autobiographical writing (500–1,000 words at most) that outlines those aspects of your professional development that were significant or important for you in becoming who you are today. Please remember that this should focus mainly on your professional life, rather than your personal life (although the two are obviously connected). It can include both 'positive' and 'negative' experiences. So, for example, you might want to include:

- what you are doing now;
- where you started professionally and how that happened;
- your career path and the various changes of direction you have taken, and why;
- accidental or unexpected changes;
- the high points of your career and achievements (for you, not necessarily the ones that advanced you);

- the low points of your career, including difficulties and frustrations;
- key influences on you professionally, including people, events, ideas, family and how they influenced you;
- what you think about where you are now and how you arrived there;
- why you want to study on the Masters in E-Learning.

The central idea is that this is a personal autobiographical reflection, written in prose. It is not a CV – so please do not itemize your career path to date!

Please have the document ready for the start of Workshop 1. You will retain control of it and may use it to contribute to activities in this workshop. You will not be required to show the story to anyone. It will be a reference point for you to draw upon in the workshop.

For some more detailed background ideas about this type of professional development you may wish to look at the enclosed paper: Bolton, G. (1994) Stories at Work, *British Educational Research Journal*, 20 (1), pp. 55–68. However, you do not need to read the paper before writing your own story.

The course has five periods of online work over the two years. We call these periods 'workshops' rather than the more familiar term 'module'. This is a deliberate attempt to engage students in rethinking their learning: workshops are places where we take part in active, participatory learning, where new ideas about learning and teaching can take place and where students and tutors can experiment and take risks in what they do. The overall timetable for the whole course is made explicit at the very beginning of the course (see Box 2.3). The design of each workshop is explicitly stated in advance of students taking it so that they have all the information about the purposes, processes, requirements and assessment methods in order to participate in knowledgeable ways (see Box 2.4). We find it important to supply this kind of information so that students can quickly grasp macro- and micro-course structures and processes, and get a much needed overview of where they are going, and more importantly perhaps, why they are going there!

Box 2.3 Overview of the Two-Year Masters Degree

Year 1

Workshop 1 *(4 months online)*
(Theme: community-building and introduction to action research)

Phase 1: Welcomes (in large community)
Negotiating collective purposes. The learning community. Action

research as a form of learning. Meanings of learning (in learning sets)

Phase 2: Plenary discussions, networking and sharing biographies (in large community)

Phase 3: The collaborative project (in learning sets)

Phase 4: Collaborative review and assessment (in learning sets)

Workshop 2 *(4 months online)*
(Theme: computer-supported collaborative learning; computer-mediated communications)

Phase 1: Review of Workshop 1. Learning set formation (in large community)

Phase 2: Personal (cooperative) assignments (in learning sets)

Phase 3: Collaborative review and assessment (in learning sets)

Workshop 3 *(4 months online)*
(Theme: the Internet as a learning environment)

Phase 1: Review of Workshops 1 and 2 (in large community)

Phase 2: Short collaborative project (in learning sets)

Phase 3: Personal (cooperative) assignment (in learning sets)

Phase 4: Collaborative review and assessment (in learning sets)

Year 2

Workshop 4 *(4 months online)*
(Theme: designing for research and evaluation)

Phase 1: Review of Workshop 3. Learning set formation (in large community)

Phase 2: Personal (cooperative) mini-action research project (in learning sets)

Phase 3: Design of personal action research dissertation project (in learning sets)

Phase 4: Collaborative review and assessment (in learning sets)

Workshop 5 *(8 months online)*
(Theme: action research dissertation)

Phase 1: Review of Workshop 4 (in large community)

Phase 2: Dissertation (in learning sets). Reviews (in large community)

Phase 3: Collaborative review and assessment (in learning sets)

Box 2.4 Detailed Timetable for Year 1 of the Masters in E-Learning 2003 Intake

Masters in E-Learning: Year 1

Workshop 1
The theme of this workshop is the development of a networked research learning community, which involves consideration of aspects of self-managed learning and action research.

Starts: Monday 6 October 2003
Ends: Friday 23 January 2004

Phase 1: Our collective purposes
Starts: Monday 6 October 2003
Ends: Friday 7 November 2003

Phase 2: Plenary and discussion
Starts: Monday 10 November 2003
Ends: Friday 21 November 2003

Phase 3: The collaborative project
Starts: Monday 24 November 2003
Ends: Friday 2 January 2004

Please note: During the Christmas holiday period the university is closed. The tutors on the MEd will not be available between 19 December and 5 January. It is entirely up to members of the learning sets to decide if they wish to continue with their collaborative project during this period.

Phase 4: Review and assessment
Starts: Monday 5 January 2004
Ends: Friday 23 January 20034
Self-study and reading period: 26 January to 9 February 2004

Workshop 2
This workshop considers cooperative and collaborative networked e-learning.

Starts: Monday 9 February 2004
Ends: Friday 14 May 2004

Phase 1: Review of Workshop 1
Starts: Monday 9 February 2004
Ends: Friday 20 February 2004

Phase 2: Cooperative (personal) assignment
Starts: Monday 23 February 2004
Ends: Friday 23 April 2004

Phase 3: Review and assessment of course work
Starts: Monday 26 April 2004
Ends: Friday 14 May 2004

All course work to be completed by Friday 14 May 2004, at which point two copies of assignment, with covering sheet and transcript of self-peer-tutor review, should be sent to the Department of Educational Studies.

Self-study period: 17 May to 28 May 2004

Workshop 3
This workshop is about the Internet as a learning environment.

Starts: Monday 31 May 2004
Ends: Friday 17 September 2004

Phase 1: Review of Workshop 2
Starts: Monday 31 May 2004
Ends: Friday 11 June 2004

Phase 2: The collaborative project
Starts: Monday 14 June 2004
Ends: Friday 23 July 2004

Phase 3: The cooperative (personal) assignment
Starts: Monday 26 July 2004
Ends: Friday 27 August 2004

Phase 4: Review and assessment
Starts: Monday 30 August 2004
Ends: Friday 17 September 2004

All course work to be completed by Friday 17 September, at which point two copies of assignments, with covering sheet and transcript of self-peer-tutor review, should be submitted.

There are three important structural elements to the course:

Workshops   The workshop is the place (and time) where we collectively take part in activities designed to inform us about one particular aspect of course content. Each workshop has a theme around which much, but not all, of the activity takes place. We have designed each workshop so that it has an action research 'rhythm' to it, in which issues for discussion or examination, or problems, are introduced, sometimes by tutors, sometimes by students. Members of the set engage in discussing 'solutions' to the issues or problems. This may lead to other activities, after which students are encouraged to reflect on the experience and share their understanding of what took place. This underpinning action research methodology is sometimes more obviously present than at other times. It is an approach to the work of the groups and community that is introduced early in the course and that resonates with the students, many of whom come to find it a powerful mechanism for carrying out their studies and supporting each other.

Phases   Each workshop is divided into three, four or five phases, each of which has clearly demarcated start and stop dates. Students know in advance what the purpose of the phase is, when it starts and when it is due to finish. Sometimes the phases are designed to be incremental, so that they contribute to the development of a larger activity associated with the purpose of the workshop. Sometimes the phases are set up in ways that help the students and tutors focus on getting to know each other and develop a sense of community. Sometimes everyone in the community participates in the work of a phase. At other times the phrases are designed to allow smaller groups, which we call learning sets, to come together to work on a project or some other collaborative or cooperative learning activity. The activities in each phase are underpinned by the use of strategic scaffolding in which we provide a loose but highly visible initial structure that is gradually reduced as the activities, and the phase, develop, so encouraging student self-management.

Activities   Each phase is made up of a series of exploratory activities designed to engage students and tutors. These may take the form of e-seminars where we discuss research papers relating to the theme of the workshop. They may be collaborative activities such as working on a project or negotiating the focus of a learning event. They may involve students in reflecting on their learning, and sharing their experiences with members of the set. Whatever the specific activity is, students are encouraged actively to participate in the spirit of cooperation and mutual support and to engage in open, self-managed ways.

In designing the course as a whole we have also tried to link each workshop through the 'rhythm' of action research mentioned above. This occurs at both the macro-level and the micro-level. So for example, in Box 2.3, which shows the outline of the five workshops, we can see that at the start of each new workshop there is a review phase where students and tutors reflect on their experiences in the previous workshop, share them in community spaces and take time to consider what they have learned from them. Wherever possible we then try to take account of the outcome of these reviews in the design of the up-coming workshops.

Before the start of the course, we provide background information that covers the aims of the course, the expectations we have of student participation and some information about the 'role' of the tutor (see Box 2.1). We do this so that students can begin to consider the nature of the course and how they might relate to the learning and teaching processes.

Preparing students for each workshop

As we have seen, each workshop has a theme and students and tutors engage with the theme through collaborative and cooperative learning processes. The phases of the workshop, and the associated activities of each phase, are the places where students work with the learning resources and where they collectively and individually determine their learning outcomes. It is important at the beginning of the course to present a structure that will provide sufficient scaffolding and support, while not being overly prescriptive. Initially, students need to feel supported but not restricted in what they can do. It is necessary throughout for tutors to show that they are willing to pass on the power of control to the student, and students need to experience this in the practice of the tutors. As the workshop progresses, scaffolding is reduced and students are helped to develop the confidence to begin to provide their own structures and processes, supported by their tutors.

The detailed information about each workshop that we provide is an important source for understanding the structures and learning processes that will take place. The Appendix to Chapter 2 shows an example of the detailed information for Workshop 1. Here students can read in advance what the design of the workshop is trying to achieve, and how the individual phases and associated activities are designed to help them in their work.

Providing information of this kind is important, but not in itself enough. We have to help students interpret and understand it. This is an important role for the tutor, who, rather than teaching in traditional ways on the course, works with students to help them make sense of the purposes of the course and the structures and learning processes. Meaning occurs in context, and interpretations have to be negotiated through dialogue, participation and activity. This takes place in the discussion forums where students and tutors work together to make sense of their project.

In the example presented in the Appendix, which is the first workshop on the course, the activities in Phase 1 have two purposes: to help students and tutors get to know each other, and to introduce students to some key concepts that underpin learning processes on the course and give them time to think about them and discuss them with members of the community. By doing this we hope they will begin to understand the kind of learning that will take place on the course, and prepare themselves for adjusting to the collaborative learning culture of the course. These activities take place in the learning sets.

Phase 2 brings the members of the learning sets together and focuses on sharing biographies and community networking. Students are encouraged to consider their personal identity, to consider their identity within a community of learners, and to develop an awareness of biography as a research tool. By sharing biographies (and tutors also share their biographies) they are able to understand the identity of other members and start a process of reconstructing their biographies. This activity also underlines a key element of learning in communities, which is the nature of difference. We think it is important to highlight difference and diversity in the context of community so that we can all develop an awareness of the individual within the collective. Most students taking courses of this kind will be doing so for the first time in their lives. They will be used to learning on their own, as autonomous individuals, and will have to develop new understandings of how to learn with others while holding on to their individuality. For most students, this is undoubtedly a difficult and perhaps even disturbing shift in their values about the meaning of learning and the purpose of higher education. Later in this book I will return to a discussion of this issue when I examine the dynamics of e-learning groups and communities.

While the learning in Phases 1 and 2 is largely designed to establish the community by focusing on the development of reflective skills and cooperative learning processes, Phase 3 is an opportunity for learning set members to work in-depth on a shared project. The students choose the focus of the collaborative project themselves, in consultation with the tutor who acts as an adviser, facilitator and resource person. The information provided in the Appendix to Chapter 2 is meant only as the starting point. Students have to negotiate the project and their own individual part in it. We shall see in later chapters how this works out in practice, and how collaborative learning can help shape the character of the learning community. We shall also examine some of the problems that are encountered in work of this kind, and how members of the sets manage them.

The final Phase 4 outlined in the Appendix is the collaborative review and assessment of course work. Students are provided with information about the three course requirements for this particular workshop. They know what outcomes they are being invited to achieve within the context of this learning community, and how they should present them. They can see that they will be actively involved in making decisions about the production of each course requirement, and that participation in the work of the groups and community is the vehicle for achieving this. Students can see in advance of this phase exactly how they are to participate in their own and each other's assessment. Collaborative self-peer-tutor assessment is central to learning in groups and communities. In Chapters 4 and 5 I will provide a detailed examination of the processes involved and of students' experiences of taking part in them.

WebCT home page

In designing the two-year course, we have taken great care to provide a simple yet effective WebCT 'home page' that contains links to the course resources. In the current WebCT home page design there are three sections:

1 Resources This area has hyperlinks to a wide variety of useful resources, including pictures and biographies of each student, tutor, course secretary and technician; access to the university library where there are CD-ROMs and e-journals (individual papers can be downloaded in pdf files); links to all major search engines with evaluations of their effectiveness; access to specific e-learning Web resources and so on. We continually update and add to these resources. In addition to providing a wide range of online resources, we also send participants a resource pack of journal articles, books and so on that are not available in electronic format.

2 Content and participation Here we provide detailed information on the structure and content of each workshop, and access to a wide variety of asynchronous and synchronous forums for community work and the work of learning sets. In the community spaces there is a wide range of activities aimed at developing and supporting the community, including plenary discussions and community networking; workshop reviews and evaluations; workshop planning meetings; learning-set formation meetings; presentation of group projects; dissertation reviews and other work and activities that require the participation of all students and tutors. In the group spaces we carry out e-seminars; collaborative project work; work associated with the production of personal student assignments; self-peer-tutor reviews and assessment; scaffolded discussions, and free ranging discussions. Café areas are also widely used, mainly by students, as places to 'hang out' and chat, share photographs and exchange personal resources.

These forums are the most important areas on the WebCT site since it is here that negotiations, communications and production of course work take place.

3 Notices Here, updated information about the course, the outcomes of community decision-making and the like are posted.

Throughout the course, we strive to develop informal relations with students and encourage them to communicate using everyday, informal language. Boxes 2.5 and 2.6 provide examples of tutors' introductions to the course and to a learning set.

Box 2.5 An Example of a Workshop 1 Welcome Page

Welcome to the MEd in E-Learning, Workshop 1 (2003 intake)

It's great to have you with us, and we hope you will have an enjoyable two years studying on the MEd.

Please take time to familiarize yourself with the layout and content of the MEd WebCT Home Page, which follows once you join Workshop 1 below.

In particular, please take a moment to read the section in the 'Resources' section dealing with the following:

a) How to use the discussion forums
b) How to use the various university facilities, such as the library and other facilities available to distant learners.

Please also read the 'Content and Participation section' (which can be downloaded as a pdf file) to find out about the structure and processes of the workshop, and the course requirements.

Please join the discussion forum called: 'General Introductions/ Arrivals' and let us know that you have safely arrived!

After that, please join your learning set discussion forum where your tutor will be waiting to welcome you and introduce you to the various activities in Phase 1 of Workshop 1 which are designed to help you get to know members of your learning set and start you thinking about your purposes on the MEd. The members of learning sets are given below, with the names of associated tutors.

With best wishes,

The tutor team

Box 2.6 Example of a Tutor Introduction to a Learning Set

Hi everyone: before we get into Phase 1 of this workshop, can I take a moment to suggest that you read the 'Content and Participation' section of the Home Page so as to get an understanding of how this workshop is structured, and the various learning processes and activities we have designed for the community.

As you will see, this workshop (like all of them on the MEd) has several 'phases' with particular focuses. Each phase has a start date and a finish date: this information should help you pace yourself and help you complete the work associated with that phase before moving on to the next phase. Most of the work will be carried out in your learning set (except for the Plenary Phase 2 where you will be networking with the whole MEd community).

A word about the learning sets: these are groups with a tutor and they are 'places' for you to carry out your course work, get to know course participants in some depth and offer members support for each other. We call them 'learning sets' deliberately, as a 'set' is a group of people who come together to support each other's learning and development. I too hope to learn and develop in this set, even though I have the special 'status' of course tutor.

We try to make the MEd as informal as possible, so that you can feel free to express yourself and take part in the activities in an open way. How you relate to this 'freedom' will no doubt depend on many things: but we hope you will find it a welcoming and supportive environment for your learning and development. We do hope you will see the MEd as an opportunity for you to develop in whatever ways you have in mind (or maybe even in ways that you did not have in mind!).

We also hope you will begin to feel 'free' enough to take some risks with your learning, and take time to stand back and look at what you are doing here in a critical and reflective way. We hope to offer you opportunities to look at your professional practice with 'new eyes', and take time as part of the MEd to examine what you do, and why you do that. When you do that in the company of others, it can appear a bit risky at first, but as you get to know each other and form trusting relationships over time, it will become easier. It is always though a rewarding experience.

If you have technical queries you can join the Technical Forum where help from Paul the technician is available. There's also a 'Cafe' forum for you to hang out at, get to know everyone on the MEd and do whatever you want.

Enough for now! If there is anything that is not clear to you as you join us in the next few days, please do just ask and I will do my best to help in any way I can.

Welcome again, and I hope you have a great two years with us.

Donald

The changing role of the tutor

Courses designed to support group and community-learning processes are likely to be developed by teaching tutor teams. These tutor teams will collectively plan drafts of each workshop and make decisions about the effective running of the course. Each tutor will have a learning set where they work closely with course participants.

Just as networked collaborative learners have to consider changes to their approach to learning, and 'absorb' this new culture of learning, tutors have to consider changes to their practice. There is a fundamental change in practice required by anyone tutoring online. For example, online tutors have to be content-facilitator/resource-provider, methodological support/process-facilitator, communication and collaboration facilitator, technologist, assessor, meta-cognition facilitator and adviser/counsellor (EQUEL 2004). And when students are asked to rank the significant characteristics of an e-moderator, subject knowledge comes low in their list:

1   supporting, understanding and encouraging (most important)
2   organized, efficient and effective
3   flexible and approachable
4   knowledgeability of subject matter (least important)

(Thomas *et al.* 2004)

In the context of this Masters course, we have found from years of experience and evaluation of our practice that the online tutor has to be highly skilled in facilitating collaborative learning in the learning sets. The collaborative e-tutor:

• helps to organize the group
• has good group development skills and good facilitation and intervention skills
• consults with the learners and ensures their engagement in the learning design
• guides the learners
• is resource provider
• is an 'expert' questioner, helping learners address important issues and questions relevant to their group work
• is a designer of learning experiences (not just content)
• understands how to deal with asynchronous and synchronous learning/ discussion
• critically reflects on their own practice, and is able and willing to change their practice on the basis of reflection
• can see the learning potential of a certain amount of 'chaos' in the learning process
• rarely lectures
• has an 'approachable' presence online
• is able to communicate effectively via text – they have a real 'presence' online
• supports collaborative forms of assessment, such as self- and peer-assessment

The place of the tutor in this learning community is complex. The tutor exists between the boundary of the institution, which s/he represents, and that of the learning community. In the learning community the tutor adopts the 'role' of tutor-participant. This implies at least two things. The first is a sharing of power with the students, where the tutor has to work at ensuring power is transferred to students in the community, who in turn have to come to trust the tutor in that process. Power is shared along a series of dimensions such as decision-making about the focus of the design of learning events, and assessment, which is collaborative, involving the students themselves, their peers and the tutor. The second aspect that this tutor-participant perspective implies is the concept of 'tutor as learner'. Although the tutor has particular expertise that s/he brings to the learning community as the representative of the institution, the tutor also presents her/himself as a learner, someone who is genuinely interested in learning and developing through participation in the community. The concept of the tutor as 'tutor-participant' is important as it signals to the participants that everyone on the course is a member of the learning community, and that the idea of community implies a different kind of learning relationship between tutor and student. Tutors and students relate in highly personal ways, and this relationship shapes a great deal of the learning on any such course. We shall return to the role of the tutor in Chapters 3, 4 and 5.

Quality assurance

Many teachers and organizational managers often have reservations about their institution offering completely virtual e-learning courses. Questions of quality arise. Many people ask whether online courses are of the same high quality as other courses offered by the university. How do we know if the people participating in the course are in fact the very people that have registered on the course, and how do we know if the people submitting course assignments have in fact written them?

Questions of this kind are inevitable and understandable, and as course providers we have to take account of them in the way we design and run e-learning courses. Institutional quality assurance mechanisms play a part in guaranteeing quality of all courses, including e-learning courses. In addition, each country may have its own national quality assurance mechanisms. In the UK we have the Quality Assessment Agency for Higher Education that assures quality nationally by a peer review process. A group of external university teachers and researchers visits a university department and examines the courses. The quality of the courses is assessed on a 24-point scale. The team assessed the quality of learning and teaching on the e-learning course discussed in this chapter (QAA 2001). In the general assessment process (the final score was a 24/24 'excellent') the Masters in E-Learning course was critically scrutinized. It was reviewed as an example of new forms of course delivery. In their evaluation, the assessors said that the course is a highly innovative and creative example of e-learning, and that it successfully combines all the high-quality elements of face-to-face tradition in a virtual learning setting. In mentioning this I am not wishing to praise our work, but rather to point to the need for external assessment in order to establish the credentials of e-learning courses that are designed around group and community perspectives.

Conclusion

The bridge between the theories that underpin the design of e-learning courses built on group and community learning principles, and the reality of implementation have been the focus of this chapter.

The design of e-learning group and community courses is likely to require a shift in the practice of many teachers, away from 'teacher-led' course designs to ones that aim to facilitate group work and the development of a community of learners. The place of the tutor in these new pedagogical designs is that of facilitator, resource person, participant, adviser and counsellor. Ensuring that the overall design is made explicit to the students, and that they understand the nature of the learning and teaching processes, is an important role for the tutor team. Direction on these matters starts before students begin their studies and continues by the provision of explicit, detailed guidance about each workshop and its associated phases and activities.

Students taking courses of this kind are likely to feel challenged in many ways, and will have to deconstruct their existing notions of teaching and learning and construct new ones in the light of their experience. How students relate to this form of e-learning, and the ways in which they experience learning in e-groups and communities are the focus of the next chapter.

Appendix: Detailed information sent to students about Workshop 1 MEd in E-Learning: 2003 intake

Workshop 1: Monday 6 October 2003 to Friday 23 January 2004 'Content and Participation'

Overview: An introduction to networked learning communities

The MEd programme starts by us considering our purposes for the MEd, from both the tutors' and participants' perspectives, and by developing processes and strategies for the development of the online learning community. The concept of action research in networked learning is considered, especially as it relates to reflective practice on this programme.

For this first workshop we have tried to develop a range of course work and assessment processes which, we hope, will reflect different learning purposes and offer a variety of experiences for us all to engage in.

Throughout the MEd there is considerable emphasis placed on experiential learning, accompanied by reflective processes aimed at helping you and your peers and tutor explore your experiences of learning in networked e-groups and e-communities. From these activities a great deal of learning occurs which we hope you will be able to take into your professional life/practice, and also use as a reference point on the MEd itself.

This workshop has four distinct phases which are designed to provide a scaffold for your studies. These are outlined below and are also presented separately on the MEd WebCT Home Page.

WebCT

In this workshop and throughout the MEd, we will be using the virtual learning environment (VLE) called WebCT. You will be introduced to the WebCT learning environment and should set aside time to become familiar with its main functions. Most of our activity (discussions, group work and so on) will take place in the WebCT discussion forums, which are text-based, asynchronous discussion areas. You will see these listed on the WebCT Home Page, under the section titled 'Content and Participation'. You enter these forums by clicking on the appropriate title of any one forum, which then takes you to the forum itself. Full information on using the forums can be found in the WebCT tutorials which you can download when you link into WebCT.

Learning sets

In Phases 1 and 3 of this workshop, you will work in small learning sets, made up of course participants and a tutor, where members can discuss their professional interests and develop a collaborative group assignment related to their professional interests and concerns. We choose to use the term 'learning set' rather than 'group' in order to emphasize a major purpose of these groupings, which is to offer you a place to come together to learn, share resources, discuss professional practice and generally support each other. We hope you will see the set as a place in which you 'learn', and not a place of competition.

Learning journal

During this workshop we ask you to start writing a learning journal of your experiences, problems, highs and lows. This is an opportunity for you take time out and reflect on what is happening on the course and what is happening to you. Details are given in the section on learning journal.

Planning your studies

Please take time to read about the course 'Content and Participation' for Workshop 1 so that you know what we are asking of you, and when the various activities take place. You will no doubt find it useful to put the dates for each phase of the workshop in your diary so that you can plan to give time to participating in them each week. You will gain most from this course by full and active participation. In particular, please read the sections relating to course work, which outline what you must do in order to gain a pass in this workshop.

Have you any queries?

We are always very pleased to help you in any way we can. If you have any queries about 'Content and Participation' and other academic issues, please do not hesitate to ask your learning set tutor. If you have any questions about using WebCT or other technical queries, please join the 'Technical' discussion forum. If you have any queries about your enrolment as a student at the university, please contact the course secretary.

The four phases of Workshop 1

Phase 1   Getting to know each other and sharing professional experiences

Starts: Monday 6 October 2003
Finishes: Friday 7 November 2003

Six group activities which take place in the discussion areas of WebCT:

Activity 1: Monday 6 October onwards

Focus: Arriving and saying 'hello'

We suggest you start by joining the general community discussion forum called 'Arrivals' and let us know that you have arrived. A short message saying that you have successfully managed to find your way into the forum would be sufficient to start with! Details of how to access and use the forums are given in the resources section of the MEd WebCT Home Page. There is a direct link to the forum from the MEd Home Page.

Activity 2: Monday 6 October to Friday 17 October

Focus: Joining your learning set and participating in discussions and activities; discussing the aims and educational philosophy of the Masters course

We have grouped course participants into learning sets for these activities – you will have been informed of which learning set you belong to when you joined the course. The purpose of learning sets is to give you a place to work with others in some depth and get to know members of the Masters community, including your tutor for this workshop. Learning sets allow you to develop trust between set members and to settle down into the WebCT environment.

Your purposes for taking the MEd in E-Learning, and your professional practice background.
The main activity is about sharing information of a personal nature with

other members of the course, and is also about 'listening', remembering and relating to what you read about others. It is the beginning of a process of talking about yourself – you as a person – that we hope will continue throughout the programme. It is, of course, up to you to decide how much you disclose to anyone in your learning set.

Process: Join the discussion forum in your WebCT learning set and start a new thread called 'Introduction to (your name)', and tell the learning set members about yourself, your personal background and professional interests.

- What are your reasons for taking the Masters in E-Learning? What do you hope to achieve in the two years of study? Why?
- Do you have any past experiences of networked/e-learning?

In this exercise, you might wish to draw on the material that you wrote for the pre-course activity.

In addition, tell us about any doubts, concerns and apprehensions you may have about studying for the Masters, or indeed about studying generally. We know that many of you are returning to study after some period away, so you may well wish to tell us of your feelings about this.

Please try to keep these introductions to about one page in length. Past experience tells us that lengthy forum entries are difficult to read and may be less appealing to your peers than shorter pieces. Please feel free to comment on each other's introductions, to ask questions, share understandings and generally communicate with each other.

Your personal biography

Please use the material from this activity to prepare a personal profile/ biography which you will present to the Masters community at the start of Phase 2, on Monday 10 November. This biography will then be placed in the 'Resources' section of the MEd WebCT Home Page, alongside your photograph. As well as any personal and professional information that you would like to share with course participants, you might like to provide your email contact address and any other information to help members contact you if necessary.

Please be assured that anything that you discuss on this course can only be read by other course participants and tutors. No one else has access to our WebCT environment. We encourage you to be as open as you feel able to, and to support other course members.

Activity 3: Monday 20 October to Friday 24 October 2003

Focus: Community and collaboration in e-learning

Our research into networked collaborative e-learning, and our experience of tutoring e-learners, has indicated to us that a major factor in sustaining networked e-learners is their need for community. Learning is a social process carried out in communities or groups where knowledge can be developed and negotiated in a particular learning or work-related context. To ensure this happens in networked e-learning environments requires us to design these environments in ways that support and sustain group learning and a sense of belonging to a community of like-minded (but necessarily different and divergent) people. In this activity we hope you will begin to form an understanding of this, and begin to see how it might work on the course over the next two years. Additionally, you will no doubt begin to see how it might work in your own professional practice.

On the Masters course, we view ourselves as a research learning community. You will be working throughout with others as a member of this research learning community. We believe that it is important in networked learning contexts to establish a sense of 'community' in order to help each member feel connected to other members, and to sustain the work of the learning sets.

Please read the paper by Mike Pedler on 'Learning Communities' which we sent you and consider what it says. You may wish to consider these questions: What do you find interesting in this paper? Why? How do you relate to the concept of a 'learning community'? Have you ever worked in one before? Do you find the concept attractive? Is there anything about the concept that you find unattractive?

Process: Join the discussion area in your WebCT learning set thread 'The Learning Community', and enter your comments. Once again, please do comment on each other's entries as and when you feel it is appropriate.

Activity 4: Monday 27 October to Friday 31 October 2003

Focus: You as a learner; your understanding of self-managed learning

In this activity we ask you to think about yourself as a learner and tell the community about your past learning experiences, what you like and do not like, how you 'go about learning' and so on. You might like to comment on whether you been involved in a formal learning course like this one before?

Please read the paper by David Boud on 'Autonomy in Learning' which we sent you. How do you relate to what David Boud says? Can you identify with it? How do you think autonomous learning relates to working in groups on this course?

Process: Join the discussion area in your WebCT learning set, in the thread called 'You as a Learner' and tell the set members about yourself as a learner and about your thoughts on the David Boud paper. Once again, please do comment on each other's entries as and when you feel it is appropriate.

Activity 5: Monday 3 November to Friday 7 November 2003

Focus: Action research as a form of learning on the MEd

The Masters in E-Learning is an action research degree. By this we mean that the work you carry out – both collaborative work and cooperative work – has an underpinning 'action research' basis to it. Action research (and action learning) is about critically reflecting on your learning and examining what you are doing *as you do it*. This is often described as an action research, or action learning, cycle where you proceed through a cycle of steps of imagining the problem, deciding how to examine it, examining it, reflecting on the examination, and engaging in a new cycle.

Background reading: please refer to the paper by Bridget Somekh and the paper by Winters which provide different yet complementary views on action research.

Process: Join the discussion area in the WebCT forum called 'Action Research'. Start a new thread in the forum by choosing 'compose' and enter your comments and ideas about action research as a form of learning. Once again, please do comment on each other's entries as and when you feel it is appropriate.

Using the chat areas: week of 3 November

Although we will mostly use asynchronous communications during the Masters, it will be useful to also use the synchronous (real time) chat facility from time to time, especially when you have to make decisions in your learning set, decide on the focus for your collaborative work and generally get together for quick discussion.

We will provide an introduction to the 'same time' chat facility in WebCT on the following dates this week. We will set up a new forum called 'Chat Training' where you can tell us which of these dates suits you. Each session will have a maximum of about 7/8 participants – so your first choice may not be available if you do not sign up for it soon!

WebCT Chat Training sessions:

Monday 3 November, 4 p.m.–5 p.m. GMT
Tuesday 4 November, 9.30 a.m.–10.30 a.m. GMT
Wednesday 5 November, 4 p.m.–5 p.m. GMT
Thursday 6 November, 7 p.m.–8 p.m. GMT

Activity 6: Monday 3 November to Friday 14 November 2003

Focus: Virtual learning

Here the focus is on learning in virtual environments. We are all very familiar with learning in conventional, face-to-face environments and we will all have our particular feelings about the appropriateness of learning in these environments. Does learning in virtual environments differ? If so, in what ways, and how might we begin to understand these differences?

This activity is designed to help you begin to think about this and discover if there are any significant differences.

Over the past few weeks you have been working in a virtual learning environment, perhaps for the first time in your life. Look back at the discussion threads and think about what has been happening in them: how would you characterize the learning in these threads? How did you feel when you were participating in the discussions and e-learning activities? Why? Do you feel there is a difference between the learning that has taken place in these environments compared with the learning that takes place in face-to-face environments? What is that difference about? What is the potential of this form of learning?

Process: Join the discussion area in the WebCT learning set. The thread is called 'Virtual Learning', and relate your experiences of learning in the Masters virtual learning environment.

Your biography

By the end of Phase 1, you should have prepared your biography and should be ready to present it to the Masters community members in Phase 2.

The learning journal

During Workshop 1, we ask you to keep a personal, reflective learning journal of your experiences and thoughts about networked e-learning. This might involve you in:

1) keeping notes and observations of activities on the MEd; your thoughts, feelings, reactions and observations about the learning processes and group work. This would be for your own personal use and would not be required to be handed in for 'assessment'. This learning journal should offer you the opportunity to reflect on your own learning experiences, and provide a vehicle for exploring your own experiences on the MEd. The journal should not just be descriptive, but we ask you to 'step back' from it and reflect on it in a critical way. This skill of being reflective and critical will, we hope, be something that you will develop throughout the course. Your tutor will say more about this in your learning set.

We hope that you will feel able to share some of this online with the members of the course during the Review of the Workshop; this is a valuable piece of 'content' which can be used to take you forward in your personal and professional development.

2)   from the above we ask you to hand in your **overview** or **meta-analysis** of the learning journal, indicating what the major learning issues were for you, how you handled them, how you thought other people related/learned/worked on the Masters, what the 'significant' learning events for you were and why. Please mention any other features that seemed of relevance to you and your personal learning. We cannot be prescriptive about the shape and content of this – it is very much up to you to decide how you want to approach this written, formal part of your journal. Your tutor will of course discuss it with you online.

The overview or meta-analysis should be submitted at the end of the Workshop 1, that is by Friday 23 January 2004. Two paper copies with the appropriate cover sheet are required. This is not assessed – but submission is a course requirement.

Phase 2   Plenary and discussions and networking

Starts Monday 10 November 2003
Ends Friday 21 November 2003

This two week phase is designed to help you consider and establish links between the following three interrelated course issues:

- group identity and the Masters degree
- personal identity
- the role of biography as a form of research

The purpose of the activities in this phase are to allow you to:

a)   begin to communicate with the other members of the Masters, share your biography, read theirs and begin to network;
b)   give you the opportunity to reflect on your own personal and professional identity. By reflecting on a range of biographies you will be accessing a range of experiences and information that may be of help and relevance to you in constructing your own identity, and of understanding that of others in this community;
c)   appreciate that biography can be a form of research that may inform your understanding of the relationship between learners' identities and their learning.

Please note: The content and processes of this phase may be drawn upon by members of any of the learning sets in Phase 3 activities and beyond.

Activity 1: Sharing biographies/personal profiles

Process: Join the new forum called 'Plenary' and start a new thread called 'Biography of (your name e.g. "Biography of Jamie Nelson")' and paste-in your personal biography (as an ordinary text entry, not a Word document please) for others to read. Take time to read the biographies of the members of the other learning sets and get to know the members of those learning sets. You might wish to ask members some questions about their profile/biography, or share experiences with them.

Phase 3   The collaborative project

Starts: Monday 24 November 2003
Finishes: Friday 2 January 2004

This phase has two major purposes:

1   learning to work in collaborative learning sets in virtual learning environments;
2   production of an assignment or 'product' as an outcome of the collaborative learning.

You should rejoin your original learning set for this work, in the new discussion forums set up for Phase 3. Your learning set tutor will help the set in carrying out its work.

The collaborative group assignment is due to be submitted to the other learning sets by Monday 5 January 2004.

1   Collaborative group project assignment

Each learning set chooses a topic, which they wish to collectively work on, relating to some aspect of networked collaborative e-learning. Phases 1 and 2 emphasized the relationship and tensions between the personal and the social in learning for personal and professional development. This should provide you with a starting point for your collaborative project.

Possible topics might include the following (but please negotiate a suitable topic with your learning set members and tutor):

• networked e-learning groups and communities
• virtual learning
• self-managed learning
• action research as a form of learning

Your tutor will help the members of the set decide on a suitable topic, if required.

The focus of the collaborative work will be on both the process of group work, with reflection on how the learning set works together and supports each other, and the product, which you will collectively produce.

Some of the purposes that we envisage for the collaborative project are given below:

- to give you the opportunity to work with others on a project which you all wish to explore/investigate;
- to provide you with an experience of working collaboratively in 'virtual' learning spaces. In Phase 4 of this workshop you will be asked to reflect on that experience and draw out some learning points for yourself and for your learning set;
- to help you begin to think about the dynamics of group work in virtual learning environments. By dynamics we mean aspects such as how you organize yourselves; who does what on the project (and maybe also why), and so on. Dynamics of learning groups is a topic of interest for those involved in running networked learning events. It is also a research issue, and can cover all sorts of issues, including gender issues;
- to help you think about the protocols that may have to be established for the learning set to work effectively, for example how often do you anticipate being available each week to communicate about your work? How often do you wish to have chat sessions? You can plan in advance for chat sessions once you have decided on an overall structure for the completion of the project.

We are sure that you will have other ideas about working together that you might want to share with the members of your learning set.

Each set should choose a meaningful task to work on, and it should be a topic that can actually be carried out in the time available (approximately five weeks: so a relatively **small-ranging, well-focused project** should be chosen). Each learning set will present their work to the other sets in WebCT.

This work requires each learning set to carrying out the following (we suggest you meet with your tutor in the WebCT 'chat' area to discuss the task and decide on a focus for the work):

- Set up a time for a chat session early in the week beginning 24 November, and formulate the focus for the task. Make sure it is well defined and is 'do-able' in the time period.
- Decide who will do what in order to achieve the final product.
- Pay attention to the way in which the set will work and support each other during the process.
- Decide on how you will put together the final product (this will require one person finally to put it together).
- Decide how you will present it to the other learning set.
- Formally reflect on the processes of the group during the period of the collaborative project.

Time-scale:

- Complete the work by 2 January 2004.
- Present your work to the other learning sets from 5 January onwards (we will set up a new forum for this).

Phase 4   Review and assessment of course work

Starts: Monday 5 January 2004
Finishes: Friday 23 January 2004

This phase is concerned with collaboratively reviewing and assessing each participant's contribution to the completion of the collaborative project in each learning set. Please see the details below concerning Course Requirements and Assessment.

The Workshop 1 course requirements and 'assessment'

There are three course requirements for Workshop 1:

1   The collaborative project 'product'

Each learning set must submit their collaborative project as a course requirement. At the front of the document there should be a statement from each member of the learning set stating clearly what work/ contribution they made to the production of the collaborative project. Each contribution should be approximately equal in time and effort and quality of content, amounting to about 2–3 thousand words or the equivalent.
  Time-scale:

- Complete the work by 2 January 2004
- Present your work to the other learning sets from 5 January onwards. (We will set up a new forum for this. You should compose a new thread to present your learning set project and attach it to the thread, or provide the URL if it is produced as a website. By 'present' we mean make the collaborative project document available to the other learning sets, and answer any questions and discussion issues that may arise about it.)

Two paper copies of the collaborative assignment should be sent to the university (see below for address). They should be posted on or before Friday 23 January 2004.
  One person in each learning set will have to collate all the material for this collaborative project and submit it on behalf of the learning set.

Please Note: Each learning set member should individually complete and sign the Assignment Cover Sheet and post it to us.

2   Personal, peer and tutor review ('assessment') of the collaborative project processes and work

In common with all other assignments on this course this assignment is not graded. As long as you fulfil the course requirement and submit the assessment document as described, you will be awarded a pass on this aspect of the course work.

There are four components to your self-assessment. These are:

1   product achievement
2   communication skill
3   social relationships
4   reflective skills

Fuller details are attached, and your tutor will explain the components in your learning set, where the whole process can be discussed with members of the set and the tutor. We recommend that you write up to about 300 words under each heading. Contributions from your two peer reviewers might be up to 200 words per heading. Your tutor will also add his/her short review.

Two copies of the full review from the WebCT forum (your own, peers' and tutor reviews) should be submitted by the end of Workshop 1.

Please attach the appropriate cover sheet to the front of the copies.

3   The learning journal

The final course requirement is submission of an overview or meta-analysis of the issues arising from your personal learning journal which you have been asked to keep during Workshop 1. Two copies are due by the end of Workshop 1, that is it should be submitted by Friday 23 January 2004. It is likely that this document will vary in length depending on the extent of the issues emerging about your learning that you wish to address, but a guideline is about up to 1,000 words in length.

Please attach the appropriate cover sheet to the two copies.

3

The experience of e-learning groups and communities

Collaboration is the focus

The previous chapter considered the design principles for establishing e-learning courses based on groups and communities. This chapter turns to the important concern of the students' experience of learning in e-groups and communities.

In designing for e-learning groups and communities, we are encouraging students and tutors to engage in meaningful practices through cooperative and collaborative learning processes. We are trying to ensure that knowledge developed is demonstrated in the context of the student's professional practice. In doing this, we have to develop a climate where commenting on each other's work, and giving and receiving feedback, is an integrated and normal part of the community's day-to-day existence. In this form of learning, there is a high degree of experiential learning (for example, learning about working in distributed problem-based learning groups by taking part in such groups), and students are encouraged to be reflective and use this as a major source of learning (Boud and Walker 1998; Moon 1999).

In achieving this, the collaborative student has to reconsider their approach to learning and move away from seeing learning largely as an individual cognitive process, to one that is socially based, that requires dialogue and negotiation with other students and tutors, and which is about developing new ways of building knowledge. This can be highly challenging for all involved, but as we shall see later in this chapter, it offers novel and exciting opportunities to work closely with others and share practices. Learning of this kind produces high-quality learning processes and outcomes.

To achieve this, the collaborative student is encouraged to:

- learn together with others through discussion, debate, questioning, problem-solving and supporting each other;

- develop their own questions and search for their own solutions;
- share resources, knowing that this will be of benefit to everyone;
- share the learning task, bringing different viewpoints, skills and knowledge;
- cooperate and reciprocate cooperation;
- not compete: excessive competition leads to self-centred learning;
- understand that they can have full and equal access to academic rewards: everyone can win;
- understand the educational benefits of group work;
- understand that they can 'construct' their own knowledge and will be rewarded for doing so;
- tolerate and support multiple perspectives;
- enjoy diversity.

The experience of e-learning in groups and communities

How do students experience this? The quality of the student's learning experience is possibly the central issue of importance in assessing the potential of e-learning in higher education, and in particular in assessing distributed networked e-learning of the kind described here. We need to understand how students experience learning that takes place in e-groups and e-communities. The students' perspective helps us develop new conceptualizations of learning, and from this we can develop new conceptualizations of teaching. Our aim is to get better understandings of the educational process, and from this improve the effectiveness of teachers and students.

This section presents a detailed analysis of students' views of e-learning. Particular focus is given to their evaluation of the quality of work in the e-learning groups (or learning sets), and of the collaborative group process in the sets. Student perceptions of the quality of work carried out in the learning sets and on the course generally give us an important indication of the educational benefits of this form of collaborative group and community online work.

There is some equivocation on the benefits of online e-learning in the literature. Some researchers report positively on the quality of online e-learning (Banks, Lally and McConnell 2003; Dirckinck-Holmfeld and Fibiger 2002; Goodyear, Jones et al. 2004; Goodyear, Banks et al. 2004; Salmon 2000). Others suggest the medium is impersonal (Keisler 1992; Wegerif 1998), that it is too difficult to engage some students meaningfully and productively in the online learning process (Jones 1998, 2000; Ragoonaden and Bordeleau 2000; Tansley and Bryson 2000) and that the medium makes no contribution to learning (Veen et al. 1998).

Research into computer-mediated communications (Hiltz 1984, 1986; Henri 1992; McConnell 1988), audio-teleconferencing (Short et al. 1976), shared screen teleconferencing (McConnell 1986) networked learning (Goodyear, Banks *et al*. 2004) and social networks (Haythornthwaite 2002) has focused on user experience and perceptions. Particular attention has been given to perceptions of the process of the meetings, the eventual outcomes and products of the meetings, and the social presence of the meetings. These characteristics have been examined to help compare these technology-mediated meetings with more conventional face-to-face meetings, and to examine the unique characteristics of learning via these media.

In the following sections, students' experiences of learning in e-groups and communities are examined with reference to these three characteristics. The data was collected from a questionnaire distributed to students after they had completed their e-learning courses.

Questionnaire methodology and analysis

The questionnaire was developed from three main sources:

- the literature on collaborative learning and computer-supported cooperative learning;
- the literature on socio-cultural theories of learning;
- my own and colleagues' experiences of designing and tutoring e-learning courses.

The questionnaire covered a wide range of issues concerning students' experiences of learning in collaborative and cooperative e-learning groups and communities. These are listed in Table 3.1.

Table 3.1   Issues Covered in the Questionnaire

Quality of discussions/work in the learning sets

Group collaborative processes in the learning sets

Collaborative processes in the large community

Collaborative assessment processes

The contribution of this kind of learning to students' personal learning

The action research/learning process

The role of the tutor in e-learning courses

Students who had taken the two-year Masters in E-Learning were invited to complete the questionnaire after they had finished the course. A total of 50 students out of 59 returned the questionnaire, which is a response rate of 85 per cent.

Most of the items in the questionnaire were closed, in which students were asked to respond on a five-point Likert scale of the following kind:

Strongly Agree, Agree, Neither Agree nor Disagree, Disagree, Strongly Disagree. Open-ended questions were used to allow students to comment on their answer or provide additional information.

The results provide a comprehensive view of the experience of learning in e-groups and communities over a six-year period of time, covering 20 separate e-learning workshops each lasting between four and eight months. The respondents were therefore students who spent a considerable amount of time studying in e-learning groups and communities, and who were able to develop deep and authentic insights into the experience. Their views are therefore extremely important and valuable in helping us understand what it is like to study in this way.

Analysis

In presenting the data, the responses to the five-point Likert scale have been simplified in order to make it easier to assimilate the data. In doing this, an estimate of data below and above a certain criterion observed is provided by the calculation of simple percentages (Choy 2003). Half the value of the 'Not Sure' category is redistributed to the 'Strongly Agree' and 'Agree' categories, and half is redistributed to the 'Disagree' and 'Strongly Disagree' categories. For example, if the percentage distributions to the hypothetical statement 'I enjoy working in groups' are as follows:

	SA	A	NS	D	SD
I enjoy working in groups	5%	10%	20%	60%	5%

we can provide the following simple calculation:

Agree   = 15% + half of 20% (i.e. 10%) = 25%
Disagree   = 65% + half of 20% (i.e. 10%) = 75%

The percentage responses can be interpreted in the following way:

80% or more = very high percentage value
70%–80%   = high percentage value
60%–69%   = moderately high percentage value
50%–59%   = moderate percentage value
40%–49%   = moderately low percentage value
39% or less = low percentage value

In the above hypothetical example we can say that a low percentage of students indicate that they enjoy working in groups, while a high percentage indicate they do not enjoy working in groups.

Learning in e-groups and communities: students' views

Process

The process of group work is defined by such attributes as the student's ability to have an in-depth discussion, raise points, contribute to discussions and group work, and generally participate as fully and openly as possible. Table 3.2 shows students' perceptions of the processes of group work.

Central to the educational purposes of this form of networked e-learning is the requirement that students engage in dialogue, discussion and communication as a way of fostering deep and meaningful learning. From these results we can see that a very high percentage of students (93 per cent) think that it is possible to have an in-depth discussion online. They

Table 3.2 The Process of Group Work

	Agree	Disagree
It is not possible to have an in-depth discussion online	7%	93%
It is often too difficult to follow the thread of a discussion	24%	76%
The asynchronous nature of discussions often means that by the time I get round to responding, the discussion has moved on to a new area/topic	59%	41%
I often go back and look over/review the discussion thread	78%	22%
I can get my ideas heard and discussed quite easily	80%	20%
I feel I have not contributed as much as I would have liked to the discussions	68%	32%
Compared with face-to-face meetings, I feel I contribute more to online discussions	40%	60%
I feel I can communicate as effectively online as I can face-to-face	67%	33%
I find there are just too many discussions occurring at the same time for me to keep track of them all	59%	41%
It is hard to find the time to participate adequately in the discussions	87%	13%
We need more pressure put on us to take part in the discussions	56%	44%
Having to produce a course assignment gets in the way of the discussions	53%	47%

report often going back over discussion threads to review the discussions and debates. However, some of them find it too difficult to follow the thread of discussions, and a moderate number say that by the time they are ready to respond, the discussion has moved on to new ground (although 41 per cent do not think this).

Being able to get your ideas 'heard' and discussed in any learning context is vital to ensuring you feel engaged. This acts as a positive motivator for students and contributes to maintaining their presence in the e-groups and to their cognitive development and socio-emotional well-being. A very high percentage of students say they can get their ideas discussed quite easily in the online groups, even though only one-third of them feel they have contributed as much as they would have liked to the discussions. This latter point may be related to the phenomenon of multiple, simultaneous discussions in online environments. Although the phenomenon can act positively by allowing multiple voices to be heard, which can support diversity and difference (McConnell 1997; Hodgson and Reynolds 2005), it does mean that students often find they do not have the time to participate in all online activities. This can lead to feelings of guilt about not contributing to the work of the group or community. Students need to develop a robust and practical relationship to this phenomenon to ensure they do not withdraw from the group's activities due to feeling unable to contribute as fully as they think is necessary. The open nature of e-learning group work needs to be managed sensitively by the members of the group and the tutor. The community needs to work at developing strategies and processes that support the purposes of the community and what it is trying to achieve. In the context of this study, the groups and communities strived to promote and support as much diversity and difference as possible. At times they faced difficulties in pursuing this, but (as we shall see in later chapters) rose to the challenges this brought and addressed the issues in an attempt to engage and support all the members of the community.

Students were asked to compare their contributions in face-to-face meetings with those of online meetings. Two-thirds feel they can communicate as effectively online as they can in face-to-face contexts, which is a very positive result that bodes well for the potential of this medium for supporting learning based on dialogue and communication. Forty per cent feel that, compared with face-to-face meetings, in online contexts they contribute more. This result does not suggest that the remaining 60 per cent of students feel they do not contribute online: we know they do. They feel that this medium does not necessarily allow them to contribute more. But, for many, the medium seems to allow them to make greater contributions compared with face-to-face contexts. This may be related to many factors, such as the openness of the medium, the possibility for multiple simultaneous discussions and activities, greater opportunities for people of different genders to have a voice online, and so on.

Finding the time adequately to contribute to online discussions and group work is clearly an important issue for these students. They are all part-time students, and most have busy and demanding jobs. A very high number say that it is difficult to contribute adequately to their satisfaction. Finding a solution to this is not an easy or simple matter. When asked if they think more pressure should be put on them (by the tutor) to take part in discussions, opinion is divided, with a moderate number thinking this may help. But in the context of adult learning where there is openness and diversity in the learning community, and where students manage their own learning and support others in their learning, it is perhaps antithetical to ask one member of the community to take responsibility for encouraging participation. It has to come from the community members themselves. They have to manage this process, alongside the tutor.

A final issue in considering group process is the relationship between the online discussions and the production of course assignments. In the design of the course, we anticipated that the two would complement each other. The discussions and online group work would support and help the development of course assignments, and vice versa. It is not clear if this is happening. Opinion is divided on whether the production of course assignments gets in the way of discussions and other group work. Since distributing this questionnaire, we have redesigned certain aspects of the course to try to ensure the discussions relate more closely to the production of course assignments. But many online discussions have a purpose of their own, unrelated to the act of producing an assignment and anyone designing e-learning should not be too quick to make everything utilitarian in this way.

Outcomes/product

The post-course questionnaire asked students about their perceptions of the outcomes and products (production of course assignments, ideas picked up, amount learned and so on) of the group work and discussions (Table 3.3).

The first and perhaps most important thing to be said here is that students are in nearly total agreement that the online discussions are central to the outcome of their course of study, and a very high number say that the online discussions have helped them produce their assignments This is an important finding as it tells us that the social constructionist design of courses like this 'works' for most of these students. The central role of discussion, dialogue and debate, and other forms of communication that are considered so important in the literature on constructionism (for example Hodgson and Watland 2003; Packer and Goicoechea 2000; Salomon and Perkins 1998) are here verified by students to be important in the eventual outcome of their learning. We can be assured that networked e-learning course designs built on these ideas do result in

Table 3.3   Outcomes and Productivity of Groups

	Agree	Disagree
When needed, I can give time to preparing thoughtful contributions to the discussions	84%	16%
I feel online discussions can be more productive than face-to-face discussions	56%	44%
The depth of analysis possible online is not as great as in a face-to-face environment	21%	79%
I like to share information and ideas with others	100%	0%
I feel the discussion forums have given me the information/ideas that I needed	75%	25%
The online discussions have really helped me produce my assignment	72%	28%
The online discussions are not central to the course	9%	91%

quality learning outcomes that are very acceptable to the students and their needs.

Similarly, a very high percentage of students think that the depth of analysis possible online is as great as that achievable in face-to-face environments. This finding flies in the face of other research suggesting it is not possible to engage students meaningfully and productively online (Jones 1998, 2000; Ragooonaden and Bordeleau 2000; Tansley and Bryson 2000) and that the medium does not contribute to learning (Veen *et al.* 1998). The experience of these students indicates that it is possible to achieve a high level of analysis in online group discussions and group work, even though they are not working together face-to-face. They are, however, not saying that online group work is necessarily more productive than face-to-face work. The results of the questionnaire are equivocal on this point.

Finally, all the students enjoy sharing information and ideas with others online, and three-quarters feel the discussion forums give them the information and ideas they need. And when needed, most feel they can give time to preparing thoughtful contributions to the discussions (see Table 3.3).

Social presence

Social presence, which is the way we feel about who we are communicating or working with, the 'closeness' to others, the level of anxiety felt in the groups and so on, is another important feature of collaborative learning.

Although it is not always necessary for students to get on well with those with whom they are collaborating (Axelrod 1990), a positive social presence is important in ensuring the well-being of a group. If students enjoy discussing issues in the groups and community, they are likely to participate fully and feel really engaged in the learning process. Very high percentages of students say they enjoy the online discussions and are always excited to see what is happening in them. However, they feel that some people do tend to dominate discussions, although students can set up new discussion threads to avoid this. In relation to this, though slightly tangentially, it is interesting to see that students are divided on the emphasis given to tutor comments in discussions. In a learning community it might be argued that what the tutor says should not be given any special or particular status compared with other community members. Everyone's views are worthy of being heard.

Getting an acceptable balance between a serious and focused academic discussion and one that is perhaps 'light' enough to be enjoyable to take part in is not easy. Over two-thirds of students think that the discussions in the e-groups are not too serious; nearly one-third think they are and that the community needs to lighten up a little (see Table 3.4). Those students who have a high need to be very academic in their approach to online work may not always be attractive to others who are less at home with an academic tradition or less willing to participate in debates on theoretical issues. We have found that different kinds of group work, and different forms of discussion and debate are needed to engage everyone at different times. This is another aspect of designing for diversity in the learning process.

When the balance of group participation and group work is not given attention, students may begin to feel isolated in their studies. Here, nearly

Table 3.4   Social Presence

	Agree	Disagree
Some people tend to dominate discussions	77%	23%
Tutor comments/entries are usually given more attention than those from anyone else	46%	54%
I am always excited to see what is happening in the conferences	74%	26%
I enjoy discussing issues in the conferences	93%	7%
The discussions are often too serious – we need to lighten up a little!	31%	69%
I often feel vulnerable 'exposing' myself/ideas in the discussions	41%	59%
I have often felt isolated	31%	69%

nearly one-third express the view that they have felt isolated at some time, and similar numbers have felt vulnerable exposing themselves and their ideas in the discussions. This is a concern, although it is perhaps inevitable when studying online. And it has to be said that it is certainly not peculiar to learning online: students can feel isolated and vulnerable in face-to-face contexts too. Feelings of isolation can be alleviated to some degree by designing group work in ways that pay attention to the individual within the group. If someone is feeling isolated, the members of the group always, in my experience, try to find out why this is happening and see if anything can be done to help or to ensure it is less likely to happen in the future. However, we should not have a simplistic or overly romantic view of e-learning groups and communities. They are as much places of conflict, struggle and isolation as they are places of harmony and social conformity (Hodgson and Reynolds 2005; Greener and Perriton 2005). We have to accept that these are social places, and that the full span of social activity takes place in them, 'positive' and 'negative'. Looking after students is, however, central to each group or community, and this should constantly be at the forefront of our minds when designing and running these events.

Group collaborative processes in the learning sets

The previous sections considered students' perceptions of the process, outcomes and productivity, and social presence of work in the learning sets. This section will consider perceptions of group collaborative processes in the learning sets.

The constructionist design of e-learning courses requires students to work together and collaborate in a variety of ways and on a variety of activities of benefit to them individually and collectively. In designing for this, it should not be taken for granted that they will easily adapt to this form of learning and participate in it. Great care has to be taken to foster collaboration in the learning sets, and to produce positive incentives that encourage, support and reward the act of collaboration. Collaborative learning is not a selfless pursuit. It is not an act of unconditional giving. It is by and large a very practical pursuit with the purpose of promoting quality learning processes and outcomes which, when it works well, can be seen by those involved to be of real benefit to them.

Organizing students in small learning sets where the focus is on sharing, supporting, discussing, collaborating and carrying out self-peer-tutor assessment is a deliberate attempt to scaffold their learning and develop a sense of shared purpose and community.

What is at play when students work in collaborative groups and learning sets? What factors contribute to someone's willingness to work collaboratively in e-learning settings? In order to answer these questions it will be useful to understand the ways in which learning sets are formed.

Forming learning sets is an important process in the life of students and tutors on these e-courses. It is a time when students and tutors make decisions about who they would like to work with, and why. A variety of methods can be used to assist in this process. For example, we devote two online weeks to set formation, with a special area set aside in the VLE for this activity. The process starts with a brainstorm activity devoted to sharing ideas on methods of forming the sets. The results of the brainstorm are often summarized and presented in the forum by a tutor or student and then discussed by the community. For example, members may wish to congregate on the basis of shared topics of interest, or to work with people they have not worked with before. Or they may wish to work with other members who wish to take some risks in their learning. Although it is important to try to find a method that everyone feels comfortable with, it is sometimes necessary to try several different methods as a way of ensuring different voices are heard.

The outcome of these activities leads to the community agreeing on one of several methods for forming sets. New threads are set up, and members cluster in possible learning set formations and assess the likelihood that the clusters will 'work' in practice. This again involves members of the new sets in dialogue and negotiation, and often some change of membership occurs as a result of this. Finally, the membership of sets is agreed, and the members choose a name for the set. New forums are formed for each set. These forums are open to all members of the community, but non-set members are asked not to write in them but only to read and observe.

This process of set formation raises some important questions. In making choices about how to form learning sets, does it matter if students know the other members of the set, and do members of the set have to share common interests in order for them to be able to work effectively together? Students were asked about this in the questionnaire, and the results show that they are divided on whether or not their willingness to collaborate depends on who the other members of the set are. Almost equal numbers think this affects their willingness to work collaboratively as think it does not matter. Similarly, they are equally divided over whether the members of the set need to be interested in similar areas of study. However, there is a slight shift in their willingness to work together, with nearly two-thirds saying it depends on how well they know other group members (see Table 3.5).

From their experience of working in collaborative learning sets, students are able to make judgements about other aspects of collaborating in sets that they bring to the learning set formation process. So for example, they nearly all believe that it is important that the work they put into collaborating with members of the sets is reciprocated. This is an important issue that has to be faced in collaborative learning: reciprocation is central to sustaining a culture of sharing and collaborating. If a

Table 3.5   Students' Willingness to Work Collaboratively in the Learning Sets

	Agree	Disagree
My willingness to work collaboratively in my *learning set depends on:*		
the level of participation of others in the group	79%	21%
how well I know the other group members	61%	39%
the degree of 'openness' in the group	96%	4%
the degree to which my efforts are reciprocated by others in the group	91%	7%
the way in which the tutor facilitates the group	75%	25%
whether we are all interested in similar areas of study	50%	50%
who the other group members are	51%	49%

student's efforts are not reciprocated, they may withdraw them in the future. Similarly, the level of participation of others in the group is also another very important factor, and can shape the dynamics of any collaborative group. The degree of 'openness' in the sets is also extremely important, as is the way in which the tutor facilitates the group.

When the community takes part in the learning set formation process, each member (student and tutor alike) brings issues such as these to play and may use them as a way of judging their peers and tutor. Forming learning sets can therefore be a demanding process to carry out effectively. It is perhaps the one time on courses of this kind when members of the community are forced to make judgements about their peers and tutors based on who they like and who they feel they can get on with.

Organization, learning processes and well-being of learning sets

The next section is divided into three components that are important when considering the group collaborative learning process, namely the way in which the sets are organized, the learning processes that occur in them, and the support and well-being of the members of the sets. Students were asked about these issues in the questionnaire, and the results are considered in turn below.

Organization of learning sets

The organization of e-learning into groups and communities requires considerable advance planning and careful course design to make it a reality. Does the arrangement of learning in small groups work? Are learning sets needed? Could the work of the students and tutors be conducted in one large community setting?

When asked about these issues, students show that they have very strong views on them. Their experience tells them that learning sets do work and are needed, and that the possibility of organizing all learning in the larger, 'whole' community setting would not be an acceptable method of working (see Table 3.6).

Organizing all learning in the large community groups does, however, have a certain appeal as it offers the opportunity for everyone to network and create a diverse working space that should, in theory, support everyone's needs. We have occasionally tried to organize learning in the large community and have experimented with this arrangement in order to understand the dynamics of collaborative learning in larger settings. The result has often been exciting, but very challenging. The possibility for high levels of creative thinking within the community is enhanced: ideas abound and are shared in an intoxicating and sometimes chaotic way. Students and tutors form clusters on the basis of emerging personal and professional interests. To this extent, this arrangement works extremely well. But the information overflow is often too much to handle, and the speed at which

Table 3.6 The Organization of Learning Sets

	Agree	Disagree
To make the learning sets really work well, students MUST choose the members of the group	28%	72%
The process we use to form learning sets is vital to their success	40%	60%
I feel I can work with anyone in a learning set: who the members are does not matter	80%	20%
I think learning sets could work well without a tutor in them	37%	63%
Learning sets need more direction from the tutor	50%	50%
I would prefer us not to have learning sets, but for us all to work as one large group	2%	98%
We need to change the members of learning sets more often	17%	83%
When we are not 'forced' to collaborate we often don't bother	45%	55%

the discussion threads develop, with members opening new threads in order to organize their ideas and invite others to discuss them, is extremely difficult to manage and navigate. Often clusters break off and set up completely new forums and are in effect breaking away from the community.

The potential for creativity within chaos can be powerful and attractive (Greener and Perriton 2005; You 1993). We have found that managing such an arrangement in an online setting such as this is too time consuming for all involved, and can sometimes lead to students and tutors feeling isolated and lost. However, it could work in other settings where members of the community are willing to devote time to managing the process and engaging in the creative chaos that can often emerge.

We have seen that students feel they can, on the whole, work with anyone in the learning sets. Who the members are does not seem to matter too much to the majority. There is, however, some division of opinion on the importance of the way in which the sets are formed: 60 per cent of students think that the way they are formed does not influence the success of the sets, while 40 per cent think it does. Courses of this kind need to be organized so that students are given the opportunity of changing membership of learning sets at the start of workshops. The vast majority of students think that the members of learning sets do not need to be changed more often than they are at present (see Table 3.6).

Finally, what do students think about the role of the tutor in the learning sets? Do collaborative learning groups need a tutor? The experience of these students suggests that the question is open for debate. Two-thirds think learning sets could not work well without a tutor, while one-third think they could. On the issue of the tutor having to provide strong direction to members of the set to ensure they collaborate, opinion is divided. Nearly half feel that if they were not 'forced' to collaborate they may not bother, while just over half feel that they would collaborate no matter what. These views are interesting, and indicate a degree of ambiguity in the perception of the importance of the tutor in collaborative learning groups. If learning sets are organized so as to allow maximum freedom in the choice of their activities, it might be argued that the tutor role will in some ways be marginal. The tutor may perhaps act as a facilitator or resource provider. This suggests members of the set are in control of the focus of their learning and can be left to manage the process of their work. But two-thirds of the students think the sets need a tutor. So from the perspective of the students, the role of the tutor is still something of an open question.

In conclusion to this section we can say that student views on the organization of learning sets are not always as clear-cut as are their views on other aspects of networked collaborative learning. Although students are in very strong agreement that learning sets are needed to support the collaborative process, and they feel they have learned a great deal in the sets and that they are creative places to work in, they are divided on other issues to do with the formation of sets, the role of the tutor in them, their need to choose and know the members of the sets and so on.

Learning processes in the sets

All students think that organizing learning so that it takes place in learning sets is a good way of running collaborative e-courses. However, a moderately low percentage of them (40 per cent) say that it has been difficult for them to adjust to working collaboratively (Table 3.7). This is perhaps not surprising, given that most students have been brought up to think of learning as a purely personal act. However, the rest of the students appear to find working in these ways relatively easy. Irrespective of whether it has been difficult to adjust to collaborative learning processes, students are very clear on one thing: the majority prefer to learn in the collaborative company of their peers. However, one in five students thinks that they learn better on their own. It is regrettable that the questionnaire did not ask these students to say why.

Very high numbers say they have learned a great deal in the sets, and high numbers think the sets have worked well for them. A very low percentage of them say the sets have not worked well for them. Unfortunately we do not have any information as to why they hold this view.

Students were asked about the productivity of sets and the achievement of learning goals in them. A high percentage of them think the sets are very productive, and a very high percentage say the sets achieve their goals. High-quality learning in groups and communities is often characterized by close, intense relationships, and these are often built on learning processes that empower students to take risks and open themselves to the members of

Table 3.7 Group Learning Processes

	Agree	Disagree
I think learning sets are a good way of organizing the course	100%	0%
It has been difficult for me to get used to working collaboratively	40%	60%
I feel I learn better on my own	23%	77%
I have learned a great deal in my learning sets	93%	7%
The learning sets have not worked very well for me	23%	77%
My learning set(s) have been very productive	79%	21%
My learning set(s) have achieved their goals	85%	15%
I have noticed others in my learning set(s) 'taking risks' in what they discuss/mention online	76%	24%
I feel the collaborative learning process has made me more likely to 'expose' myself/ideas online	76%	24%

the group. If relationships of this kind can be facilitated, we can be reasonably sure that good-quality learning will ensue. When asked about this, three-quarters of the students say they have observed their peers taking risks in what they have discussed or worked on in their sets, and similar numbers indicate that they have personally felt empowered to be open, and expose themselves and their ideas in the sets. This indicates that the collaborative learning processes that underpin learning in these sets are highly effective from the perspective of those taking part in them.

We can say that students' views on the group learning processes show that the majority, on the whole, are very satisfied with the learning processes in these online learning sets. There is, however, a persistent minority who are not always satisfied and it would have been extremely useful to know why this was the case, but unfortunately the questionnaire did not ask them to say why. It would be important in any future studies of this kind to ensure students are given the opportunity to substantiate their answers with written comments.

Support and well-being

Giving and receiving support, and the feeling of 'well-being', are central to the life of effective collaborative groups (Haythornthwaite 2002; McGrath 1990). In order to gauge the presence of this in these e-learning contexts, students were asked about the support that individuals require in order to be able to work effectively in e-learning groups, and their feelings of well-being when working in the e-groups.

Nearly every student thinks their peers have been concerned for the well-being of the members of the sets, and high percentages say they have supported the members of their sets as much as they were able to, and have been supported by others in turn (Table 3.8). A very high percentage

Table 3.8   Support and Well-being

	Agree	Disagree
I think learning set members have been concerned for the well-being of each other	99%	1%
I feel I have supported learning set members as much as I can	73%	27%
I feel I have been supported by others in the learning sets	88%	12%
I feel we have been successful in developing a sense of community online	88%	12%
If my online contributions are not responded to, I feel I am not valued	82%	18%

feel they have been successful in developing a sense of community online. Offering support to one's peers and looking after each other's well-being takes time in face-to-face contexts, and probably more time in e-learning contexts. So it is gratifying that the design of these e-learning courses encourages students to look after the community in these ways, and ensures most students are supported.

Collaborative processes in the large community

The organization of learning by the use of small groups, or learning sets, is a practical arrangement designed to make it possible for students to participate in forms of learning that develop from the presence of strong intimate ties. When students work in close collaboration on shared topics, the communication overhead (i.e. the effort required to sustain textual communications) is high and can best be dealt with in small groups. Small groups also encourage high levels of risk-taking and openness because members can develop trust in each other.

But in arranging learning in this way we run the danger of fragmenting the larger community. We have already seen that the students are not in favour of all their learning occurring in the larger community settings. But opportunities are needed for all members of the community to come together to develop and sustain the large community. This may involve making decisions about the role of the larger community, planning their collective work, reviewing and evaluating the workshops and planning for future ones, forming new learning sets, sharing experiences and insights, and participating in shared activities where access to a wider set of views and opinions may be useful, such as in e-seminars and discussions.

All of these activities provide an alternative to the very focused and highly productive work carried out in the sets. But they may also detract from that work and may appear too time-consuming and unfocused for some. A balance has to be struck between the two, but it is not easy to do so. On these courses, two-thirds of students think this balance has been achieved (Table 3.9), but the other third clearly think it has not. When asked if they would like more opportunities to work with others in the large community, over two-thirds of students said no. At the same time, a very high number indicated that they would not prefer all the work and discussions to take place in the small learning sets. These apparently contradictory views may be due to their feeling they do not have the necessary time to devote to both the large community and the smaller learning sets. Indeed, two-thirds feel they have not had sufficient time to participate in the activities of the work of the community. Consequently perhaps, almost as many say they enjoy working in the large community as say they do not.

Despite this, a very high number of students feel the community meetings are useful for carrying out general group discussions and work,

Table 3.9   The Collaborative Process in the 'Community' Groups

	Agree	**Disagree**
The balance of work between the learning set group and the large groups is about right	62%	38%
I would like to have more opportunities to work with everyone in the large community	31%	69%
I would prefer all discussions/work to occur only in the small learning set groups	18%	82%
I have not really had the time to participate in the large group work	67%	33%
I enjoyed working in the large groups	48%	52%
The large community is useful for carrying out general group discussions	80%	20%
The large groups have been productive in their own way	75%	25%
We don't use the large group forums/spaces very effectively	77%	23%
The balance between structured and unstructured discussions in the large groups is about right	63%	37%
I would like to see more structured activities in the large groups	77%	23%
The *structured* discussions in the large group forums/ spaces have worked well	56%	44%

and that they are productive in their own way (Table 3.9). However, students think the community meeting spaces are not used very effectively, and the balance of structured and unstructured activities is thought not to be correct by one-third of students. Is this a matter of providing better, more structured activities where the large numbers can participate more effectively? Some of the activities that are used were described in the previous chapter. Providing more structure may be part of the answer, although students are not in agreement that the existing structured activities work well.

So, overall, although students appreciate the opportunity to come together in the large community and forge new identities by participating in activities alternative to those that take place in the smaller learning sets, they do not hold strong views about community work in the way they do about working in the sets. My personal view on this is that students often do find the community work exciting, and they see the need for it too. But as we have seen, the large numbers involved and the consequent difficulty in managing the communication overhead makes working in them hard going at times. Alongside this is the perception that it is in the smaller sets that work that can readily be applied in their personal and professional learning is carried out.

So, are the large community meetings seen as being a necessary but time-consuming distraction? Or is there more to them than this? Do they add a necessary additional dimension to the students' overall experience, one that 'cements' the community and in reality makes it possible for everyone to feel free to go off into their learning sets in the knowledge that they have 'taken care' of the large community? More research into these large groups is needed to understand their role in collaborative learning of this kind.

The contribution to students' personal learning

We have seen in Chapter 1 that, although collaborative learning has benefits for the group, it also has benefits for the individuals in the group. What benefits do students themselves think working collaboratively brings to their personal learning?

The questionnaire asked students about their perception of the potential benefits of learning in groups and communities to their own individual learning. First of all, they were asked how collaborative learning might support the development of self-awareness, and awareness of learning how to learn. Second, they were asked about the effects of this kind of learning on their ability to manage and direct their own learning. Finally, they were asked about their views on the educational philosophy of collaborative and cooperative group and community e-learning.

Development of self-awareness, and awareness of learning how to learn

The development of an awareness of one's own learning is a key lifelong learning aim. If students can learn to be aware of how they learn, they are likely to become better learners. Collaborative and cooperative learning designs should foster self-awareness and help in the development of learning-to-learn skills. They are inherently reflective in their processes and require students to 'stand back' and assess their learning. When asked if studying in this way made them more aware of the strengths and weaknesses of their learning styles, a very high percentage of students said yes they thought it did (Table 3.10). They feel this form of learning gives them the time to re-assess their own learning, and they indicate that this form of learning has made them more aware of learning how to learn. For many, their motivation to study has been positively affected by participating in the range of activities and processes that underpin group learning.

Working in groups where they are invited to 'expose' themselves and their ideas is a challenge to many students, but it is a process that they feel is beneficial to their learning development (Table 3.10). They feel they have learned a great deal on these collaborative learning courses, even though for two-thirds of them the openness and self-managed learning approach has at times made it difficult to determine the 'correct' level of work required. But the learning philosophy of collaborative groups and communities has significantly changed the views of learning of a large number of these students.

Finally, the effects of this kind of learning on the development of professional practice have been considerable too. The course readings have played an important role in helping them assess their own practice, and a very high percentage indicate that they are aware of using ideas from the course when carrying out their own practice. This is a point that I will return to in a later chapter when I consider the groups as examples of communities of practice.

Overall, these results suggest a very positive relationship with the kinds of learning fostered by collaborative and cooperative group work, with real evidence of students developing skill in learning-to-learn and in the transference of learning to other contexts.

Table 3.10 Development of Self-Awareness, and Awareness of Learning How to Learn

	Agree	Disagree
Studying in this way has made me more aware of the strengths and weaknesses of my own learning process	91%	9%
I feel I have had time to reassess my own learning	88%	12%
This form of learning has made me more aware about learning how to learn	77%	23%
This form of learning has positively affected my motivation to study	72%	28%
I feel that having to 'expose' myself/ideas has been beneficial to my learning and development	87%	13%
I feel this learning philosophy has significantly changed my view of learning	76%	24%
I feel I have learned an awful lot on this course	91%	9%
It has been difficult to determine the 'correct' level of work required for this course	64%	36%
The course readings have helped me reassess my own practice	89%	11%
When carrying out my own teaching, I am aware of using ideas from this course	96%	4%

Effects on managing and directing one's own learning

Is there a relationship between this kind of learning and students' ability to manage and direct their learning? Learning in groups requires students to be self-managing. For example, they have to make decisions about how to work in the groups, how to manage their own and others learning processes, how to negotiate the focus of their learning within the group, how to plan their work and meet deadlines and so forth. These skills have to be developed within the context of the learning community and the work of the learning sets.

It is no surprise, I think, that nearly every student says they enjoy the freedom of 'self-managed learning' (Table 3.11). When students are empowered to be self-managing and to make decisions about their own learning, they quickly find it both exciting and satisfying. The vast majority say they have indeed managed their own learning and, moreover, have helped others manage their learning. A very high number now feel more able to direct their own learning as a consequence of being exposed to these kinds of learning processes. Although over two-thirds say they do not prefer to be directed more in their learning, nearly one-third say they would prefer this. It is not possible from the results of this questionnaire to say what form this direction should take.

There are, of course, challenges to learning in this way. A large percentage of students feel this form of learning requires more discipline than 'traditional' forms of learning, but it is ultimately more beneficial. And despite the requirement to work in groups and collaborate in a

Table 3.11 Effects on Managing and Directing One's Own Learning

	Agree	Disagree
I enjoy the freedom of 'self managed learning'	93%	7%
I feel I have indeed 'managed' my own learning to a large degree	91%	9%
I feel I have helped others manage their learning	73%	27%
Having studied in this way I now feel more able to direct my own learning	82%	18%
I prefer to be directed more in my learning	29%	71%
This form of learning requires more discipline than 'traditional' learning	91%	9%
This form of learning is, ultimately, more beneficial to me	80%	20%
I have been able to study the course at my own pace	67%	33%
I have been able to study the course when it suits me	75%	25%

variety of different ways with their fellow students, two thirds of the students surveyed feel they have been able to study the course at their own pace, and when it suits them. This is evidence of the benefits to the group and to the individual of these kinds of learning processes.

The educational philosophy of group e-learning

Collaborative e-learning courses of the kind discussed here are built on general educational principles, or philosophies, of teaching and learning. These include, for example, the belief that learning in groups and communities has wide-ranging educational benefits for those involved; that structure in the learning process has to be kept to a minimum in order to allow groups to manage and develop their own structures and processes; that knowledge can be built from information in relatively effective ways, and that students can develop in their own way, in their own time, while still benefiting from working in the company of others.

Do students relate to these general principles of learning? How do they think the principles relate to the reality of e-learning? The questionnaire asked students about these course attributes and the results are given in Table 3.12. Once again, the students confirm that the principle of organizing learning into learning sets is a very strong and positive one. They also confirm, but to a slightly lesser degree (but still a large majority opinion) that incorporating the concept of 'community' in the design of e-learning works in practice and that it is not just a theoretical idea. It has real relevance to their learning. On the issue of the use of structure in the design of the groups, there is some disagreement that this kind of learning is too loosely structured for their liking, although they are divided on whether or not they could have learned more in a structured learning environment. It would have been interesting to ask for clarification on this as it would be useful to know what sorts of things they feel they could have learned in more structured environments.

But a majority (77 per cent) say they have not found it difficult to learn effectively this way, though it would of course be useful to know why the remaining 23 per cent think it was difficult to learn this way, and if learning in this way actually prevented them learning what they wanted to learn, or what they felt they should be learning. For most (67 per cent), learning in collaborative groups and communities turned out to be better than they had expected, and a slightly higher percentage go as far as to say that the course is one of the most interesting they have taken part in. The 'just-in-time' benefits of access to information and knowledge in e-learning contexts, which in this case also include the benefits of knowledge-sharing and co-production with peers in the learning sets, are seen to be effective by most students, although as we have seen many times so far, students feel they have not had the time to participate as much as they want and take full advantage of these benefits. Is this perhaps due to the particular design

Table 3.12 Views on the Educational Philosophy of this Kind of Learning

	Agree	Disagree
I think that working in learning sets has helped in my learning	93%	7%
The concept of the learning community is good in theory, but in practice it doesn't really work	25%	75%
This kind of learning is too loosely structured for my liking	25%	75%
I think I could have learned more in a more structured learning environment	47%	53%
I have found it difficult to learn effectively this way	23%	77%
Learning in this way has turned out to be better than I expected	67%	33%
This course is one of the most interesting courses I have taken part in	77%	23%
Compared with other methods of obtaining information and knowledge THERE and THEN, this course has been more effective	67%	33%
Throughout this course I feel I have just not had the time to participate fully	71%	29%
We have been asked to do too much work on this course	37%	63%
A course like this allows participants at different stages of learning to develop in their own way/pace	85%	15%

and requirements of this course, and not perhaps a general attribute of this kind of learning? Over one-third of the students say they have been asked to do too much on the course. So it may well be that for some students our particular design requires them to do too much. It would be worthwhile to examine this issue more at a later stage. Nevertheless, it appears from the result of the final question in Table 3.12 that courses of this kind, which are built on group work, do not necessarily make it difficult for individual students to develop in their own way and at their own pace.

The action research/learning process

The previous chapter discussed how an action research (AR), or action learning, methodology is incorporated into the design of the workshops and the course as a whole. The AR approach is designed to introduce a reflective, analytical rhythm into the work of the collaborative learning sets and the community. It permeates the course and becomes part of the culture of learning. Early in the course, students are introduced to some of the literature on action research and action learning, and are given the opportunity to discuss the ways in which these approaches might be used to underpin their work. At other times, the influence of AR can be seen in the various activities and processes embedded in the course.

How do students experience this? Does the action learning process add anything to students' learning? The students appear to think it does (see Table 3.13). A large majority of them agree with the statement that the AR process gives them a foundation for carrying out their course assignments, and they believe the process made them reflect critically on their course assignment and course work. However, similar numbers of them also think that they should have spent more time considering the role and purpose of the AR process. This is not to say that they feel the process has not worked: 77 per cent of them feel it has worked, and similar numbers disagree with the statement that 'the use of an action research method restricts too greatly what is possible for course assignments'. They confirm the usefulness of the approach when 72 per cent disagree with the statement that they did not bother much with the AR methods and processes.

All of this indicates that, for the vast majority of these students, the use of an action learning model to guide them in their work has been highly beneficial. We can see that the rhythm of action learning appears to be something that students are aware of and appreciate as a vehicle for supporting, and at times directing, their learning. It seems to permeate the course and is an important part of the culture of learning.

Table 3.13   The Action Research/Learning Process

	Agree	**Disagree**
The AR process gave me a foundation for carrying out my course assignments	80%	20%
The AR processes made me reflect critically on my course assignments/work	77%	23%
We should have spent more time considering the role and purpose of the AR process	65%	35%
I don't think the AR process has worked	23%	77%
The use of an AR method restricts too greatly what is possible for course assignments	22%	78%
I did not bother very much with the AR methods and processes	28%	72%

The role of the tutor

We saw in Chapter 2 that the place of the tutor in e-learning groups and communities is complex. With the emphasis on 'community', the tutor has to consider her/his place within the community and work towards being a tutor-participant, rather than a conventional tutor whose role it is to ensure students address a curriculum or syllabus that has been devised by others for their benefit. This implies a collegial relationship based on sharing power over such things as course content, methods of learning, learning processes and structures, learning outcomes, assessment and evaluation.

The development of this relationship with the student members of the community (and indeed with the other tutors on the course) is important and occurs at different levels and in different ways. For example, in the large community meetings mentioned in a previous chapter, where for instance members network and share biographies, the tutor also participates by sharing her/his biography in the company of students and other tutors. When the community reviews each workshop to reflect on their learning experiences, the tutors also take time out to reflect on their experiences. In the smaller learning sets, tutors also contribute as members of the set while also contributing as 'tutor'. This dual role has to be worked at to be effective and authentic. The tutor acts as 'custodian' of the course as s/he has been actively involved in the design process. They are also the representative of the university and have to ensure standards are met, quality assured and that effective administration of the course occurs. At the same time they are participants in activities such as the self-peer-tutor review and assessment process (to be discussed in some depth in later chapters). They may also participate by sharing their professional and research interests with members of the community, and interact with the student members in e-seminars and discussions. They do this at the same time as assisting the members of the set in carrying out their personal and collective projects.

Students have many formal and informal opportunities throughout the courses to comment on the role of the tutor. The questionnaire asked them to comment on a few issues relating to the place of the tutor in the groups and communities. Given that the role of the tutor is different from that on 'conventional' courses, did the students understand what role the tutor had in this community-focused setting? This question was asked because from time to time early in the course some students did query the role of the tutor and seemed unsure about the relationship they had with their tutor. However, a very high percentage of students (88 per cent) completing the questionnaire disagreed with the statement that, at the end of the course, they still did not understand the role of the tutor (Table 3.14). Of course, they did have two years to work with their tutors and become familiar with their role on the course, so it is perhaps not surprising that they should feel they understand the tutor role by the end of that time!

Having said this, many of the students (78 per cent) feel that the tutors need to discuss their role more openly. This, I think, illustrates the need for tutors to be constantly open to discussing with students what work they have to accomplish on courses of this kind and how that work may at times take on the formal 'tutor' role, and at other times take on a participatory role. It has to be said that some tutors find this dual role difficult to act out in practice. They sometimes feel vulnerable being 'open' in the community. Others are extremely comfortable with it and relish the freedom to participate that it brings. But we do have to be aware of the possibility of tutors taking a privileged view of themselves in order, perhaps, to protect themselves. The community does discuss such concerns from time to time, for example in the reviews of the workshops, and that helps enormously. And the tutor team also pays attention to these, and other, issues in their team meetings.

How influential are tutors in these learning environments? Students are divided on this issue (Table 3.14). Nearly equal numbers agree and disagree with the statement that 'despite the rhetoric, tutors are MUCH more influential in the learning sets than anyone else'. Some tutors have said that, realistically and despite their best efforts not to be, they are bound at times to be more influential than the students. There has to be some truth in that: no matter what democratic relationship we wish to adopt as tutors, some students will occasionally defer to the perceived authority of the tutor. But tutors have to strive to exist on the course as if they are members of the community, and strive to accomplish that in their actions, words and relationships. As tutors we each have to reflect on our

Table 3.14   The Tutor Role

	Agree	Disagree
I still don't understand the role of the tutor on the MEd	12%	88%
I would like the tutors to discuss their role more openly	78%	22%
Despite the rhetoric, tutors are MUCH more influential in the learning sets than anyone else	58%	42%
The tutors should participate more	67%	33%
The tutors need to be more directive	48%	52%
I think the tutors should keep to the background and intervene only when really necessary	15%	85%
I think the tutor role in the learning sets is just about right for this kind of course	67%	33%
It must be easy tutoring on this MEd	7%	93%
I think we should have the same tutor in each set throughout the course	20%	80%

practice, and make every effort to develop practices that are congruent with the values and beliefs we hold about this form of learning.

Being a member of the community requires participation in the work of the community. Two-thirds of these students express the view that the tutor needs to participate more. It would have been useful to enquire in what additional ways students think tutors should or could participate. Adopting a more directive approach could be one form of greater participation, but students do not agree that the tutors should be more directive: they are nearly equally divided on this issue (Table 3.14). Should tutors therefore keep to the background and only intervene when necessary? A very large majority (85 per cent) of students think not. This call for tutors to participate more and not keep to the background points to students' real concern that the community should be made up collectively of students and tutors, where everyone participates on an equal footing. These student views are good news and indicate that the value tutors place on community in the design of the course has been taken up and 'owned' by the students. It is, however, the tutors who seem, at times, not to be practising what they preach as much as students would ideally like. When we meet as a tutor team, the question of our participation is often discussed and is one that each of us has different views on. We do not disagree on the need for tutor participation, but we do sometimes argue about the extent of participation and the forms of participation that are expected or are needed in order to help develop the community perspective of the course.

The questionnaire also looked at students' views on three other issues to do with the role of the tutor. They were asked: 'is the tutor role in the learning sets 'right' for this kind of course?', and two-thirds responded by saying it was. Unfortunately the questionnaire did not allow for those who disagreed to say in what ways this could be corrected. Students were asked if they thought it was easy to tutor on this course, and over 90 per cent said they thought it probably was not easy. This item was added to the questionnaire because some observers of this kind of e-learning hold the opinion that because there is a high degree of self-management and group work in this form of e-learning, tutors must have little if anything to do. This is of course far from the case: in my experience, tutoring in these contexts is extremely demanding, complex and at times time-consuming. Students clearly appreciate that it is not easy, and that the tutor role is certainly not a move 'from the sage on the stage to the guide on the side' (Jones and Steeples 2002: 9) as some commentators suggest it could be. Given this, it might be thought that the tutor should stay with their learning set throughout the course in order to sustain the work of the set and develop familiarity. The questionnaire therefore asked the students if they should have the same tutor throughout the course, and a large majority of them disagreed. This suggests that there is a desire among students to work with different tutors and that the variety of tutor styles, backgrounds, interests and experiences is attractive to them. It also suggests that, despite the time required to participate in set formations, where students and tutors take part in forming new groups, many students see the benefits of working with different tutors (and, in case it is forgotten, the benefits of working with different peers).

Conclusion

This chapter has focused on the results of a questionnaire distributed to students after they had completed their studies in the e-learning groups and communities. The questionnaire was designed to gain insight into students' experiences of learning in e-groups and communities and covered such issues as the quality of discussions/work in the learning sets, group collaborative processes in the learning sets, the collaborative processes in the large community, collaborative assessment processes, the contribution of this kind of learning to their personal learning, the role of the action research/learning process, and finally their view on the tutor role in e-learning courses.

The importance of understanding how students experience networked e-learning cannot be understated. It is important for us to know if the e-learning designs we employ, and the various methods chosen to help develop the groups and communities, work in practice. The design of e-learning groups and communities is complex and requires a holistic approach that aims to provide truly integrated learning experiences where each element of the course structure and course process makes sense to those involved, and provides them with a satisfying and demanding encounter.

Students experience these pedagogical attributes in different ways. A questionnaire of this kind helps provide us with an overview of their views. It helps distil viewpoints and offers us the chance to focus on the major issues from the viewpoint of the learner. The results can be taken alongside the results of the other research approaches and methods described in other chapters of this book used to investigate students' experiences of e-learning, each adding another perspective to our understanding of the overall student experience.

As we have seen, students' views on learning in collaborative learning sets and communities are, on the whole, very positive. There is, however, a small minority, sometimes one in five, who are not so enthusiastic and do not always hold such positive views on the nature of this kind of learning and teaching. It would be surprising, I think, if everyone was supportive of every aspect of this kind of learning, and it is to be expected that learning in e-groups and communities will not appeal to everyone or meet their expectations or learning needs.

But no learning and teaching method 'works' completely or is 'perfect'. Face-to-face methods have many imperfections, and we know that students and teachers face considerable problems when using them. This questionnaire did not set out to compare face-to-face methods with e-learning methods. It was designed to assess the experience of students who had been involved in e-learning groups and communities for a considerable amount of time (two years in fact), and who were therefore extremely well placed to evaluate the potential of this form of learning. The results are extremely encouraging, showing that when e-learning courses are designed with some care and attention to the meaning of learning in groups and communities, students' experiences can be very positive. This should be taken as a huge endorsement by students of this form of learning, and should encourage us confidently to proclaim the potential of courses designed on e-learning group and community principles.

4

Assessing learning in e-groups and communities

Introduction

In Chapter 1 I said that the design of e-learning groups and communities must address the important issue of assessment. I turn to the issue in this chapter, and the argument is that if we are serious about designing e-learning so that it takes place in collaborative and cooperative groups and communities, we must design assessment processes that support and reward learning of this kind.

The case for involving students in some form of self- and peer-assessment in higher education is well established (for example, see Boud 1995, 2000; Boyd and Cowan 1985; Broadfoot 1996; Heron 1981; McConnell 1999 2000; McDowell and Sambell 1999; Shafriri 1999; Somerville 1993; Stefani 1998; Stephenson and Weil 1992). Student involvement in their own assessment is an important part of the preparation for life and work. Although by no means universal, there is now a wider belief in the educational and social benefits of self- and peer-assessment. The place of self- and peer-assessment in networked e-learning has, however, still to be established. In this chapter I hope to make the case for incorporating self- and peer-assessment as a central part of the learning process in e-learning groups and communities.

Why is self- and peer-assessment important?

Why do teachers want to use self- and peer-assessment processes? What benefits accrue to self-assessment processes? And why is self- and peer-assessment important in the context of designing online courses that are based on collaborative and cooperative learning processes?

Table 4.1 lists some reasons given in the literature for using self- and peer-assessment processes. They indicate a set of educational values about

Table 4.1　Why Should We Use Self- and Peer-Assessment Processes?

For teachers
To enable teachers to evaluate output of their courses more accurately
They are relevant to the process of curriculum change
They are a strong, formative educational tool
To use methods that are more student centred
To reduce time spent by teacher in marking student work
To get feedback to students more quickly

Reduce power differentials
They help to remove student/teacher barriers
They give students greater ownership of the assessment process
Students become less dependent on their lecturers

Future work situations
To allow students to assess and evaluate their own work in ways that are
　applicable to their future professions
To use methods appropriate to the demands of employers and society as a whole
They help students develop enterprising competences

Democracy
They are part of a wider move to more democratic approaches to teaching and
　learning

To promote wider skills
They help promote interpersonal skills
They increase responsibility and autonomy
They help students develop useful problem-solving and thinking skills

Improve the quality of learning
Students become more critical and perceptive about their own learning
They bring about changes in students' learning processes
They help students take a more active role in their learning
They help students take more control over their learning
They help students have a greater understanding of how to improve their own
　performance
They promote reflective learning
To develop skill in self-awareness
Their use can lead to 'deeper' forms of learning

To sustain student learning
Their use can lead to greater motivation
To make students consider the whole learning process

the role and nature of assessment in higher education: they are beliefs and wishes. They highlight a major concern by some educators to provide a more egalitarian and fairer system of assessment than unilateral teacher assessment.

Not all of these reasons are derived from or based on empirical evidence. It would probably be possible to test each reason by empirical research, but would probably not be entirely conclusive:

It is difficult to prove conclusively that the use of peer assessment will improve the quality of students' work. Even if it does not, it is still a valuable exercise as it clarifies the learning goals for students through the development of criteria for assessment.

(Searby and Ewers 1997: 381–2)

Some form of self-assessment is also part of a philosophy of, or approach to, education that seeks to work with students as self-managing people who can take responsibility for their own learning:

I have long argued that an educated person is an aware, self-determining person, in the sense of being able to set objectives, to formulate standards of excellence for the work that realizes these objectives, to assess work done in the light of those standards, and to be able to modify the objectives, the standards or the work programme in the light of experience and action; and all this in discussion and consultation with other relevant persons. If this is indeed a valid notion of what an educated person is, then it is clear that the educational process in all our main institutions of higher education does not prepare students to acquire such self-determining competence. For staff unilaterally determine student learning objectives, student work programmes, student assessment criteria, and unilaterally do the assessment of the students' work.

(Heron 1981)

What effects, if any, does self- and peer-assessment have on students' approaches to learning? We know from research into the effects of assessment on learning that many students are cue seekers: they actively seek out information about how they are to be assessed and try to find out about aspects of the course that are likely to be addressed in the assessment process. This knowledge helps to guide them in what they focus their learning on, and often determines what they study towards for the course assessment (Miller and Parlett 1974). Indeed, it has been argued that students' view of university life is largely governed by what they think they will be assessed on (Becker *et al.* 1968).

The importance of all of this in situations where students work as collaborative and cooperative learners and where they are involved in collaborative assessment seems clear. If students are actively involved in decisions about how to learn and what to learn and why they are learning, and are also actively involved in decisions about criteria for assessment and the process of judging their own and others' work, then their relationship to their studies will probably be qualitatively different from that of students who are treated as recipients of teaching and who are the object of others', unilateral, assessment. Because students in cooperative and collaborative learning situations make important decisions about their learning and assessment, there will be less need for them to seek cues from their teachers about assessment or seek to find ways of 'playing' the system.

They help determine the system themselves, in negotiation with other students and teachers. Ramsden points to the way in which assessment processes inform students of what is important to learn and what is not: 'The evaluation process provides a signal to students about the kind of learning they are expected to carry out; they adapt by choosing strategies that will apparently maximize success' (Ramsden 1988).

It has been suggested that collaborative assessment is central to changes required in making learning less instrumental and more participative: 'assessment is arguably the most important aspect of an educational programme in which to introduce collaborative principles. It is this intervention that develops the design from the instrumental to a more fundamentally participative approach' (Reynolds, Sclater and Tickner 2004: 256).

Collaborative assessment is particularly important in the context of e-learning groups and communities, where an ethos of collaboration and cooperation exists. In this context, the expectation is for students to engage in helping each other develop, review and assess each other's course work. It is the collaborative learning and assessment process itself that signals to the students what form of learning is expected of them (McConnell 2000). It can therefore be anticipated that collaborative assessment will be a central process in networked collaborative e-learning and will influence students' relationships to learning. In such a context it might be expected that students will adapt to a learning situation that requires them to share, discuss, explore and support.

Background

Collaborative assessment should be a central learning process on any e-learning course based on learning community principles. Although assessment has the dual function of certification and evaluation of learning outcomes, we need also to emphasize the potential of assessment as a central learning process, as part of the 'content' of the course. This can be done by building in time throughout the course for collaborative review and assessment.

In contexts where e-learning courses are run on a learning community, or 'community of practice' (Wenger 1998) basis, it is necessary that the course is designed to ensure that students and tutors engage in meaningful practices through cooperative and collaborative learning processes, and to ensure that knowledge developed is demonstrated in the context of the student's professional practice. This can be achieved by the development of a climate where commenting on each other's work, and giving and receiving feedback are integrated and normal parts of the community's day-to-day work.

Assessment of cooperative learning

Assessing learning in cooperative and collaborative contexts requires methods that validly evaluate the different kinds of learning that take place in each context. There are differences in the methods that can be used to assess cooperative and collaborative learning processes, but the *collaborative assessment process* where students and tutors work together in carrying out the assessment is central to them all.

Let us first consider assessment of cooperative learning. Cooperative learning involves students and tutors in supporting each other in the development of each student's own, individual piece of work. This is a convivial shared experience where students take time to think through an issue or problem that they would like to investigate, and discuss it with their peers as they proceed. Unlike collaborative learning, students in cooperative learning do not negotiate a shared focus for their collective learning. There is no product that they are collectively trying to achieve. The focus is on the individual within the community.

Several methods can be used to facilitate collaborative assessment in cooperative learning contexts. One method that we have used extensively and evaluated as being highly valid, involves course students, their peers and a tutor in a process where they review each student's assignment, and use a set of criteria provided by each student, and a set provided by the tutor, to guide them through the assessment process.

This takes place within a wider collaborative and cooperative learning environment where students work together in e-learning groups of up to twelve students and a tutor. The group members explore their practice as it relates to the focus of the course, and produce individual products that are the focus for collaborative review and assessment.

The process of developing skill and understanding about collaborative self- and peer-review and assessment takes place in a wider supportive learning context. It is highly unlikely that this process can be introduced into e-learning courses that do not function as a cooperative learning community. Learners and tutors have to develop a sense of trust and a common purpose. They have to develop the belief that they are a community of learners, before they are likely to believe that self- and peer-assessment will really be taken seriously, and will work effectively. They are, after all, going to 'reveal' themselves in this process.

The process of collaborative review and assessment of cooperative learning typically involves the following:

- An extended period of negotiation, in which each student and their peers and tutor discuss the focus of the assignment topic, from an initial tentative idea to a fully confirmed topic. Each student offers suggestions on what they would like to do for their assignment. This is done by their setting up a personal thread in the asynchronous electronic forum. Other students and the tutor offer comment, and discussion evolves.

Students' approaches to their assignments often change as their proposals are discussed. We feel it is important that each student choose their own assignment topic, which is usually a real problem or issue related to their professional practice.

- A period of asynchronous discussion of issues, problems and viewpoints surrounding the topic follows. This usually moves between short, exploratory discussion entries to more fully formed entries that focus on substantive conceptual and methodological issues.
- At the same time, there is a sharing of resources related to the topic, such as students and tutors sharing research papers and useful website addresses. In addition, students provide personal and professional experiences and ideas that are hugely helpful.
- Often incomplete drafts of the assignment are provided to the group, followed by short collaborative self-peer-tutor reviews. The extent to which students and tutors engage in review at this early stage depends very much on their interest in the topic, and the time they have available. But this can be a valuable exchange of ideas and critique that can be built on in the following stages.
- The final document is then submitted to the group (for example as a Word file or a website), which is subjected to self-peer-tutor review and assessment. Criteria for assessment are mutually agreed, and the group thinks through what is involved in assessing each other's work. Prior to this in the e-workshops we have collectively discussed the nature of a learning community, part of which involves each student being willing to review and assess other students' assignments. This is an important role for students to play on the programme, and (as we shall see later in this chapter) they do it willingly and with much enthusiasm once they have experienced it. The group tutor is also involved in the review and assessment exercise.
- The review process starts by giving and receiving feedback. The exact way in which this occurs depends largely on the members of the group. Sometimes the writer of the document begins a review of their work, mentioning those aspects they see as being in need of clarification or modification, or talking about some of the learning issues that emerged for them in writing the paper. Sometimes the writer asks for others to start the review. What is focused on depends to some extent on the wishes of the writer and the interests of the other students, including the tutor.
- Each assignment is finally assessed on a pass/refer/fail basis (self-peer-tutor assessment) with reference to the student's set of criteria and the set of criteria supplied at the beginning of the course by the tutor.

Throughout the whole process it is necessary to develop and maintain a shared power relationship between the tutor and students. Ensuring that students develop their own criteria for self-assessment is important as it can enhance the validity of the whole process (Falchikov and Goldfinch 2000).

The review and assessment process is meant to be truly open and collaborative, with the tutor having no more or no less a role to play than the students. Tutors should strive to work in negotiation with their students and not use their power of assessment unilaterally (McConnell 1999). We shall look at an example of the process later to see how it works out in practice.

Assessment of collaborative learning

In cooperative learning the group processes focus on support that helps each student develop their own individual project. The social economy is relatively simple: each member of the group freely provides support that is then reciprocated. Each student is then collaboratively assessed according to their own and the tutor's criteria.

The social economy in collaborative learning is more complex. The members of the group negotiate a shared problem or issue that they want to investigate, and each student plays an important role in helping the group achieve its aim of producing a 'product' that could not be produced by any one individual on their own. In these circumstances, the issue of what to assess causes some debate among students.

Should participation be assessed?

Many students think that their participation in the work of the learning set/group should contribute to the overall assessment of their course work. This signifies a need for their participation in the group work to be formally acknowledged and taken into account. It is my impression that those students who fully participate in the online discussions and group work are sometimes the ones who wish such activity to be taken into account in the assessment procedures. Those who do not participate quite so fully, for whatever good reason, are naturally concerned about this being a criterion in assessment.

This raises a question about collaborative learning generally: what criteria, if any, can we apply to help define the nature and extent of participation that is necessary for us to be able to say that 'collaborative' learning is occurring? Some students say that, even if they are not 'participating', they learn a great deal by reading others' comments and responses and by following the work of the group. The incidence of vicarious learning has been shown to have useful learning potential in computer-mediated communication environments (McKendree et al. 1998). But in a collaborative learning environment, where participation is expected and necessary for the work of the group to take place, what are the role and limits of vicarious learning? Can a student's participation be infrequent and still be counted as 'contributing' to the work of the group?

At what point do we say that the level of contribution is so minimal as not to be sufficient or acceptable? When course tutors try formally to define the level of required contribution – for example, by indicating how many times each student should log on to the VLE per week, or by indicating how many comments students have to make each week – some students inevitably use this as a minimum criterion and only participate to this level and not beyond it. By defining the level of participation, we may reduce the possibility of its occurring, or encourage a mechanistic relationship to participation.

Is all participation the same, and is participation always a 'good' thing? In a community of learners, where critical reflection on the issues being investigated and discussed is encouraged, what are the limits of participation? One student made this comment:

> Should we assume that, as people have volunteered to be members of the community, then they will tell us if they want to leave and that unless we hear otherwise we continue to assume they are still part of the community ... [snip] I feel that 'participating' means different things to different people. I personally think that we need to give each other some space. After all reflection is meant to be at the heart of what we are trying to do and this can be difficult if people feel they are compelled to respond. I realize that people are different in the ways they like to work and therefore I don't want to be prescriptive about this – vive la différence! But perhaps 'looking after the community' includes giving people space if they need it.
>
> (Interview quotation)

We do not always know what is going on when a student is observing. It is likely that they are as cognitively involved as other students:

> Why should observation ever be better than actively participating? First note that there are two distinctions in play – voyeurism versus participation and consumption versus construction. These two are not independent but neither are they identical. The voyeur as well as the student may be actively engaged in construction, checking them against those of the students. The student may be merely engaged in fact consumption.
>
> (McKendree *et al.* 1998: 117)

If this is the case, and students are observing and not participating in the knowledge construction process, then they may well be benefiting from the experience. The issue is: how acceptable is this to those students who are actively participating? In a collaborative learning context most students are willing to support non-active participation of others from time to time. It is unlikely though that such behaviour would be accepted as the normal form of participation.

Assessing participation

As we have seen, collaborative learning and assessment rely on reciprocation: each person involved has to give to their peers in addition to receiving from them. Without this reciprocal relationship, goodwill diminishes and competition is likely to take over (Axelrod 1990; McConnell 2000).

The place of individual accountability in the collaborative work of the group needs to be addressed by the community: tutors and students alike. The group often leaves it to each individual to determine what they can offer the group, or what workload they can carry. And it is the responsibility of the group to look after itself and its members and to find a level of performance (and therefore also individual accountability) that they feel is acceptable to them. When learning groups work with such an open contract, the degree to which it is successfully achieved can vary from group to group. In some groups there can be a tangible feeling of discontent due to the marked differences in contribution and performance of individuals. And although this may never get in the way of the group's completing its work, it is sometimes commented on in the review and assessment periods:

> there has been another person who just hasn't contributed a darn thing ... I think. And he has come back online a few weeks ago and everybody said it is great to see you back, don't give up, hang on in there which is wonderfully encouraging stuff but I didn't respond at all because if I had I would have said what the hell are you doing? Which is not the thing to say at all of course but I just felt well you actually haven't contributed to anything.
>
> (Student quote)

In these circumstances, some students ask why the process of the collaborative work itself (that is, each person's participation) cannot be formally assessed. They correctly point out that a great deal of their time, thought and energy goes into the procedural work of the group, and this should be rewarded, like anything else they do.

In cases where this is an issue, there is residual resentment of some kind towards those who, for whatever reason, do not participate as much as others. Some students may think that by assessing participation, rewards can be given for 'good participation' and those not fully participating can be censured. Although no students have ever discussed the matter in these terms, I suspect that from time to time it is an underlying unresolved element of the relationship of members of some groups.

In a self-managed learning environment, one way of approaching the issue of participation (and accountability to the group) is to ask each group to manage the process themselves. This is achieved by involving students in forms of self- and peer-assessment of individual participation. This can be challenging for them but also surprisingly useful too. Students are asked to review their contribution to the work of the group against a set of criteria. Their peers and tutor also present their review of that person's contribution against the same criteria. The various 'triangulated' reviews of those involved are shared within the group and become the basis of a discussion about the nature of participation.

This open, reflective process helps each member say why they participated in the way they did, and this helps other members 'hear' those explanations while also providing their own feedback on the nature of that person's participation. This has the beneficial effect of forcing discussion of the issue while reducing the possibility of anyone 'accusing' someone about lack of participation without knowing the particular background and circumstances of that person.

It also has the benefit of members approaching the issue as a learning event, from which they can learn about the various ways in which students participate and the reasons for that. From examining each person's experience of the group work, members make suggestions about future group work processes, and begin to define a set of procedures or protocols – grounded in the experience of real group work – that suit the various personal needs and requirements of the various members.

By addressing the issue in this way, those group members who have participated less frequently than others are sometimes encouraged by the discussion to participate more fully in future group work. Similarly, those who are inclined to participate in great volume can reflect on the consequences for others of their high level of participation!

Components of collaborative assessment

Over several years we have developed with our students a model for reviewing and assessing collaborative learning in e-learning contexts. In developing the model we were aware that any scheme aiming to assess collaborative learning has to be capable of assessing the wide variety of forms of participation that can take place in an e-learning environment, with the purpose of allowing students the opportunity to indicate how they contributed to group processes as well as to the group product.

There have been several iterations and evaluations of the model to refine and validate it, involving the views of both students and tutors. The construction of the model has involved a theoretical analysis of the literature, examination of the actual process of collaborative assessment as it takes place in the e-learning environment, and evaluations with students of their use of the model. The final model has four components that can be used by each student, their peers and the tutor to assess collaborative learning. These are: product achievement, communication skill, social relationships and reflective skills (see Table 4.2).

Table 4.2   Assessment of Collaborative Learning: Components and Indicators

Component	Indicator
Product Achievement	1 Contributing to project ideas
	2 Contributing to the research process
	3 Contributing to the analysis of the research
	4 Building on comments and on help received from others
	5 Helping to produce the report, essay or other product
	6 Meeting deadlines
	7 Stating problems or goals
	8 Taking initiatives
Communication Skill	1 Initiating dialogue and discussion
	2 Seeking information from others in the group
	3 Giving information to others in the group
	4 Helping to clarify what is happening in the group
	5 Summarizing the work of the group
	6 Seeking consensus
	7 Describing one's own feelings
	8 Observing others
	9 Being brief and concise
Social Relationships	1 Being sympathetic
	2 Encouraging members of the group
	3 Showing interest in the members of the group
	4 Praising others
	5 Expressing friendship
	6 Dealing with one's own emotions
	7 Sensing and dealing with other's emotions
	8 Coping with conflict and different opinions
	9 Acting dominant
	10 Being protective
	11 Competing with others
Reflective Skill	1 Analysing the group's behaviour
	2 Noting reaction to comments
	3 Summarizing
	4 Learning about oneself
	5 Learning about others
	6 Sharing knowledge

Product achievement

For many (but not all) students, producing the final 'product' will be the most important aim of the collaborative learning process. Product achievement is therefore a central component when defining the outcomes of collaborative learning.

There are eight indicators of product achievement. The members of each group spend considerable time developing a collective focus for their project, and the contribution that each student makes to the ideas of the group are therefore an important area for consideration. Their contribution to the research process itself is also a central component in the work of the group and usually involves taking responsibility for carrying out specific parts of the work. Third, contributing to the analysis of the research that the group carries out, perhaps by analysing data or evaluating online resources or carrying out some other analytical activity, is an activity that all students can be encouraged to participate in. A fourth indicator involves students building on the comments of other students and being open to receiving help from others in the group. The fifth indicator involves student participation in the final stages of the project, when the report, essay or other final product is being put together. The final three indicators are generic to all activities in the production of the group product: meeting deadlines is seen by students to be absolutely key to successful achievement of their project; being able to state problems and bring them to the attention of the members of the group is another key indicator; and finally taking initiatives, and perhaps taking risks, are actions that often help move the project forward in unpredictable yet hugely beneficial ways.

Communication skill

The achievement of the final product is dependent on the members of the group successfully and effectively communicating with each other. Communications largely take place in the asynchronous forums and the synchronous chat rooms, but occasionally one or two students also communicate via other electronic means such as personal email, faxes and telephone calls.

There are nine indicators of communication skill that can be taken into consideration in the collaborative assessment process. In collaborative learning contexts, communication is largely about sharing understandings of the task and helping keep the group working towards its shared objective. Success in this context is about initiating dialogue and discussion and seeking information from others, and reciprocating this. Students have to develop skill in helping the group clarify what is going on so that it can learn from its processes. Being able to summarize the work of the group is also important, and working towards consensus (but not closing down on the possibility of difference) helps move the group forward. Working together is an emotional experience and students benefit in their learning and group relations if they are able to communicate their own feelings and observe what others are doing and describe their feelings. In a context where communication is by text, being brief and precise is usually considered beneficial, though there will be times when extended textual communication is needed in order to provide greater clarity and meaning.

Social relationships

Whereas group communications may directly assist in the development of the final product, all work of the group is underpinned by social relationships. Although collaboration need not require those involved to like each other, or to feel close to each other (Axelrod 1990), we have found that collaborative learning can benefit from good social relationships. Students usually feel more able to be open and to confidently support each other if they have good social relationships (and we shall see in a later chapter what may happen when this is not the case). Some indicators of this revolve around the support that students can offer each other: being sympathetic, encouraging, showing interest in others, praising their efforts and expressing friendship are all key indicators. Other indicators are about working with emotions, one's own and those of others. Being overly dominant is often seen as unacceptable behaviour that can disrupt the group's relationships, as can excessive competitive behaviour. Sometimes in such situations, students have to be protective towards others.

Reflective skill

In a learning situation, the development of reflective skills is an important attribute. The expression of reflection in collaborative groups not only helps students be aware of what is happening in the group, it also indicates to the members of the group that one is thinking about what is taking place. This can have real benefit to the social and working relations of the group.

There are six indicators of reflective skill (see Table 4.2). The first is a student's ability to analyse the behaviour of the group and make those observations available to the members of the group in order to assist their work. The second indicator is the ability to note members' reactions to what is being said in the group. The third indicator is a student's ability to summarize this, and summarize the work of the group generally, and make it available to the group. This can be highly beneficial to the group and assist in its development and in its achieving its goals. The fourth indicator of reflective skill is learning about oneself, and sometimes making that knowledge available to others in the group. The fifth is one's ability to learn about others. The final indicator is a student's ability to share knowledge of many different kinds – emotional, theoretical, procedural and so on. This requires considerable reflective skill.

Self-review and assessment

Developing a list of shared components and indicators of collaborative assessment is only one step in the overall process. It is important not to encourage a mechanistic use of the components and indicators: they need to be used as mainly a guide to what students might refer to in their reviews. There should be no requirement that students address all indicators, or that they should restrict their self-reviews only to these components and indicators. There may be other components and indicators that they wish to refer to, and this should be encouraged.

It is helpful to offer students some simple questions to address in writing their reviews. These questions relate to the components and are offered as a way of helping students draw on the indicators under each heading in their personal reviews. Table 4.3 presents the four components and the associated questions. Each student assesses him/herself under each heading, and is assessed by two peer learners and their tutor. The self-, peer- and tutor-assessments are posted in the discussion forum, and a discussion of the assessment of each student then takes place.

Table 4.3 Writing the Reviews

Component	Questions for students to consider in writing their own review
Product Achievement	What goals and products were agreed earlier with my peers and tutor that I should achieve? Did I achieve the goals and products that were agreed earlier with my tutor and peers? *(Please provide details.)*
Communication Skill	Did I understand the contributions made by both peers and tutors and did they understand me? What was the quality of my contributions? *(Please provide evidence from the group discussions and group work to support this.)*
Social Relationships	On the whole, how do I feel I communicated in the social learning environment of my learning set? And how did I view the social relations generally in the set?
Reflective Skill	Is the collaborative process one in which I have 'learned' and enjoyed and have I contributed towards others' learning and enjoyment? *(Please provide evidence from the group discussions and group work to support this.)*

Evaluation of the use of the model in practice

The next chapter considers the students' experiences of participating in collaborative self-peer-tutor assessment. Here I would like to provide some examples of the use of these models of collaborative assessment. First I will present two examples of the process of collaborative assessment of students' personal assignments to illustrate what is involved. I will then present some examples of the assessments that are given by the students themselves as part of their review of the collaborative project work.

Two examples of the process

Example 1: Sharing thinking about course assignment proposals   This relates to the development of a supportive learning environment, where students come to feel they are working within a trusting learning community where they can offer tentative thoughts and ideas concerning the course assignment they wish to work on.

As we have seen, students' relationship to assessment does not start at the point where they hand in a piece of work for assessment. Most learners are engaged in a complex relationship with assessment from the moment they join the course. We know that the assessment process can be central to the way that students engage with learning. We have seen that how they are to be assessed often determines what they learn, how they learn it and how they prepare for their assessment (Becker *et al.* 1968; Miller and Parlett 1974). If we are to develop deep processes of learning, and authentic, meaningful learning, we have to produce, as early as possible, an environment where it is possible for us all (students and tutors) to share our thoughts and feelings about the development of course work that is to be assessed. If this is achieved, then students are likely to be in a better position to bring some self-determination into the process, and feel they have some control over it. This in turn helps them develop a more secure relationship between themselves, their tutor, peer learners and in their assignments and their assessment.

An example of how this starts in a networked e-learning environment may help. Below is a summary of an online discussion of how one student started to engage co-learners and tutor in thinking about the production of a course assignment (S stands for 'student' and T for 'tutor').

S1   makes a statement about the possible focus of his assignment (which is about 'facilitating IT/networked development of teachers in schools). He asks if this would be appropriate for the assignment.

T   makes a supporting comment; asks a question relating to the assignment; observes that it could be quite a complex piece of work to carry out; asks how S1 might go about developing the idea.

S1   provides details and acknowledges that he should keep the assignment 'simple'.

T   makes a supportive statement; asks more detailed questions; offers further support and requests S1 keeps the learning set informed of his work.

S1   provides a long entry describing his contacts with the school he is working in and their enthusiasm to be involved; mentions how he is becoming more focused in what he wants to write about; mentions a Web resource he has found and gives the URL for others in the learning set to examine; mentions a relevant DfEE (Department for Education and Employment) document found on the Web and quotes from that in order to illustrate the need for teacher development in this area; asks T for specific help on the issue.

S2   makes a supportive comment; copies parts of what S1 has said to reflect back to him (as quotes) and asks some questions; finishes by saying she is puzzled about how this will relate to his own practice.

S3   points S1 in the direction of a computer-mediated discussion system freely available on the Web (gives the URL) that might be of use in his assignment; asks him to let her know what he thinks of it.

T   makes a supporting comment; copies something S1 said earlier, quotes it back to him, and makes some detailed comments on it; makes a cautionary statement to S1; poses some questions about S1's proposed assignment.

S1   says he recognizes the need to be 'cautious' in what he is attempting for the assignment; restates his reworked assignment proposal; gives more background information about IT resources available at the school; describes whom he is working with in the school; discusses how the development work at the school that he is planning to carry out will 'fit' into the Masters assignment and his own practice. Thanks others for their comments and resources.

T   quotes back to S1 something he said earlier in order to elaborate on it; makes a supporting statement; makes a further possible suggestion concerning S1's proposal; provides some ideas on how to carry out educational evaluations; makes a supporting statement concerning the role of the learning set in helping S1; ends by making another supportive statement.

S1   (*some time later*) reports back on work already carried out on the project; gives some thoughts on what is involved for school teachers taking part in the project; says he has now set up a virtual classroom and is examining his own roles (his practice) in the project as part of the assignment.

S3   makes a supporting statement; expresses her interest in seeing the

> results; asks a question about something he said which isn't clear to her.
>
> S1   thanks S3; answers her question; makes a further statement about what he is trying to achieve in the project.

This sustained, focused discussion about S1's proposed assignment topic occurred over several weeks. The asynchronous nature of networked e-learning allowed him time to think about and reshape the topic while receiving detailed comments from the members of the learning set. His struggle to make sense of what he was trying to achieve was carried out in a supportive learning context. Because of the asynchronous processes involved, he was able to take time to think about the comments others made, go off and find Web and other resources to help develop his thinking, and bring some of that back to the group to share with them. Even though some time elapsed between some of the entries in the discussion, S1 was able to pick up the thread of the conversation whenever he needed to and could count on the other learning set members to 'be there' for him whenever he needed to talk with them.

By examining the transcript of the discussion it is possible to 'see' S1's ideas and knowledge developing, to see him pick up on other students' and the tutor's points and use them. By working in this way, students are able to develop their understanding of the importance of a supportive online learning environment by directly *experiencing and participating* in it.

> One great positive from this course for me has been the invaluable insight I have been given into the issues through the views of others – wonderful after having worked on my own for so long. It has really helped to examine my own viewpoints.

(Student quote)

The extended period of discussion and development of the course assignment also sets the context in which the assignment can finally be submitted for self-peer-tutor review and assessment. Those involved in this process know what S1 is trying to achieve and why, and know something about his thinking around the topic. They have been prepared in advance for receiving his assignment, and are already in a different position with respect to understanding how to approach assessing it from that which would have been possible had they not been involved in this process. The process is a necessary precursor to the assessment itself.

Example 2: developing learning relationships through assessment processes   The opportunity for students and tutors to share their criteria for making judgements about the learning that is evidenced in a course assignment can also be a fruitful arena for learning.

When the focus of the assignment is on issues relating to the student's own professional practice, they can be encouraged to reflect on their practice, critically examine it and carry out small-scale action research interventions into it. Such assignments often have a dual role for them. It is a piece of work that has some real use in their practice, for example it may lead to a document that can be used in their institution for some aspect of staff development or organizational change. At the same time the work also forms the basis for their course assignment.

One issue that sometimes emerges is how to write for different audiences when using the same material. There can be a tendency for students to prepare just one document for the two purposes (for their paid work, and their Masters degree studies). This often leads to a discussion about the form of a document that can be used for submission as an academic piece of writing, and the form of a document for work-related purposes.

An example of this will help to illustrate the complexity of this learning relationship and show how beneficial it can be for a student to be able to challenge the tutor's judgement on their work – within the wider social space of the collaborative learning set. For reasons of clarity, reference is made here only to discussions between the tutor and the student, leaving aside the peer comments on the assignment.

S   presents her assignment to the set for self-, peer- and tutor-review and assessment; she offers her criteria that she wants to be used by others in reviewing her assignment.

T   reads the assignment, makes several supportive comments; raises several issues, including his view on the explicitness of the critical perspective that the student has taken on some issues in the assignment (he suggests her critique is sometimes 'implicit' and not made explicit).

S   says she is confused and doesn't understand his comment; she challenges him to give some examples of 'explicit critique' so that she can understand what he means by 'implicit'; she says she thinks she has been 'explicit' in her critique; she points out that T does not raise this concern in the reviews of other Ss' assignments (which are being reviewed at the same time) yet from her analysis of them they offer no fuller explicit critiques in their assignments.

T   reads the assignment again and agrees she does carry out an explicit critique, to some degree; he goes on to try to explain what he means by 'explicit' and 'implicit' critique, and why explicit critique is so important in assignments; the T is somewhat defensive on this point.

S   (*sometime later*) says she still needs to be clearer about implicit and explicit critiques before the end of the workshop; she copies and pastes selections from the assignment that she thinks shows that she was being explicitly critical; she asks T what he now thinks.

T   reconfirms his view that she has been explicit in her critique, to some degree.

Once again, this discussion occurred over several weeks. The summary of the discussion does not capture the strength of feeling that was clearly evident in the student's comments to the tutor. She made it clear that she wanted to challenge the tutor on the issue. However, there was no sense in the discussion of either one of them taking the view that one was 'right' and the other 'wrong'. There was also no sign of the tutor resorting to a differential power relationship in order to retain his status. Both took time to 'listen' to each other, to re-read the assignment in the light of the discussions and their new understanding of it, and offer new insight and comment on it. They were engaged in what might be called a 'learning relationship'.

This extract indicates the possibility of a deep tutor–student learning relationship in networked e-learning. The tutor's comments on the assignment are challenged and dissected in an open way by the student. The other students in the learning set follow the discussion and participate as and when they see necessary. This high degree of openness contributes to the students' growing understanding of their role on the course, and the possibility for them taking control and managing the learning process. Of course, different students engage with the process in different ways, and to varying degrees. But the sharing of power does become something that is real to them all, and not just rhetorical. They come to see that, through this process, they do have power, and that it counts.

The student's final comment to the tutor shows something of her orientation:

> Thanks for your comments [T name] and clearing up the implicit/ explicit confusions – there is a lot to think about in words like explicit critique! It was really useful to think about it. I re-read my assignment ... and could see how the critique was more to the fore in some places than others ... [snip]. It is interesting as the bit I found most difficult (brain wise) to write was the section where I was trying to be more explicit in my critique with reference to theoretical ideas as well as 'how they work in practice'. So looking at your initial comment about it being explicit has really helped me develop my thinking about this in evaluating my own work, and other things I'm evaluating, and of course being clearer about academic concerns ... [snip] ... The process – i.e. my difficulty in writing [the] assignment for work and the MEd, and your difficulty in commenting on something geared around my practice, has been a total pain but again really useful in terms of taking my thinking further around the distinctions and overlaps around professional and academic awards. Sooooo ... all in all a really useful learning and assessment process ...

The collaborative project: self-, tutor- and peer-reviews and assessments

Turning to assessment of the collaborative projects, an example of self-tutor-peer review of the collaborative project in Workshop 1 is given in

Boxes 4.1, 4.2 and 4.3. This review involved three students from one learning set who lived in Greece, United Arab Emirates and New Zealand, and the tutor who lived in the UK. The student Marianna presents her self-review, which is followed by the tutor review and then two peer reviews, by Lucilla and then Roger. This example is neither typical nor atypical. It was chosen randomly from the many reviews available. I have not edited the reviews in any way, leaving them exactly as they were written and presented to the members of the set. I have, however, changed the names of those involved and any other information that may reveal who they are.

Student self-review The self-review is a very detailed piece that covers this student's personal reflections on the four components of the collaborative assessment process, that is, product achievement, communication skill, social relationships and reflective skills (Box 4.1). The four-digit numbers refer to messages in the discussion threads. There is much one could comment on here. A few examples will suffice:

- This student presents a confident, upbeat review of her work in the set.
- She shows she was committed to the project and states her role in the project.
- Clear evidence of her participation in the project is provided.
- She refers to discussion threads/messages in support of her claims.
- She indicates how she paired up with others to carry out her work.
- She shows she took initiatives, offered help to others and generally contributed to the well-being of the set.
- She criticizes some members for their poor communication and intermittent presence.
- She indicates she has learned from the process: about group work as well as about herself.
- She is quite hard on herself at times, though realistic too.
- She says use of the medium helped develop her writing skills.

**Box 4.1 Example of Self-Review:
Workshop 1 Collaborative Project**

**Self-assessment of the Collaborative Project
Workshop 1
Marianna**

Project achievement
I was committed to this project and reliably participated in the development and the completion of the project. My role, in collaboration with Agnes, was to research and produce a report on the social, pedagogical roles of the online tutor.

I feel fortunate that I was able to contribute to the project right from the inception stage by proposing a few ideas towards both the goal and the process. Following a chat meeting between Agnes, Lucilla and myself (chat log 14) the topic of motivating online learners was selected and I continued with a proposal in the discussion forum on the organizational structure and follow up of progress for the collaborative project (3709 & 4315). At that stage I began my work within my sub-group with Agnes on the tutor–learner relationship. I proposed a structure on our sub-task which with Agnes's help we were able to finalize and begin the actual work. At this stage I sought research publications on the topic which I shared with the other team members (3368 & 3828). I took the initiative in the production of the first draft of our sub-task (4151) which was followed by negotiation with Agnes for a shared decision on how to structure and finalize the report. We reviewed each other's work offering creative and constructive input. Following a chat discussion (log unavailable) between Agnes and I, we agreed that Agnes would merge the two drafts and I would produce our part of the Power Point presentation. I produced the first draft of our Power Point presentation (4789). Nige's encouraging comments and formative feedback (4945) helped us complete our task successfully. We completed work on time (4746). I wanted to help other team members, but was very cautious not to infringe on their responsibilities. I offered help and made myself available for help (4746). I took the initiative in editing part of the collated report (4802 & 5120).

On the whole my accounts of the collaborative project were very positive. I was fortunate to work closely with Agnes who was always supportive and responsive.

Communication

The fact that we could do a detailed project in a step-by-step fashion and be able to coordinate every part of it has been very satisfying and rewarding experience.

Of course, as with every other task, this one has had its hassles. I did not understand why some members did not communicate with the rest of us, which I also found frustrating to deal with. Getting the group together was not the primary goal but having input from every member was imperative. I sometimes wondered whether I should be more forceful. But then I decided that such actions are not within my domain and I went on with the project with those who were most responsive, thus my communication was limited to certain members which I would like to extend to other members in the future.

I have had responses from all and had appreciated all; the greetings and the social interactions are as equally pleasing to the project completion. I observed others and gave feedback (4645) and initiated dialogues with every member of the set (4315) but then at times found myself talking to a vacuum. It was discouraging at times when postings were ignored (3817).

Due to the lack of responses from certain set members and the social interaction and other external pressures, I expressed my feelings to others (3598). I found myself becoming abrupt, intolerant. For example one time (3817) I had no other means of expressing my anger and frustrations except to shout. Ultimately, I believe my reactions stem from the fact that I cared and wanted clear directions towards achieving our goal, I was seeking cooperation and compromise for considering mutually convenient time for our chat meetings.

Overall, I learnt more about communication. It is now easier for me to initiate communication than it used to be. The process has become an exchange for me. I have always been a highly verbal person, but orally. Writing did not come easily to me. Today I write with more energy and openness. And I see writing serving an online group dynamic, whether in chat rooms, private emails or discussion threads I sought information, asked questions for further clarifications (4685), also elaborated and offered information (3938 & 3618).

In many ways this medium of communication has enhanced my writing skills, which in turn enhanced my online social interaction.

Social interaction
Like the project we have embarked on, social interaction is a process. It can be intense, mellow or varied. My interaction with this group of individuals has been developing in some cases (4800 & 4817) and has been stagnated in others (4817 & 5121). I can't say that it is always the other person's doing or fault, for when a person does not respond to me, I lose interest and find it difficult to make the effort to interact with them.

Social interaction exists at different levels simultaneously. It is at its best when the social/professional and academic merge into a natural flow of give and take. When I write to a member of the team, my 'hello, how're you?' I'm expressing my enthusiasm and interest about the project, about our progress (4095). My questions about a team member's family are also questions about his ability to work within the pressures of daily life (4817, 4072). Likewise, when I talk about my work and my family (3598), I could be expressing frustration over time constraints or pleasure about small successes. It is as if I take a small step forward each day. Talking about my weekends and holidays (4800, 4817, 4095) allows me to experience these frustrations and successes, allowing me to understand myself while I communicate with others. In this sense, the communication is a mirror of my achievements, which I nurture and value.

On many occasions I was supportive, encouraging to peers for their dedication and effort in completing tasks, this is evident in many messages (4850, 5121, 4878, 3003 & 4800). Then there is the attempted social interaction with those who are less active. During the early stages of the collaborative project, I was sympathetic when I emailed (29 November, email) Jim updating him with work encouraging him to come and informed him that he could easily catch up and he hadn't missed much. I informed the set members of my communication with Jim (3709).

Reflective skills
Every time that I am engaged in a task, I find two strands of thinking going through my mind: thinking about the task and reflecting on my performance. That is my understanding of the term reflection, different here because it is handled self-consciously on paper.

I am a person who seeks improvement, and to improve my performance I have to evaluate myself as well as others – evaluate not to judge but to understand and create options in behaviour, in writing, in teamwork, in approaching this course work. An example illustrates my attitude. I once had the opportunity to observe a chat room interaction – where for the first and the only time all set met – without me actively participating in it. I wanted to get to know other participants in real-time conversation, who wanted to do what and so on. It gave me a good view of the interaction of the group and how that could influence my functioning.

The process also helped me understand the dynamics of our group. I used to think that I was rigid in my approach to work, always working backwards when planning projects, course syllabus, etc. but I found that I am flexible, that I can adopt the systems adopted by others, as happened with our collaborative project. I went along with whatever other set members suggested and successfully completed the tasks (3122 & 3198). That shift opens new possibilities. The less positive side of things, at times I accepted other ideas but not willingly, although I believed that our report and Power Point presentation could have been improved, I made no additional suggestions. This is one of my weaknesses which I need to work on in the future.

Working on the project has led me to a better understanding of myself. In my effort to balance my family commitment, my demanding work and this course, I find that I have to evaluate the time I spend on tasks, the time I have to complete tasks, both short term and long term. Deadlines make me tense even when I have time before the work is due, I try my utmost to complete tasks on time because I do not want to let other members down (4746 & 4817).

I enjoyed most of the actual work and the interaction with other participants. I learnt to engage myself in the learning discourse, and I am able to give and take, to balance my contribution (4817). I understand that when a participant is not active, the team loses.

Philosophically, though, I am able to accept loss, but also to focus on the positive and to keep moving ahead.

I am more critical of myself and of my work than others are of me. I always want to do more, to do better and demand a lot of myself (chat with Agnes, log unavailable). I do recognize my skills and achievements but they are usually not enough. Of course this negative is always a positive, for had it not been for this characteristic, I wouldn't have been doing this course.

On the whole my first experience in the online collaborative project has been very positive, it had an element of the spontaneous which does not exist in traditional environment. Because of that new ideas occur. The limitations are – it is only as good as the people involved in it and how much time and energy they are willing to commit to the learning activity. You can have high-energy participants who are ahead of the project and those of low energy who participate infrequently.

This student's self-review shows, I think, that she was very aware of the four components of the collaborative review and assessment process in advance of participating in the collaborative project. Her review is so focused on these four components that it is difficult to imagine it being written by someone who did not take them into consideration prior to the learning event. This is exactly what we would hope for. The review and assessment criteria are provided in advance so that students can read them and consider if they wish to take account of them during the set's work. They have a dual role: they alert students to the assessment criteria that each of them is to apply later to themselves and to each other; they also provide a guide to students about how they may participate in the collaborative project by giving examples of the kinds of personal participation that can be drawn on to help them work effectively in the set.

Students take this awareness of the four components with them into other workshops as part of a process of absorbing the culture and values of the course.

The tutor's review   The tutor review (Box 4.2) is extremely positive and supportive. He starts by immediately congratulating Marianna on her successful contribution to the work of the set. In addition to letting her know he is aware of her contribution to the collaborative product, he lets her know that he is aware of the contribution she has made to the well-being of the set by referring to such things as her use of humour, the anecdotes she made in the conversations, and the warmth of her communications especially when it was a member's birthday. He notes that she brought many resources to the work of the set, and he finishes by saying he has no hesitation in awarding her a pass.

Box 4.2 Example of a Tutor Review

Tutor Review for Marianna, Workshop 1

Hi Marianna,

I shouldn't need to tell you that you have passed with flying colours. On any reckoning you have made an outstanding contribution to the set as a learning community and contributed as much to the social climate as to the excellent working atmosphere that developed over the course of the collaborative project.

You were supportive of others in general comments, in the way you researched and contributed resources and ideas and in the way you put yourself out for others. In addition life was not easy working in a new environment with relatively unknown others and working across time zones as you did. I am well aware that you were willing to attend chat sessions in the small hours in order to help the set work towards a successful conclusion. That kind of attitude and disposition towards others make a huge difference to the success of a set and to the generally warm working atmosphere that developed.

Your communication skills are excellent. Many times you signalled to others in the set that they were doing well and that their input was welcomed and understood. You offered praise to others (for instance in message 3003) and returned the hard work put in by others with an equal input by yourself.

Your contribution towards the end-product and to the task being achieved was significant indeed. You were happy to summarize and report on progress being made by reflecting and reviewing chat sessions and the conversations unfolding (message 3122 for example). You searched for resources and brought them back to share with others in the set and you also did background reading to help improve the quality of the end-product.

Your contribution towards the social climate was tremendous. This ranged from wishing others happy birthday through to chasing up missing members of the set to ask about their welfare. You shared personal anecdotes for example sighting a leopard out on a day trip and you were thoughtful towards me and some of my difficulties. This was personally appreciated and I can't but imagine others in the set felt similarly appreciative of your comments and friendly disposition.

It is a pleasure having you with us on the course Marianna. You come over as a warm, caring and humorous person who is both sociable and intelligent. You also worked tirelessly for the set and the experience was all the better for your contribution and your presence. I award you a very strong pass. Well done and good luck with the rest of the course.

Cheers,

Nige

The two peer reviews   Like the tutor, Lucilla and Roger provide very supportive reviews, but at the same time show their willingness to be frank, and point to some of Marianna's 'weaknesses' (Box 4.3). Mention is made of Marianna's willingness to stay up late at night in order to participate in the real-time chat sessions: evidence of her commitment to the project. They refer to the discussion threads as evidence of her work in the set, pointing out that she took initiatives, supported others, could be relied on, consulted others throughout the time of the project and so on. They note that Marianna was particularly concerned about the quality of communication in the set: she considered the opinion of others and was 'brave' enough to express her feelings; she was not afraid to 'listen' to others' opinion, and she had a great need for reciprocal praise. They both say Marianna was a key member of the set.

Box 4.3 Examples of Peer Reviews

**Marianna's Assessment
By Lucilla**

Marianna, I judge that your contribution to the collaborative project has been of great value and importance. You were one of the persons who showed commitment to the final goal and a high level of disposition and consistency. Apart from all, I think that your most outstanding qualification is that you are extremely sensitive and responsive to other people's problems, helpful and supportive. Your contribution to the warm and friendly atmosphere that was finally created in our virtual classroom is indispensable.

Project achievement
You helped a lot at defining the subject of our project, by posting proposals and ideas from the first moment that our collaborative work started (Mess. No 2927). You were building on the other members' comments, by researching and expanding their ideas (Mess. No 3599). You have contributed equally to the whole team and your subgroup (which worked in social and pedagogical aspects of motivation). You analyzed the subject that you worked for, in a very thorough and precise manner (Mess. No 4315). You produced very interesting material, using supportive and inventive methods

(Mess. No 3889). You were always there to state the problems that the group confronted (Mess. No 3618) and proposed possible solutions. You took initiatives, as to schedule and organize the group work (Mess. No 3709). As soon as you took over a job, I knew that you would be very consistent and WOULD keep the time limits that we set. This made me feel safer. Finally I must explicitly refer to your commitment, which is indicated by the fact that you often stayed up late at night, in order to participate to the chat sessions.

Communication skills

When it was needed you created new discussion threads (Mess. No 3368), stimulating the rest of us to contribute the best we could, in the whole process. You gave information for the wealth of your subgroup (Mess. No 4660) and also provided information to the other subgroups, even if you weren't obliged to do so (Mess. No 4171). You sought for information and your questions always helped all of us to define more accurately the context of our work (Mess. No 4685). You expressed your ideas in a very clear manner and provided adequate clarifications to all of us, when it was necessary (Mess. No 3534). You elaborated on the ideas of the rest of the group (Mess. No 3198). You took initiative in summarizing proposals and tensions that were expressed in the group, an attitude that led to a better organization of our work (Mess. No 3122). You often asked for consensus on various issues that arose (Mess. No 3831). You didn't hesitate to express your feelings in an intense and very sincere manner, when you had no other way to show your anxiety and the difficulties that you confronted (Mess. No 3817). In parallel with your work within your subgroup, you observed the work of the other subgroups and the most important is that you offered for helping when you felt it was needed (Mess. No 4572). Overall your participation in the threads was very dense, but you kept your messages brief, making it easy for the rest of the group to read them.

Social relationships

Marianna, I think that you are one of the most sensitive persons within our group (or at least one of those, who are brave enough to express their sensitivity). You often expressed your feelings along with your understanding and sympathy to what was happening to the other persons (Mess. No 3332). You showed interest, when someone had been absent from the threads for a long time and you tried to contact personally with him through mail (Mess. No 3706). You encouraged your partners to feel comfortable in expressing their thoughts (Mess. No 4151). You often praised the efforts of your colleagues (Mess. No 3003), not being in the least competitive (Mess. No 4170, No 4315), but rather supportive and helpful (Mess. No 4171). You were protective, encouraging your partners not to hesitate to ask for any help (Mess. No 4572) and you were very cooperative, always taking into consideration other people's opinion, avoiding to show any dominance (Mess. No 4151). You are a person full of emotions and you are sincere enough to express them even if they are negative (anxiety and frustration). I don't believe that you ever exaggerated on this expression, but even if you did, you are mature enough to be aware of these exaggerations (Mess. No 4095).

Reflective skills
You have exercised a lot your reflective skills. Whenever I posted a message to you, I knew I wasn't talking to the vacuum. You always reacted in any comments that referred to you, or to the group as a whole (Mess. No 4817). Maybe that's why you kept on learning a lot about yourself, not being afraid to listen to the opinion of other persons for you (Mess. No 4817). It is very important that you often made criticism to yourself, within the discussion threads (Mess. No 4095). You were willing to learn about the other people's character and expressed your positive and encouraging feelings about them (Mess. No 5056). Nevertheless, in general you avoided making any criticism and analysis of the group's behavior and attitudes, or at least you didn't express it in the threads, except for the slight cases (Mess. No 3618) that you refer most to organizational aspects.

So, like the rest of us, you felt comfortable in sharing knowledge about project matters, but not about issues that had to do with our relationships within the group.

Overall, I think that your presence has been very positive. More important, I think that you are a person who is constantly improving, so I do believe that in the future you will be even better.

Peer Review for Marianna by Roger
Workshop 1 Collaborative Project

Project achievement
Marianna, I think you should take a bow and feel very pleased with the contribution you made in ensuring we firstly had a focus for the project and secondly in getting the project finished. Whilst I don't and can't detract from the excellent work of others, your willingness to propose ideas (2927) and then discuss other ideas further (3198) shows your commitment to the success of the project. This is also apparent in your willingness to engage people in discussions as seen in your participation in the chat rooms (chat logs 14 and 20) at anti-social hours!

I also liked and appreciated your willingness to organize the learning set by summarizing the areas of interest (3122) to ensure clarification. I also liked the way you took the initiative by starting new threads (3368) showing an understanding of keeping discussions separate in this new environment. This same posting also shows your willingness to research relevant sources for the whole group.

In working with Agnes it is also clear that you wanted your contribution to be of the highest quality through an open and honest exchange of ideas and information (4315, 4643 and 4919).

Communication skills
This I think is another of your strengths Marianna. I have noted several examples of you seeking consensus in the group for the project topic (3198) and also for clarifying the roles that needed to be assumed to ensure the project kept moving (3527 and 3709) with timeframes and deadlines.

It is also clear that at times you do get frustrated and angry (3817) although your frustration subsides almost immediately with an apology. I think possibly in the future you should make your feelings known earlier about chat times for example, as I for one would readily accommodate you. It is clear though that your frustration stems from wanting the best outcome for the group. Indeed your motivation seems to be driven by not letting people down – possibly a negative starting point. I personally think that you should turn your thinking around so that you realise how important and positive your contributions are to the dynamics of the group and its ongoing and final success. This will hopefully come in time as I think it is our job to encourage your participation so that we benefit from your skills and qualities and you see your contribution as positive.

In your work with Agnes, it is clear that you enjoyed working together in a relaxed, informative and productive manner. You often give praise (4315 and 4531), which is always greatly received. You are very capable of clearly expressing your own ideas and thoughts yet in a way that allows the group to comment on them in an honest and open way if needed.

Your assistance at the end to ensure the project was edited and the way you supported Lucilla through a difficult time was appreciated by all of us I'm sure.

Social relationships
Whilst many of us concentrated on work related issues you managed to find the time to wish Nike a happy birthday, enquire about Nige's daughter, ask after Jim's welfare and wish us all a Merry Christmas despite working on Christmas Day! My impression of these interactions is that they are extremely important to you and this is how you like to build social relationships. I for one would like to develop these personal anecdotes with you as I think they are what you look for and gain immense pleasure from – even in the stressful phase of putting a piece of work together!

I find that your comments are full of praise when needed (4643) especially towards Agnes and fiercely supportive towards Lucilla (4572). In the same posting you again give reassurance and ask if there is anything else you can take on – reminding us all that it is a collaborative project!

In rereading your comments to Nige – you not only express genuine concern for his family but also a genuine appreciation to him for keeping you in the course (5056). This could I feel have been to any one of the group at any time.

Reflective skills

I do believe that you have very strong skills in reading how the group is developing not only in a task but overall. I think you are able to analyse and assess the 'mood' of the learning set and its direction and skilfully do whatever is required to ensure it keeps moving. This is evidenced by a lot of work you seem to do behind the scenes in terms of looking for resources or finding articles for comment. You are willing to share your thoughts and knowledge in a humble fashion whilst at the same time inviting comments and criticism only to develop yourself further.

Whilst you do this for the group I think you are also trying to assess your own contribution – its value and effect. It seems to be very important to you to give praise but it's also important for members of the learning set to reciprocate through ongoing interactions to allow you to develop sound social and work related relationships. In many instances you take the initiative in these relationships but need affirming responses to develop the relationship further. If you don't receive them you naturally and understandably 'cool off'.

It has been a real pleasure to work with you on this project Marianna and I look forward to working with you further. You bring many strengths to this group, which we have benefited from enormously and which I think I understand much better.

Thank you!

All these reviews are provided in a rather self-conscious way. This is the first time these students have ever been involved in a self-peer-tutor assessment process. They are naturally a little cautious and wish to be as supportive as they possibly can. They therefore take great care to acknowledge Marianna's contribution to the work of the learning set by providing supportive and generally very positive reviews using each of the four criteria as guides to their comments. However, they do not shirk from pointing to areas they think require attention, or which they think Marianna is not being completely 'honest' about. There is perhaps an air of attentive pleasantry to the whole process, but the reviews are highly believable and from my analysis of the work of this set, present authentic and valid views on Marianna's work. It is evident that everyone involved was being honest in what they said. Some banter about the reviews took place later, in which Marianna and her reviewers shared perspectives on the nature of what they had been involved in, and the benefits to their learning from taking part in the process (see Box 4.4).

These self-peer-tutor review and assessment events occur at regular stages throughout the course and represent points in the course when the members of the community are requested to formally present their views on each other. They can be a risky, challenging and emotional time for everyone, but they also represent points in the work of the members of the community when they feel they are really engaging with each other and deeply learning about themselves and the nature of working in an e-learning environment. For many, they are the high point of the course. As one student put it, the reviews reveal a member's character: 'Wouldn't it be better if all these comments that we exchange now about our character, have been exchanged earlier? I think that our cooperation would be even better in this case.'

Box 4.4 Exchanges about the Reviews

Message no. 5308
Posted by Marianna on Sunday, 12 January 2003 8:23 a.m.
Subject: Marianna's self-evaluation
includes attachment
Hi all
For your review, attached is my self evaluation on the collaborative project.
Not sure if I've done it right, at some point I felt I went into meta analysis a little.
… [snip] …
Grateful thanks
Marianna

Message no. 5362 [Branch from no. 5308]
Posted by Nigel on Monday, 13 January 2003 1:19 p.m.
Subject: Re: Marianna's self-evaluation
includes attachment
Hi Marianna, I'll have a look asap at your review but in the meantime here's the tutor review to go with it. Well done!
Cheers, Nigel

Message no. 5405 [Branch from no. 5362]
Posted by Marianna on Tuesday, 14 January 2003 5:04 a.m.
Subject: Re: Marianna's self-evaluation
Hi Nigel
It felt good reading your review. I'm fortunate to work with such a group.
Thank you
Marianna

Message no. 5453 [Branch from no. 5405]
Posted by Nigel on Tuesday, 14 January 2003 8:55 p.m.
Subject: Re: Marianna's self-evaluation
Hi Marianna, I wonder if i've finally developed a good bedside
manner. Pity it's only in text (smiles).
I'm glad you liked it anyway and i think it was an accurate picture.
We're all fortunate to have worked together so well and in such a
warm atmosphere aren't we?
It was great and thanks to everyone. Good luck and well done.
Cheers, Nigel

Message no. 5461 [Branch from no. 5453]
Posted by Marianna on Wednesday, 15 January 2003 6:35 a.m.
Subject: Re: Marianna's self-evaluation
Nigel – Your bedside manner was so good to an extent I did not feel I
needed it. (smiles)
Cheers
Marianna

Message no. 5468 [Branch from no. 5461]
Posted by Nigel on Wednesday, 15 January 2003 12:13 p.m.
Subject: Re: Marianna's self-evaluation
Wow!! (smiles)
Nigel

Message no. 5457 [Branch from no. 5308]
Posted by Roger) on Wednesday, 15 January 2003 3:19 a.m.
Subject: Re: Marianna's self-evaluation
includes attachment
Hi Marianna   I've completed my peer review – and like Nigel it was
a pleasure! Many thanks Roger

Message no. 5460 [Branch from no. 5457]
Posted by Marianna on Wednesday, 15 January 2003 5:15 a.m.
Subject: Re: Marianna's self-evaluation
Hi Roger
Glanced through your review of me and couldn't resist replying so
quickly. That's what I call constructive criticism! Thank you so
much Roger. I'll study it further. You've made me think critically &
deeper of my behaviour.
Well done for the excellent observations, Roger.
I'm afraid my review of you is bland compared with yours.
As for our Thursday chat, Let me know what happens with your
schedule. if not we'll arrange some other time.
Do take care
Marianna

> **Message no. 5527**
> **Posted by Lucilla on Thursday, 16 January 2003 6:21 p.m.**
> *Subject: Marianna's evaluation by Lucilla*
> includes attachment
> Hi Marianna,
> here is my evaluation. I hope I am not hard on you and yet I hope I
> will contribute something to what you already know about yourself.
> Cheers, Lucilla
>
> **Message no. 5561 [Branch from no. 5527]**
> **Posted by Marianna on Saturday, 18 January 2003 5:19 a.m.**
> *Subject: Re: Marianna's evaluation by Lucilla*
> Hi Lucilla
> Why do you think you've been hard on me in the review?
> I'm not that sensitive believe me. When I told my husband that I'm
> seen as the most sensitive person within the group, he laughed his
> head off. Interesting how some people portray themselves via this
> medium!
> As for your last point in the review Lucilla, you're quite right I do
> seek improvement and if it wasn't for that, I wouldn't have been
> doing this course. There is room for improvement for each one of us.
> Thank you so much Lucilla for your review. It's been very interesting
> to read.
> Talk to you soon
> Marianna
>
> **Message no. 5577 [Branch from no. 5561]**
> **Posted by Lucilla on Saturday, 18 January 2003 7:22 p.m.**
> *Subject: Re: Marianna's evaluation by Lucilla*
> So you are not so sensitive as I thought?!!! Yes it is interesting to
> know what other people think about us and our character. Yes may
> be Internet is a very tricky medium but yet remember that we have a
> lot of personalities as well. And they are all real!
> Cheers, Lucilla
>
> **Message no. 5608 [Branch from no. 5577]**
> **Posted by Marianna on Monday, 20 January 2003 7:10 a.m.**
> *Subject: Re: Marianna's evaluation by Lucilla*
> Maybe not as much as you thought, Lucilla.
> Talk to you later Marianna

Conclusion

Collaborative e-learning groups and communities make it possible for
students and tutors to develop relationships based on collective

responsibility, shared repertoires and common purposes. Each member of the community is engaged in personal and collective development. Environments of this kind affect the quality of learning. I have argued in this chapter that we cannot ignore the effect that assessment has on these learning processes, and that we must incorporate forms of assessment that support and reward those involved in these settings.

Collaborative assessment of cooperative and collaborative learning has been advocated here as one method of doing that. I have shown how such methods can be devised in cooperation with students to ensure their validity to assess these forms of learning as authentically as possible. I have also indicated how they are used in real e-learning settings, and provided some examples of their use by students and tutors in online learning environments.

Assessment is so central to students' orientation to learning. Tutors cannot afford to jeopardize the development of the community by retaining unilateral control over it.

5

Assessment: the view from inside

In the preceding chapter I made the educational case for collaborative self-peer-tutor assessment in e-learning groups and communities. I indicated that if we ask students to participate in collaborative e-learning we must acknowledge their contribution to the group's work and reward them for it. There is little point in unilaterally assessing them: we must involve them in some form of collaborative assessment. I outlined some approaches to carrying this out that have been successfully validated, implemented and evaluated.

In this chapter I want to move to a discussion of how students experience and perceive collaborative assessment. This is such an important aspect of working with e-learning groups and communities that it is vital we examine the potential of this method for enhancing the overall e-learning process. Understanding students' experiences of collaborative assessment is important in itself: it will help us gain an understanding of who the students are, and about their identity. More practically perhaps, it will also help us develop and improve collaborative assessment processes.

Methodological approach

In exploring learners' meanings, experiences and perceptions of collaborative assessment, we are trying to describe the lived experiences of individuals in real contexts. To achieve this we have to adopt a research approach that predominantly seeks to 'tell their story'. In doing this, I have drawn on three sources of data relating to the experiences of students:

1 face-to-face interviews with students about their experience of this form of learning;
2 an examination of online forums and group work where students discuss the collaborative learning and assessment process;
3 data from a questionnaire distributed to over 50 students who have

taken e-learning courses based on group and community principles, in which they respond to (among other things) questions about their experience of collaborative assessment and learning.

This approach has much in common with the phenomenographic approach described by Richardson (1999), and of that described by Asensio, Hodgson and Trehan (2000) in their research into the experience of online learning. In addition, I also draw on ethnographic approaches to researching. For example, in the analysis of the online work, which was carried out by an examination of transcriptions of the asynchronous and synchronous discussions, I am doing what an ethnographer would be doing: seeking to explain 'what is going on' as the groups carry out their collaborative assessments (Davies 1999; Hine 2000).

From a grounded theory approach to the analysis of the data (Glaser and Strauss 1968; Strauss and Corbin 1990) two broad analytic categories were developed under which the experiences of students can be considered: (1) the appropriateness of collaborative assessment; and (2) collaborative assessment as a learning event. Each category is sub-divided, as shown in Figure 5.1.

Appropriateness of collaborative assessment
Appropriateness and fairness
The role of the tutor
Who chooses the assignment topic?
Appropriateness of the medium

Collaborative assessment as a learning event
From unilateral to collaborative assessment
Enjoyment, frankness, anxiety and tensions
Responsibility to others
The development of collaborative assessment skills
Insights into assessment
Access to others' learning
Reflection on learning
Motivation to learn
Intrinsic v extrinsic validation of learning

Figure 5.1 Perceptions of Collaborative Assessment: Analytic Categories

The appropriateness of collaborative assessment

Appropriateness and fairness

When asked about the appropriateness of collaborative assessment in their studies, the overwhelming majority of students (94 per cent) are in agreement that the collaborative assessment process is a very appropriate form of assessment. They are, however, in much less agreement over the general appropriateness of this form of assessment for any course. The number of students who think that it is appropriate to apply collaborative assessment techniques to any course is approximately equal to the number who think it is not appropriate. This may be related to the perception of 'fairness' in the application of collaborative assessment. A major criterion for using collaborative assessment is the degree to which it offers a fairer form of assessing student work in e-learning groups and communities.

Compared with unilateral teacher assessment, collaborative assessment allows for (a) multiple views on each student's learning; and (b) the application of several sets of criteria for judging learning (tutor's criteria, each student's own criteria, and those of their peers). The majority of students agree that this is a fairer way of being assessed, especially in e-learning groups and communities.

The role of the tutor

When asked about the role of the tutor in the assessment process, students overwhelmingly agree (94 per cent) that the tutor alone should not be the one to assess their course work. Any suggestion that it is perhaps 'unprofessional' to involve students in their own and each other's assessment is completely dismissed by them. As we saw in the previous chapter, the literature also suggests that assessment need not be the domain only of teachers. For example, Stefani (1994) looked at the reliability of student-derived marks to determine the extent to which peer and self-assessment could be used in formal grading procedures. The results suggest that students' self-assessment can be as reliable as that of teachers.

However, some students seem to differentiate between the role of their peers and the role of the tutor in the assessment process:

> I don't think I would like it if there was just a tutor involved, it would be so sad ... The tutors are useful, but its more useful in a way of actually showing that your work is ... the only word to use is 'rigorous enough', and that your use of theory is appropriate and that you are not missing bits ... because of course you are working in fragments of time ... could miss a huge area which is essential.
>
> (Quotation from interview)

Allowing themselves to become free of the constant need for unilateral tutor validation indicates the development of new relationships with the 'authority' of tutors:

> It's been an 'eye opener' for me about how much I was stuck in a traditional model of assessment. In the past it was almost as if I couldn't quite believe an assignment had passed until I got it back from a tutor with a big red 'PASS' stamp on it. I think it says a lot about my own need for external validation of work.
>
> (Quote from online discussion)

Despite the wishes of the tutors to dismantle the major power differences and relations between themselves and the students, some students do still look to the tutor to take a firmer stance in the assessment process than they would take:

> I think saying the really hard things is the responsibility of the tutor, because despite the fact that I know how keen you (tutors) were on dismantling those differences, the bottom is not possible, and there were times when I thought 'no I want tutor intervention here'.
>
> (Quote from interview)

This particular student understood the benefits of self- and peer-assessment, and thought this form of assessment was exactly right for him and others on the course. But he had very little experience in critiquing the work of his peers. From my experience of working with him I knew he was in fact quite good at critiquing others' work. It is possible that he misunderstood the difference between criticism and critique. His comment does, however, indicate the potential fragility of peer-review and assessment in a setting where students are working as a learning community. I will return to this issue later.

Who chooses the assignment topic?

The vast majority (88 per cent) of students involved in collaborative assessment also believe that having to decide on their own assignment topics in negotiation with their peers and tutor (rather than having to write to a topic provided by the tutor or course team), and decide on the way of carrying them out, is very beneficial to their learning.

> I really like the freedom of choice and the assessment techniques devised for this course ... keep 'em coming. I employ them in my own practice where I have the control to do this. but most of the time I don't, which is incredibly frustrating ... but I know I'm not alone in this context.
>
> (Quote from online discussion)

Changing who chooses the assignment topic, from tutor alone to student with tutor, seems to provide the learner with some major benefits. The new tutor–learner relationship tells them that they are in charge of managing this aspect of their learning. Because they choose the topic for their assignment, it is nearly always a topic that is highly relevant and appropriate to them in the context of their particular interests and professional practice. The topic is usually situated in their practice, and is often defined as a problem, a concern or an important issue that they wish to investigate. Because of this, it is not approached merely in an academic or theoretical way. It has a basis in their professional 'practice' or personal interest, and through investigating their practice they are in a position to relate that to theory – rather than the other way round. This starting point is not trivial: by situating the focus of their learning in their practice (Lave and Wenger 1991; Wenger 1998) they are deliberately grounding their writing and thinking in a real working context. In doing this, they ask themselves important questions about their practice, or the context of their work or interests, and then proceed to examine these questions in their assignment.

Appropriateness of the medium

How appropriate is the 'online' medium for carrying out collaborative assessment? Carrying out this form of assessment can be a complex process no matter what the medium. Reading and reviewing someone else's work – offering comments and insights on it and commenting on the appropriateness and degree of achievement of the assessment criteria (those of the learner themself, and those given by the tutor) – all this requires a high degree of online communication skill, and an equally high level of supportive, yet critical, judgement. It might be assumed that carrying it out in an 'online' medium, where students and tutors cannot see each other, and where all communications are reduced to the textual medium, could prove to be a major barrier to its effective execution. As we shall see later, it is not problem-free; but the overwhelming feeling of the students surveyed (82 per cent) is that it is not too complex to carry out online. This is an important outcome. It indicates that despite the narrowness of the textual communication medium and all the missing social cues that can help one understand what is being communicated, it is still possible to participate in a process that can be damaging if not carried out sensitively.

In fact, the online medium seems to add important dimensions to the collaborative assessment process: asynchronous communication supports reflective learning, allowing students time to read and reflect on what is going on in their learning sets, and to contribute thoughtful comments. The textual nature of the medium also allows them directly to manipulate each other's communications by incorporating sections of each other's text into their responses, permitting direct links to what has been said and using that to build an argument or summarize a series of different points by highlighting who has said what.

The comments and reviews that form the basis of the collaborative assessment process are embedded in threaded discussions that can be re-read and manipulated in various ways (for example, to find out who said what about a particular topic). Students can see the relevance of this compared with similar verbal face-to-face processes:

> When writing a response to someone's posting you are recording your comments which can always be referred back to. Any of us can look back through the postings from October and restart a debate. Can you remember any conversations that you had back in October – in detail?
>
> (Quotation from online discussion)

Using a system that logs everything you 'say' and makes that available for anyone to revisit and remind you about may, however, be somewhat intimidating to newcomers to this form of learning. Ensuring that students feel safe in doing this is important:

> Students can have a real fear about posting up information for others to read and comment on. Can you remember what it felt like the first time you posted a message to Notes (the discussion system) and awaited someone to respond! The need for a safe environment is very important.
>
> (Quotation from online discussion)

In addition, in an online environment anyone who has been away from the group for a period of time can easily catch up on the proceedings, and continue their contributions in the knowledge that they know what has been happening while they were away.

Collaborative assessment as a learning event

From unilateral to collaborative assessment

A major purpose of collaborative self-peer-tutor assessment is the wish to change the focus of assessment from unilateral tutor assessment (which is usually a summative evaluation, after the event) into a formative learning event – one that allows students to learn from the event itself, and incorporate what is learned directly into the piece of work they are currently writing. This takes the form of a review of the assignment in which peers and tutor thoughtfully read the piece and comment on it in ways that help the student who wrote it gain alternative insights into it. Having a definite audience can make all the difference:

> I really, really like the cooperative stuff. Partly because there was a definite feel of audience, do you know what I mean? I mean this

wasn't 'basket' work. This was stuff that genuinely was going to be read and reflected upon. Some people I felt were ... very thorough and that was really helpful. When they reviewed my stuff that was great, I mean to get all that feedback, to think that someone has not only read what you have written but thought about it. It becomes really valuable. It is not just a 'red tick', you know 8 out of 10 or whatever ... that's the effect of peer reviewers on me and cooperative learning on me, the way other people contributed, the way other people could dismantle your thinking for you and assist in your reflection.

(Quotation from interview)

These insights are used to help the learner rethink the piece. They are used in editing and rewriting the assignment before finally submitting it as a finished piece. These reviews can also be the basis for discussion of the substantive issues covered in the assignment, so contributing to the learning of all those involved and not just the person who wrote the assignment. It is not surprising then that nearly all students (94 per cent) think that collaborative assessment is a learning event as much as an assessment process. Students comment on it favourably:

You knew you were going to be assessed. You knew you were going to get criticism on your work but I suppose the way it was done is that ... because you were putting up different versions you would get feedback: 'I am not happy with this, this is too long' – so by the time you got to your finished product you had had a lot of positive feedback already and it was your work. Again that was just so refreshing. It was your work, but at the end of the day the fact that other people had seen it, read it, commented on it and you had changed it in light of what they had said, that was just nice as well just to be able to allow that to happen. Because again that was just something completely new, we had never experienced that before. It was all about learning at the end of the day and the end result was what had you learned and the fact that you had learned something and it had also come from your peers that the finished product was better than what you could have done on your own.

(Interview quotation)

The student herself is at the centre of this form of assessment. The collaborative assessment process focuses on them and the assignment they are writing: it is for their benefit. As well as peer and tutor reviews of their work, the learner also reviews their work and has to assess what they have learned:

I think the assessment has been a breath of fresh air. For me it was just what I needed. It was nice to experience a situation where you weren't getting graded ... I have never been happy with grading but this presented ... what is the alternative ... well this was the alternative. You don't need to be graded, we are graded as league tables and things like that for somebody else's benefit but for using individually, for me as an individual it was nice not to be graded because it meant that you had to assess your own learning and that was what was important – what you felt you had learned not what somebody who was marking your work felt you had learned ... I knew what I had learned. Not having somebody saying well you got a B+ or a C–. That was really a refresher because, you know, you get B+ or C– or whatever, and you think ... and you might agree or disagree. But [here] you have gone through processes, sort of self-assessment and I think that has been one of the strong features of this course, the fact that as far as I was concerned I had to look at what I had learned during that workshop and that was good.

(Interview quotation)

Enjoyment, frankness, anxiety and tension

Collaborative assessment processes appear to be positive, enjoyable events. Many students spontaneously talk about how pleasurable it is to have their work read and assessed by peers:

We were required to mutually assess ... Again I was worried about this, but I feel it turned out to be an interesting and useful experience. I generally hate being assessed – but found it not to be a problem in this case – in fact I rather enjoyed it!

(Quotation from online discussion)

and

I wonder how many of us were really *not* looking forward to this aspect of the course? And yet having more than one pair of eyes cast over the work did seem to allow for genuine criticism and – even better – the chance to put things right. Luxury. I haven't seen any negative comments on this as yet.

(Quotation from online discussion)

Although the vast majority of students say they enjoy the collaborative assessment process, it has to be noted that it can be an uncomfortable event. Students are not unaware of the potential of a process that puts them and their work 'on the line' to 'go wrong' or to cause pain and anxiety:

It was good to get feedback from your peers because I think people were genuinely truthful but in a sort of positive sort of way and it was again ... there is a skill to that and I think everybody I have worked with handled it really well because it could have gone drastically wrong.

(Quotation from interview)

As this student observed, the process is generally very positive and the comments students make of each other's work are generally insightful and to the point.

But it can happen that they are sometimes unwilling to offer really critical comment in case it offends. One person said that when he felt a peer's assignment was not very good, he sometimes felt 'incredibly uncomfortable' in giving feedback. He coped with this by trying to be ultra-positive ('I tried to make really constructive comments, and that stretched me'). But he felt he was being dishonest: 'Well the dishonesty was not actually turning round and saying what I would want someone to say to me: this [piece of work] isn't good enough' (quotation from interview). So in this case he avoided saying that the piece of work was not 'good enough' by providing only positive, supportive comments. Throughout the course, this particular student had voiced concern about the quality and 'Masters level' of his own work: he was never sure that he was working at Masters degree level. One way for him to learn about 'quality' and standards was to compare his own work with that of his peers: '... if I compare somebody's work to mine and I find it a lot worse then I think they have got a real problem because I'm assuming that I'm down there in your Cs and Ds ... that's to do with me, that's a "Graham" thing' (quotation from interview).

Another student believes that the comments given by some are not always as frank as they might be:

> Oh yes, there is no way that educationalists can say, well they might, the way you are doing it is completely wrong. Maybe in a scientific approach to something: but scientists tend to be a bit more dead-set in their ways whereas anything in the arty ... area – everything is open to interpretation and I think that is where our peer reviewing has been – I wouldn't say exactly 'too kind', but each peer reviewer has come in with very, very constructive remarks indeed, if you left something out ... or your references aren't very good. But who is to say that everybody's slant on anything is wrong? I mean you would have to actually ... if you were to actually try to fail somebody you could really only do so on the basis that they haven't put the work in in the first place ...
>
> (Quotation from interview)

This particular student thought that it is impossible to offer 'correct' views on someone else's work. There are no right and wrong ways of writing or doing something: it is all a matter of interpretation. She felt that it was therefore sometimes 'impossible' actually to provide comment on someone's work. This, in my experience, is an extreme case. But it does perhaps point to the need for students to develop understandings of how to go about reviewing and assessing their peers' work, a point to which I will return below.

All of this is not to suggest that the comments given and received are not beneficial, nor to suggest that they are never critical. It does, however, highlight the need to be careful in wording comments in an online medium. Those involved have spent considerable time and energy developing positive relationships online. Throughout the process they have been supporting each other as a learning community, and perhaps at the time of assessment this relationship is in danger of being damaged if they are not sensitive to each other's concerns and needs:

> if the learning environment is viewed as being 'safe' and encouraging then this fear is soon dispelled and sharing ideas becomes a very useful and interesting form of learning. I have certainly found this to be true. It is also a motivator to know that someone else is going to read and assess your work and vice versa.
>
> (Quotation from an online discussion)

It is a fine balance between continuing to work in the supportive learning environment that they have been cultivating over some months, and pushing the edges of this in order to offer critical, insightful and valuable feedback. Neither discounts the other, but getting it right is a skill that requires considerable insight into the nature of the collaborative assessment process itself, and this is something that students (and indeed tutors) usually have to develop over time:

> you know it is a fine balance between ... what level do you critique and that sort of thing, there is social relationships as well as being co-learners, you know, co-colleagues and friends. All those different roles I am talking about get mixed up in that so there is quite a lot of anxiety in people.
>
> (Quotation from interview)

Anxiety, pain and tension in a learning community can be important for the development of its members, and for the development of the community itself (Hodgson and Reynolds 2005). Helping yourself (education) and helping others (therapy) are important supportive elements of a third dimension, that of development (Pedler 1981). Development in the context of a learning community (and online learning communities are no different) suggests 'a movement away from the individualistic and personal towards the altruistic and transpersonal' (Pedler 1981). For this to occur, a real meeting of minds and personalities has to take place. Reconciliation and coexistence are sources of reflection, learning and development (Wenger 1998). They require to be worked on by the community members. The fact that students comment on this is evidence that this medium is not barren and sterile, as some commentators suggest. It can be a place of considerable social and intellectual complexity.

Responsibility to others and submission of assignments

The process of collaborative review and assessment has to be scheduled into the course timetable. A set period of time is devoted to it: usually three weeks at the end of each workshop. Each student is responsible for ensuring their assignment is submitted to the learning set/group in time for the review to take place. And each reviewer has a similar responsibility to ensure that they read and comment on their peers' work sufficiently early on in the period to allow discussion to take place, and some rewriting if that is required.

Inevitably it sometimes happens that a student is not able to submit on time (often due to the intervention of demands from their paid work). In an adult learning context it is advisable to be reasonably flexible about this, permitting late submissions. But this is an issue for the learning set to address, as late submissions affect everyone, submitter and reviewers alike. Submitting late holds up the review process. Students are busy people, and in order to meet their commitments they usually put aside time for these activities, and sometimes cannot work outside these scheduled times. When someone is late submitting, especially when they have not let their reviewers know they will be late, annoyance can ensue: 'I was thinking I don't see why I should comment on it at all. You know if you can't get it in on time that is understandable but you know, I have also got my time planned out. That is what being given a deadline is for, to help us' (quotation from interview).

Sometimes, if the reviewer is willing, the review process is extended: 'but I will still make sure ... whoever I am helping, helping with theirs and giving them feedback. You know me I will make sure I am in there giving them feedback on it because that is still a responsibility for me' (student quote). There are occasions when one of the two student reviewers fails to carry out their review. Those waiting for the review are usually good-hearted about this, but it can cause resentment. Collaborative learning survives on a reciprocal learning relationship (McConnell 2000). If this is not forthcoming, then relationships can be damaged and the goodwill associated with this form of learning can be undermined.

The development of collaborative assessment skills

Assessing your peers in learning environments is a skill that is likely to require some practice. As we have seen, students are sometimes anxious about doing it, and early on in the process often feel they do not have the necessary skills and insights to carry it out effectively. Students have different relationships to the concept, and participate in the process from different perspectives:

> You know, the comments weren't really hitting the mark. Again they were very surface level but I also, I came in ... maybe we are at

different stages of development. Me I'm a bastard when I'm reviewing anyway, I am not sort of very sensitive I don't think ... Hit hard, probably too hard, but people will think I'm at least trying to be fair. I sort of expected that a little bit as well because I am sort of used to a peer review system with my own students and within my department.

(Student quote)

Students know they differ in these respects:

Maybe James could have critiqued me a little more, I don't know. But he may not have been able to even critique me a little more. I mean there is a sort of relationship part and there is also how you see that sort of process and that is developmental. But there are two aspects of development. Development in terms of just critical thinking and commenting skills and peer review skills. There is an aspect of getting to be comfortable with each other as a group and the more comfortable you are as you are going through the programme, the more easy you find it to be quite fair.

(Student quote)

Early experiences can have a profound effect on the reviewer:

I was remembering the first workshop and I reviewed Adrian's [assignment] ... and I did quite a lengthy critique on it and afterwards I felt really, really bad. Yes I felt bad because I had seen what other people had written about other people's work and I had been ... almost as though I was marking a student.

(Student quote)

In the first review period, this particular student approached the assessment of his peers as if they were students taking one of his courses in his own university, and not as co-learners in a learning community. He reviewed their work in the way he would assess the work of his own students. It was only after the exercise was completed, and he had read the reviews of other students, that he realized how inappropriate this was in this context. It became clear to him that peer reviews needed to be carried out within the context of the wider social and learning relationships being fostered on the course, in which he was required to relate to his peers as co-learners rather than distant 'students'. He said he had been 'a bit extreme' in that first review and 'backed off' in later ones.

Insights into assessment

Another outcome of involving students in collaborative assessment processes is the opportunity for them to gain insights into assessment generally. For most students, collaborative assessment is a new experience:

I too have had my eyes opened to a number of different assessment processes so far on the MEd which if you had asked me last year what I thought about them I would have been very skeptical. I have come through a very traditional educational path. Grammar school – red brick university – FE college, and am still very much in the process of getting to grips with the theories and philosophies about teaching and learning but I do find all of this fascinating.

(Quotation from online discussion)

When this is the case, students invariably say that they now have a better understanding of the meaning of assessment generally from having to participate in this form of assessment. These insights help them in a variety of ways: they can relate more closely to their own students when they are assessing them, and they have a wider perspective on the nature and purposes of assessment. They also say that participating in collaborative assessment processes makes them more aware of the power of anyone carrying out unilateral assessment.

Participating in collaborative assessment can be a defining moment for many students. The experience can be so personal and can touch many inner emotions and feelings that they are forced to reflect on their own assessment practices. They often begin to see the problems and inequalities of traditional unilateral teacher assessment. Such is the power of this experience that, when asked if they intend to use some form of collaborative assessment with their own students, over half of them say they plan to (or have already started to) use collaborative assessment procedures in their own practice.

Access to others' learning

From the viewpoint of the learner, perhaps the most beneficial outcome of collaborative assessment – as a learning event – is access to other students' work, and the insights into the processes of learning and writing this affords. Students say they learn a great deal about other students' work through the collaborative assessment processes and through the sharing of course assignments. This in turn helps them make judgements about their own work: about its standards, the quality of the content, the quality of presentation, the ways in which they make reference to literature and the ways in which literature can be used to support arguments. They have access to the ways in which their peers think and how they approach the examination of relevant course issues and problems. Additionally, they have access to the examination of 'practice' and the ways in which their peers approach their professional practice. Because all of this is highly contextualized and grounded, it helps students go beyond the literature and begin to question it in relation to each other's practice and circumstances.

Alongside the development of skill in reviewing and assessing, students are also developing new skills in learning and writing. The opportunity to reflect on their own writing over time has clear beneficial effects:

> for me this is the big thing that has come out of it [that is, peer reviews]. From workshop one to workshop four, the fact that I have been able in a way to be far more reflective, far more prepared to be able to look at things from a different perspective, in as much that my writing style has changed and I think my view on it has changed. I think my view on it has changed by working with other people whose writing styles are quite different. Whose opinions are different and the way they look at things are different.
>
> (Student quote)

He feels it has been the challenge to be more open about his approach to his learning and writing that has helped him develop. As an engineer he was used to writing in a particular, 'objective' style. He now feels he would write the upcoming dissertation in Workshop 5 in a completely new and different way:

> I am convinced that the dissertation will be totally different from anything that I would normally write, in a way that I would be prepared to write. I think this, and I would like to do this, whereas before I would have to write in a very cool, detached view, very objective. I know now I don't have to worry about that ... And I think that has directly come out of the discussions and debates that we have had online and in fact even some of the more kind of heated debates that we have had, the middle of workshop one, about what we were going to do.
>
> (Student quote)

Reflection on learning

The architecture of asynchronous systems such as WebCT, Lotus Notes, Blackboard and other virtual learning environments supports one of the underlying educational purposes of networked collaborative e-learning, which is to offer an opportunity to students to reflect on their learning as it occurs in the groups and learning sets. There are sat least three outcomes of reflection for students:

- the production of new forms of knowledge
- learning to learn
- the development of 'deep' approaches to learning

New forms of knowledge   We only have a partial view of the learning that takes place in the discussion forums of any VLE. But the technology makes it possible for this trace to be open to analysis by the learner, who is able to view and re-view the discussion as it unfolds before them. This is surely unique to networked e-learning? Students do in fact do this, and find it highly beneficial to their understanding of the discussions. This 'written' record also allows them to develop new knowledge about the topic under discussion, as students point out:

> It gives a written record of knowledge being developed, as well as a final product of the assignment. This makes it easier to refer back to relevant entries and pick up on different points over time.
>
> (Student quote)

> One of the 'goodness' factors, for me, is that I can read the responses, reflect and respond if I feel that I have something worthwhile to say. I can be a participant or a watcher ... I can go back to the parent previews to refresh the threads of the conversations and nearly always see something new there, especially if I have been doing some reading in between.
>
> (Student quote)

By being able to access previous entries posted by members of the learning set, the student is able to develop, through reflection and discussion, new understanding which can lead to new knowledge. This might be thought of as a form of 'local knowledge' that at any moment is implicit within the evolving discussion. It requires the student to make it explicit by reflecting on it, organizing it, deconstructing it and then constructing its 'new' meaning for themselves.

Learning to learn   This 'referring back' is also a form of level two learning (Bateson 1973), that is, learning to learn. By taking time to reflect on the discussions, students are examining at a meta-level what has taken place. It can perhaps be assumed they are analysing the discussion with a view to trying to learn about their learning. This can lead to 'a change in the process of learning' (Bateson 1973: 264), a redirection concerning their understanding of the nature of their own learning. It is the dialogical nature of the networked e-learning process that makes it possible for this to occur. If there is no discussion within the learning set, then there is no trace for the learner to reflect on.

Even when active participation in some discussions does not take place, students are quick to acknowledge the benefits to them of 'vicarious' learning: being able to read and follow the discussion of others. Indeed, the community has at times engaged in heated discussion about the meaning of 'participation', with some students assuring the members of the community that their presumed 'lack' of participation does not mean they are not engaged in the discussions. This is a phenomenon observed by others (McKendree *et al.* 1998).

However, the contribution of the 'non-active' participants to the collaborative process can perhaps be challenged. Collaboration requires active involvement in order to take it forward, though, as we have seen in the previous chapter, the extent of a person's involvement is a point for debate.

Deep approaches to learning The social learning environment in which collaborative assessment takes place – with an emphasis on the development of ideas and thinking within a discursive environment, and the exposure of each person's writing to the group as a whole – can foster deep approaches to learning. This is not, however, a purely cognitive process, but a co-production process supported by the social scaffolding afforded by both the technology and the members of the learning set. What is involved here is a socio-cultural transformation of the kind Lave and Wenger discuss:

> Contemporary developments in the traditions of Soviet psychology, in which Vygotsky's work figures prominently ... [suggest that] In the context of these recent developments, a third type of interpretation of the zone of proximal development takes a 'collectivist', or 'societal' perspective. Engestrom defines the zone of proximal development as 'the distance between the everyday actions of individuals and the historically new form of societal activity that can be collectively generated as a solution to the double bind potentially embedded in ... every day actions'.
>
> (Lave and Wenger 1991: 49)

By agreeing to participate in the learning set's focus on collaborative learning (becoming situated), students and tutors contract collectively to engage in helping each other develop, review and assess their course assignments. To engage successfully in such processes requires something greater than 'surface' participation. It is the collective, collaborative assessment processes themselves that signal to the student what form of learning is expected. Students adapt to a learning environment that requires them to discuss issues in a critical way, and to be able to collaboratively review their assignments with others in an open critical way.

Motivation to learn

Knowing that their peers are going to read their assignments appears to influence students' relationship to the production of the assignment. They are motivated by the knowledge that there is an audience:

> So the learning has certainly been enhanced for me because of the collaborative element, because of the peer group, not demands exactly but the challenge of knowing that your peers are going to be looking at your work has actually been more of a spur to me to make

as much an effort as I can. And I think a traditional course where the tutor reads through, gives me a grade, puts a few red pen marks throughout. I don't necessarily agree with what he or she has said. So the peer review aspect of the course I think has been quite definitely a good influence on motivating me to try my hardest because I didn't want to let them down. I didn't want to let myself down but I didn't want to let them down either.

(Quotation from interview).

Another element of the peer assessment model that I found interesting was how much of an incentive having to show your work to other members of the group is. Do you think that standards of assignments improve because learners know that their work will be open to scrutiny by everyone?

(Quotation from online discussion)

This focuses the mind, and 'energizes' them.

Embedding assessment into the overall learning process of an e-learning course signals to the students that learning and assessment should go hand in hand. This seems to be appreciated by those involved:

The assessment process is a lot more integrated into the whole learning process. Instead of being something 'out there' and threatening, it can actually be a supportive and motivating process. For example, having peers and tutor bother to take the time to go through your work bit by bit and comment on it is a very positive experience – it certainly motivated me to make changes and do further reading, and I'm sure this resulted in a better piece of work than if I'd just handed in a final draft for marking.

(Quotation from interview)

This kind of peer support and assessment also works to help students extend their academic skills and abilities. It seems that sharing their work in this way and reviewing each other's assignments motivates them to extend their normal approaches to learning, and for some, the openness of collaborative assessment helps them become more sophisticated in their thinking:

Peer support is an excellent method of developing your own skills in an area. Like you Lorna I have been encouraged by the supportive comments and have been more active in wider reading and I am sure that I have gone through a much more sophisticated thought process whilst developing my ideas for assignments than I ever have before.

(Quotation from online discussion)

Intrinsic versus extrinsic validation of learning

Collaborative assessment methods seem to challenge learners to develop approaches to learning that are validated by intrinsic criteria, rather than solely by the more usual external ones offered in most traditional forms of assessment:

> I've set myself a personal goal to get better at self-assessment. I want to actively work on reducing my need for external [tutor] validation of work and improve in being able to judge the quality of my own work.
>
> (Quotation from online discussion)

This student said she had previously felt satisfied only when a teacher passed her work and gave it approval. Now she is much more relaxed about the need for this as she has understood the benefits of self-assessment. This is echoed by others:

> My traditional view about assessment mirrors yours about the big red stamp of approval required before being satisfied that something is worthy of a pass! This is now something that I am much more relaxed about.
>
> (Quotation from online discussion)

This is a feeling shared by all students. It would be possible for students to do the minimum and just go through the act of participating in this form of learning and assessment. But the experience of taking part in collaborative assessment helps them understand and appreciate the benefits of managing their own learning, making personal choices about what to learn and how to organize it:

> getting out of that straight jacket traditional way of assessing people. It was personal assessment. It was important to me because I knew what I had learned or hadn't learned – that is what it was about. You could have kidded yourself as well. I suppose the opportunity was there that because you weren't getting formal grades then I suppose you could have done minimum at the workshop just enough to satisfy you that you had met the course requirement. But that never happened because you knew that what you had learned was the best effort and I think that was really a positive aspect, you decided what you had learned.
>
> (Student quote)

This kind of personal knowledge is surely a requirement for the lifelong ability to judge one's own learning.

Discussion

Collaborative assessment in networked collaborative e-learning communities is not only possible, but is desirable. It supports the collaborative work of the community. It is not merely a technique to be applied to students, but a value-laden approach to learning and teaching that seeks to involve students in decision-making about the assessment process and how to make judgements about their own and each other's learning. It is an integral part of a whole with many benefits for those participating in it. Above all else, it seeks to foster a learning approach to assessment.

This research indicates that students involved in networked collaborative assessment actively and critically reflect on their learning and on the benefits of collaborative assessment. It also shows that these new Web-based electronic learning environments are well placed to support the complexity of this form of assessment. The architecture of networked/e-learning systems such as Lotus Notes and WebCT supports students in the reflective learning and assessment process.

The outcomes of this research indicate that networked collaborative review and assessment helps students move away from dependence on lecturers as the only or major source of judgement about the quality of learning, to a more autonomous and independent situation where each individual develops the experience, know-how and skill to assess their own learning. It is likely that this skill can be transferred to other lifelong learning situations and contexts. Equipping learners with such skills should be a key aspect of the so-called 'learning society' (Boud 2000).

In addition, a move towards a situation where each person comes to appreciate that unilateral assessment can often be based on the personal values of the assessor is surely desirable and necessary. Collaborative assessment strives to bring different viewpoints, and therefore different values, to the assessment process and in doing so helps to make the process of assessment more open and accountable.

The openness of the collaborative assessment process is crucial to its success. Whereas most assessment techniques are closed, involving only the student and their teacher, collaborative assessment has to take place in an open environment (cf. Ames 1992, as quoted in Boud 2000) who thinks all feedback should be private). As we have seen, learning relationships have to be fostered, and trust developed and maintained in order for collaborative assessment to succeed. The balance between critique and support is very important, yet at times very fragile. Peers and tutors are involved in collaborative learning and support throughout this course. But they are also called on to review and assess each other's work. In a learning community or community of practice this is not only possible, but also desirable. We cannot bring in strangers to this community to assess learning. That would endanger the sense of community and undermine the learning relationships that each learning set has developed. The community 'knows' itself and has developed a very strong sense of identity.

But it also has to be able to reflect on its work, and be critical of each member's learning. This, I think, is achieved with some success in our context. As this research has shown, students are aware of the possibility of deluding themselves. But it is my experience that the openness of this form of assessment, when carried out thoroughly and conscientiously, maintains a strong check on that.

There can be problems in using self- and peer-assessment processes: some students are reluctant to assign 'pass' or 'fail' to their peers. It is a time-consuming activity, though, as we have seen, the benefits to student learning can be great. In cooperative learning contexts where students are asked to provide their own criteria, not all students provide them on every occasion.

But overall this research shows the importance students attach to learning and assessment processes that take place in a social environment. This is a major theme that is constantly referred to throughout the interviews and in the online discussions. Its importance cannot be over-stated. It is not only a major factor in supporting and motivating distant learners and in helping them overcome feelings of isolation. It also points to the benefits of social constructivism and social co-participation in learning, especially in continuing professional development contexts. Not only do adult learners enjoy learning in social settings, but they are also quick to appreciate the potential benefits afforded by collaboration in the learning and assessment process – and no less so in networked collaborative learning environments.

Conclusions

From these findings, we can make three broad sets of conclusions.

First, it is clear that students are very positive about collaborative self-peer-tutor e-assessment. They see it as being fair and 'honest'. The online medium is supportive of the collaborative assessment process and supports student learning.

Second, collaborative assessment allows students to enjoy the benefits of shared insights from a real and motivating audience (peers and tutor). They like the encouragement to review and self-assess and give perceptive feedback about affective dimensions of the experience. They comment positively on community responsibility, development of skills and learning about assessment. There is a movement away from extrinsic validation of learning to intrinsic self-validation, and evidence of students developing deep approaches to learning. Collaborative assessment also helps motivate students and sustain e-groups and e-communities. The most beneficial features of collaborative assessment appear to be access to others' work at formative stages, and the insights into learning and writing this affords.

Third, many students feel participation in online discussions and group work should contribute towards assessment, that is, group learning processes should count. This is acknowledged to be problematic. In order to implement it, we need criteria for defining what 'acceptable' participation is. We need to define the kinds of evidence required to show participation has taken place. And we need to demonstrate that sufficient participation has taken place. All of this could lead to the adoption and application of mechanistic approaches to assessment if not applied validly, fairly and sensitively. We have seen that it is possible successfully to apply a set of criteria for assessing participation that requires self-peer-tutor reviews. This can be a challenging experience that requires trust and openness, but which is ultimately a true learning experience for all involved.

6

Problem-solving and action research in communities of practice

Introduction

We have seen that the work of e-learning groups and communities is often about solving problems. These problems are not chosen by the tutor but by the members of the groups themselves and are often related to real-life situations in which they are involved. Designing learning as 'problem-solving' is a powerful way of engaging students. It allows them to bring their own experiences to play in a context where they can pose possible solutions to the problem and examine methods for arriving at their resolution. The problems bring a high degree of 'reality' to their learning because they are problems posed by the students themselves.

How does this work in practice in the context of e-learning groups and communities where the members are distributed across the Internet? How do students negotiate what problems they want to examine, and how do they go about sharing the work required to 'solve' the problem?

The problems that students bring to the group can vary in scope and size. For example, they may be problems that are related to the professional practice of the students: these are often problems that the students face in their personal, day-to-day work and which are amenable to small-scale examination using an action research approach. In contrast, the problems may be related to the institutions in which the students work. For example, the problem may be about how to encourage staff in their institution to use e-learning methods and technologies.

No matter what the problem, the process of examining it may take one of two forms. If students are working on their own individual problems, they may work in cooperation with other students in their group who help them think through the problem, ask critical questions about the nature of the problem, and then support them in finding ways of examining it. When the student has carried out the examination of the problem, the members of the group act as peer reviewers in the self-peer-tutor review process described in a previous chapter, helping the student evaluate their 'solution' to the problem and helping them reflect on what they have learned in the process. The other form of problem-solving is where the group works together in collaborative learning processes to investigate a problem of their collective interest. Here the focus is on the negotiation of a problem or issue that is of interest to all involved. Students examine the problem and each brings their personal resources to bear on the problem. They share the work needed to investigate the problem, and when they are finished they evaluate their learning by the collaborative self-peer-tutor assessment processes described in an earlier chapter.

This process can be referred to as 'distributed problem-based learning', or DPBL in short. DPBL events do not occur out of context. They are embedded in the wider context of any course where values and beliefs about appropriate forms of learning and teaching are explicitly and implicitly addressed in the design of the course. As we shall see, this has consequences for tutors and learners alike.

This chapter focuses on an examination of problem-based learning (PBL) in the context of e-learning groups and communities. To conclude the chapter, I will discuss some implications for the professional development of tutors involved in supporting DPBL.

Action research and problem-based learning

To begin I need to define the two main concepts here: action research/ learning, and problem-based learning.

Action research/learning

Problem-based learning in the context of these collaborative e-learning groups and communities is carried out through an action research approach, and is based on a philosophy that acknowledges that people learn in different ways. The action learning/research focus allows students to make choices about the management, focus and direction of their learning. Students work in small groups where they are encouraged to view their work as 'action research' (Carr and Kemmis 1986; Elden and Chisholm 1993; Whitehead 1989; Winter 1989). As I pointed out in an earlier chapter, they are introduced to the concept of action research early in their studies in an e-seminar. This provides them with a model of how to work together, which helps guide them in their work.

Action research is 'a cyclical inquiry process that involves diagnosing a problem situation, planning action steps, and implementing and evaluating outcomes. Evaluation leads to diagnosing the situation anew based on learnings from the previous activities cycle' (Elden and Chisholm 1993: 124). In the context of e-learning groups and communities, students work

in learning sets to carry out this work where the focus of action research/
learning is on solving the problem and learning to learn:

> The learning set provides a balance of emotional support and
> intellectual challenge through comradeship and insightful question-
> ing which enables each member to act and learn effectively on three
> levels:
> 1 about the problem being tackled;
> 2 about what is being learned about oneself; and
> 3 about the process of learning itself i.e. 'learning to learn'.
>
> (Bird undated)

Distributed problem-based learning

Problem-based learning is conceptualized here as being part of the
tradition of adult learning (Boud and Feletti 1997). It is a form of learning
that is little understood: we know very little about what actually happens
within a problem-based learning group (Savin-Baden 2000). The
approach adopted in these collaborative e-learning groups is not the
usual PBL approach (as described for example by Colliver 2000, and Davis
et al. 1999) where a problem is defined by the teacher and given to the
student as their starting point for learning. In this traditional model,
students acquire knowledge and skills through staged sequences of
problems presented in context, together with associated learning materials
and support from teachers (Boud and Feletti 1997: 2). The kind of PBL
examined in this chapter occurs in an open adult-learning context where
learners, who are already professional people, work in small, distributed e-
learning groups and negotiate among themselves the focus of the problem.
There are no specific predefined learning outcomes. As we have seen, each
group embarks on a learning-journey that requires collaboration but
which does not define in exact detail how they should work together or
what the outcomes of their learning should be. In this respect, as we have
seen, the groups are following a long tradition of adult learning which
supports openness and exploration (Boot and Hodgson 1987; Cunningham
1987; Harris 1987), and which has a history in experiential learning
groups (Reynolds 1994; Davis and Denning 2000).

I believe that students learn best when they are allowed to choose the
focus of the problem being investigated, which is always in the context in
which the knowledge is to be used. In this way, they can work on an issue
or problem that has real significance to them in the development of their
personal and professional practice, and that can be located within their
current understanding of both their practice and their learning. The
outcomes of the problem-based learning are of real value to the members
of the group in their professional practice.

The problems researched are defined within each group through processes of negotiation. They are usually complex problems which are sometimes difficult to define, but which are fertile ground for the production of mutual understandings and the construction of 'shared resolutions' (Schon 1983). PBL is a complex and as yet little understood form of distributed learning.

Two types of DPBL are supported:

Collaborative distributed problem based learning   Where students work in small learning sets to define a problem relating to their personal or professional practice amenable to collaborative group work. The purpose of this is to help students:

• experientially understand and critically evaluate the nature and complexity of collaborative group work in virtual learning environments. This understanding contributes to the development of their own professional practice;
• work collaboratively on a shared problem which will lead to a portfolio outcome which can later be shared with other learning sets;
• critically reflect on the experience using a set of self-analysis tools. The outcome of this critical reflection is then made available to the learning set members, who also offer their 'assessment' of each student's self-analysis.

Cooperative distributed problem based learning   Where individuals within a learning set define an agenda for carrying out a course assignment chosen by themselves in consultation with their peer learners and tutor. This assignment is designed around a real problem or issue that they face in their professional practice (or which their organization faces) amenable to being carried out by action research. The focus of the problem is always around some aspect of the course being studied. This form of DPBL is based on principles of self-managed learning, as well as principles of cooperative learning.

Students work cooperatively in virtual learning environments such as Lotus Notes, WebCT, Blackboard, etc. in order to help and support each other:

• define the problem and its overall scope;
• consider its appropriateness as an assignment for the Masters course which will both illuminate some aspect of problem-based professional practice and also contribute to an understanding of the course being studied;
• offer each other support in finding resources that may be useful in considering theoretical underpinnings for analysing the problem or issue being researched, and in considering the implications for their professional practice;
• participate in collaborative (self-peer-tutor) review and assessment procedures where each student brings a set of criteria which they would

like members to use in making judgements about their assignment, in addition to the use of a generic set of criteria which are offered by the tutor. The review is an opportunity for students and tutor to read each other's assignment, critically discuss and examine the issues in it, offer insights into the meaning of the assignment as a method for examining the original problem, suggest additional references and resources that might be useful, and finally offer comment on the extent to which the assignment meets the writer's set of criteria and those offered by the tutor.

Students' work on the course takes place in a series of e-workshops on different themes, culminating in a research dissertation in Year 2. They are organized into groups of between eight and twelve members, plus a tutor. They are given a very broad brief to work to in which they have to agree on a particular problem to investigate that is acceptable to all members and that requires collaborative learning within the group. The problem is defined as anything that is important to the development of the member's professional practice or personal learning the outcomes of which can be of use in real-life settings.

Researching DPBL groups

How can we go about examining the work of such DPBL groups? The examination of group work is often carried out in artificial laboratory contexts, where group members are brought together to participate for short periods of time in some form of group work or group learning. They are often given payment for participating as an incentive to take part in the study. The research approach adopted here is different from the above and has two important elements. First, it is naturalistic rather than experimental. In terms of the frameworks and methodologies used, it employs observation, ethnography, textual analysis and in-depth interviews. Data is subjected to a grounded theory approach where theory is developed inductively from empirical sources, rather than the more usual approach where existing theory is applied to an examination of empirical data. Second, it involves the study of groups in natural settings where work is carried out in virtual, e-learning environments *for extended periods of time*, typically between four and nine months.

I will discuss two related studies of distributed problem based learning in action, both within the context of an e-learning groups and communities course design.

In the first study the ways in which DPBL groups develop over time are considered. In particular, I look at the way that one distributed group negotiates the 'problem' it will focus on, indicating how the group dynamics work and how the outcome of 'problem definition' quickly determines the life of the group thereafter.

The second study is an examination of the ways in which the work of the group implicitly and explicitly helps to develop and sustain it as a community of learners. Two characteristics of the work of this group help explain how it sustains itself as a community of learners: the first is the achievement of milestones which are pivotal points in the life of the group that appear to be central in shaping its learning. The second is the ways in which the members of the group negotiate identity and knowledge, and how this affects their perception of themselves within the group and within the place of their professional (paid) work.

The chapter concludes with a discussion of implications for the professional development of tutors involved in supporting DPBL.

Methodology

The focus of this chapter is on the following questions. How does a group of distributed learners negotiate its way through the problem on which it is working? How does it come to define its problem, choose a method for investigating it, and produce a final 'product'? What happens to members of the group as they participate in this enterprise? What can we say about the dynamics of the groups, the ways in which they communicate, share their ideas and resources, plan their collaborative work and finally produce a product at the conclusion of their task?

The work of one group of seven students (five female, two male) and a male tutor is examined. They spent 13 weeks working on a collaborative problem-based learning event, using WebCT forums and chat rooms as their meeting place. In addition, as part of their particular project, they designed and used an intranet.com site (a Web-based environment with a set of user friendly tools which can be used for meetings, learning events and so on) that became the focus of some of their research. In carrying out their distributed work, members of the group produced over one thousand separate entries in the asynchronous forum, which when printed amounts to 240 pages of text. They participated in 15 synchronous chat sessions, each lasting at least one hour, which amount to over 100 pages of text.

Two sets of data are used in this research: the first set consists of transcripts of the communications and work of the DPBL group, easily available from the WebCT learning environment. The second set consists of data from face-to-face in-depth interviews with some students. Both sets of data were analysed using a grounded theory approach (Glaser and Strauss 1968; Strauss and Corbin 1998). Grounded theory is a set of qualitative research methods for interpreting and organizing data: 'These usually consist of conceptualizing and reducing data, elaborating categories in terms of their properties and dimensions, and relating through a series of prepositional statements. Conceptualizing, reducing, elaborating, and relating often are referred to as coding' (Stauss and Corbin 1998: 12). This qualitative research approach allows the emergence of sensitizing concepts, which are 'less specific suggestive ideas about what might be potentially fruitful to examine and consider, an emergent meaningful vocabulary that alerts the researcher to promising avenues of investigation' (Clarke 1997). This procedure differs from other research methods where definitive concepts are generated from data abstracted from its social milieux. The purpose of grounded theory is to remain close to the natural world being researched, and be sensitive to the words and actions of the people who are the focus of the research (Strauss and Corbin 1998).

In analysing the online transcripts, I started by reading them and making annotations in the margins indicating different features of the group's work. This approach is rather like that of an ethnographer analysing the life of a community. In adopting a grounded theory approach, the researcher is not bringing existing theory to the analysis of data, but rather developing theory inductively from the data itself. The theory must grow out of the data and be grounded in the data (Moustakis 1994). It is, of course, appreciated that the interplay of data and the researcher's meaning-making is a creative one in which 'interpretations are the researcher's abstractions of what is in the data' (Strauss and Corbin 1998: 294). No researcher enters into the process with a completely blank mind. So in my own case, I immersed myself in the transcripts, reading them in detail and trying to understand what was going on in the groups, and why. In doing this, I was attempting to unravel the elements of experience and their interrelationships and develop theory that helped me, and hopefully others, understand the experience of this group of learners (Moustakis 1994).

This approach to analysis is both scientific and creative:

Analysis is the interplay between researchers and data. It is both science and art. It is science in the sense of maintaining a certain degree of rigour and by grounding analysis in data. Creativity manifests itself in the ability of researchers to aptly name categories, ask stimulating questions, make comparisons, and extract an innovative, integrated, realistic scheme from masses of unorganized raw data. It is a balance between science and creativity that we strive for in doing research.

(Strauss and Corbin 1998: 13)

This first reading of the transcripts allowed me to 'get a feel' for the group's work and to immerse myself in the data. By a process of progressive focusing (Parlett 1981), issues of relevance and potential importance concerning the nature of DPBL became apparent. For example, some of the issues that emerged in the early analysis included such things as the group's shared ideas, the ways in which members disclosed issues, how the group planned for chat sessions, summaries of chat sessions, the production of documents, discussions of the documents, joking, sharing professional practice, sharing resources, the production of timetables of planned work, reference to stakeholders and so on. The notes accompanying the analysis amounted to some 20 pages of hand-written text with detailed notations on each issue. As part of the procedure I also made analytical notes to myself highlighting possible interesting issues for investigation and analysis.

All the issues represent potential categories. As a category emerged from the analysis, I would make a note of it and proceed with the analysis of the transcript, trying to find evidence that might support or refute the category's being included in the final set of categories. I would then look in depth at these emerging categories, re-read the margin annotations and notes to myself, moving back and forth from the text of the transcripts to my notes. A new set of notes was made on the particular category, clarifying for example who said what or who did what, how others reacted to that, and how the group worked with members' ideas and suggestions. Typically, I would then proceed to engage in a new round of analysis in order to illuminate the category in some more detail (Parlett 1981).

In this way, categories were reworked and reconceptualized on the basis of re-readings and analyses of the transcripts with the purpose of producing the final set of explanatory categories. Sometimes new categories emerged as I reduced the data and merged categories. The rigour of this approach is a measure of the 'trustworthiness' (Lincoln and Guba 1985: 290) or validity of this kind of research. The development of the categories and emergent theory are grounded in rigorous analysis of the data (Dey 1993).

At the same time as doing this, I produced a summary flow chart of the work of the group, detailing each important step taken, synchronous chat sessions and their outcomes, asynchronous discussions and group work, milestones, the production of documents and so on (see Figure 6.1).

The transcripts show what each member of the set 'says'; and what they say is automatically indexed in the transcripts (along with dates and times and other contextual information). Because of this, I was able to follow the various threads of the discussions and group work with relative ease.

The face-to-face interviews were carried out with British students after they had completed the Masters. They took the form of an open-ended discussion with the students about their experience of learning in e-groups and communities (and sometimes about my own experiences). They were audio recorded and later transcribed for analysis. They were subject to a grounded theory analysis. Together with the online transcripts, they provided a degree of triangulation of the data (Patton 1990: 464)

The development of groups and communities

What I would like to do here is present examples of emergent issues in order to illustrate some aspects of the group's work and indicate the richness of the data and the possibilities of the methodological approach for analysing distributed problem-based learning.

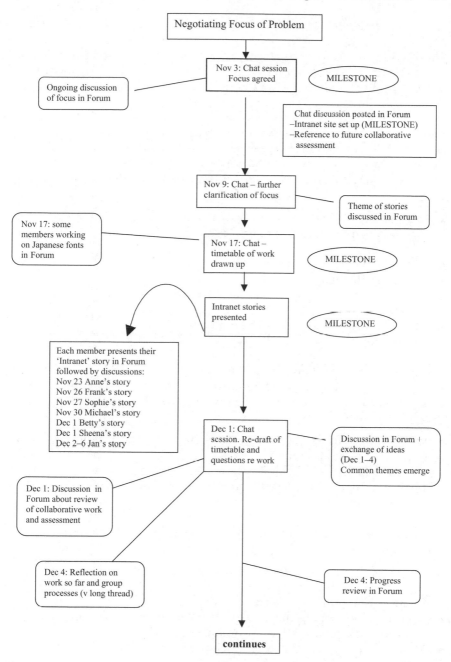

Figure 6.1   Incomplete Example of Flow Chart of Major Stages of Group's Early Work

The group's development

One of the major issues that emerged from analysing the data was the way in which the group developed over the 13 weeks. In examining the work of the group, three main phases of development can be discerned, each with several sub-phases:

Phase 1 – negotiation   There is a long first phase that is characterized by considerable negotiation between the members of the group. The work in this phase is highly collaborative and involves all the members working closely together. Several sub-phases are evident in the group's work:

- Negotiation of the focus of the particular problem to be investigated, with members communicating in real-time chat rooms and asynchronous forums.
- Setting a timetable for their work.
- Beginning the work.
- Redrafting the timetable on the basis of their experience and new evidence.
- Checking course assessment requirements.
- Negotiating the format and structure of the final product.

Phase 2 – organizing   This is a medium-length phase that is characterized by the group's organizing itself into three sub-groups, and by the members of the sub-groups busying themselves with particular parts of the research around the particular problem.

- Each sub-group has a particular focus and contribution to make towards the final product.
- Each sub-group sub-divides its work among its members.
- Members from each sub-group are invited to contribute to the work of the other sub-groups.

Phase 3 – production   This phase is short and is characterized by production.

- Drafts of sections of the product are shared by sub-groups and commented on by everyone.
- Chapter headings are finalized.
- Assurance concerning the assessment requirements is sought.
- A draft of the final product is produced and shared.
- Members take part in a final chat session to polish the finished product.
- The product is submitted to the wider e-community for review and discussion.

Phase 4 – Reflection This is the point in the work of the group when members reflect on their learning and review what they did. This has several sub-phases:

- Each member takes time out to reflect on their contribution to the work of the group.
- Each member compiles 'evidence' on their own and each other's participation.
- Submission of review and assessment reports are submitted to the group.
- There is general discussion of the reports.

Although these four phases occur over the 13 weeks during which the group is working together, they are not completely discrete. There is movement within each phase, especially in Phase 1 where there are many iterations of the negotiations sub-phase, and drafting and redrafting of the timetable (see Figure 6.1). Additionally, as the DPBL work moves from one phase to another, there is a blurring of one phase with another.

The division of labour in Phase 2, where sub-groups are formed in order to carry out particular aspects of the group's overall work, is a point where collaboration is occurring at two levels: within the group as a whole, and within the sub-groups. As there is no concern that every student should learn the exact same material according to a set curriculum of predefined learning objectives, or that they should all research the exact same topic, this does not present a problem in this particular context.

Negotiating the focus

Negotiation is the central driving force of this group. Throughout their work, they make a conscious and collective effort to maintain a climate of support and negotiation. Of particular interest is the way in which the group negotiates the focus for its project. In this group, negotiating the problem to be investigated occurred over a short (one week) but highly communication-intensive period of time.

After some very positive comments from members about how much they were looking forward to working together, they immediately begin to negotiate the focus of the project. There is considerable manoeuvring among the members to try to establish the focus of their topic. Three brief edited excerpts from the transcripts will serve to illustrate this. I have edited the transcript to make it easier to follow, indicating where edits occur by placing the word 'snip' in the text.

Excerpt 6.1

Day 1

Anne: ... [snip] ... I am personally interested in exploring the potential for using computer-mediated communications in learning (the second topic mentioned as a possible project for workshop one) –

What sort of technology is available? How can we implement it effectively for learning? etc ... [snip]

Frank: [snip] ... I agree with you that Computer Mediated Communications in Learning, offers us an opportunity to move quickly to the main business of this course. There is no shortage of material or issues to be explored. Perhaps the chat session will help us decide on the most suitable topic ... [snip]

Betty: [snip] ... I am certainly happy to go along with Computer Mediated Communication in Learning ... [snip]

Day 4
Frank: [snip] ... perhaps we should prepare for the chat session by attempting, between now and then, to choose ... [snip] the general topic for our project and, if possible post some ideas as to how we might proceed. Perhaps we could decide in advance how the issues of substance that will arise will be decided on and shortlist the type of issues that can be dealt with in the chat-room. [snip]

Frank: (**New thread**) I apologise if I seem to be jumping the gun a bit but I think it's easier to focus on the task of formulating a proposal if there is something on the table that can be replaced or amended. That's the purpose of this draft proposal ... [snip – *goes on to present his draft proposal*].

This excerpt shows how quickly members of the group start negotiating the focus of their problem-solving project. Although Frank acknowledges the need for discussion and collective agreement, he nevertheless starts a new thread to post his detailed proposal. Therefore, within a few days of starting their work, one particular proposal has been given a significant place in the negotiations.

This is followed by a period during which members ask Frank questions about his proposal and offer additional viewpoints on their proposed work. Frank takes considerable time to answer them in detail while also taking the opportunity to expand on the details of his proposal.

Excerpt 6.2

Day 5
Betty: [snip] ... I've been thinking about the project and chasing some websites that are incorporating computer mediated learning ... [snip] Carol Cooper's website is interesting ... [snip – *she goes on to explain her proposal and how it might relate to her professional practice*]

Frank: [snip] ... Carol Cooper's site is excellent ... [snip] However, what I'm thinking of is creating a Guide [*the product of their project*] ... [snip –*he goes on to describe in more detail what he is proposing*]

Sophie: ... [snip] ... I've had a quick look at the site you mentioned Betty – it's brilliant. I've immediately got stuff from it that I can use in my teaching. Many many thanks. I love the colour/ease of use etc. I'm still thinking about your proposal Frank. One concern I have is ... [snip – *she goes on to discuss her misgivings about Frank's proposal*]

Another member comments:

Day 6
Michael: [snip] ... Frank – thank you very much for taking the initiative in this. There are obviously lots of ideas regarding topics to discuss in our chat session on Friday morning. Perhaps one way of helping to agree a topic is for us to think about what topics we would like to look at in the other assignments in phase [*workshop*] 2 and 3 of year 1 and the dissertation and how this one might feed into those. [snip – *he goes on to offer some suggestions*]

Frank: ... [snip – *some discussion and elaboration of Michael's points occurs*] I feel that the end product of the [*his own*] proposed project for this workshop fits with reasonable comfort into what is presently known of the requirements of WS2 [*Workshop 2*] and WS3 [*Workshop 3*]. [snip]

Here Betty elaborates on Anne's original CMC (computer-mediated communications) proposal by incorporating her own research findings to develop a new proposal. Frank acknowledges Betty's proposal but immediately restates his own, making a strong case for its being generally more applicable to the group's proposed work. Sophie acknowledges Betty's proposal and thanks her for the Web address. She also raises some concerns over Frank's proposal.

Excerpt 6.2 shows the group managing itself around several proposals. Michael later intervenes, acknowledging Frank's hard work at trying to get them started while also restating that the upcoming chat session might allow them to explore all possible ideas.

Excerpt 6.3

Day 7
Sheena: [snip] ... I like Frank's proposal and the idea of writing a guide at the end. [snip – *she goes on to discuss it*] ... Is this the sort of thing you (collectively) had in mind? [snip]

Frank: [snip] ... I think that you've identified a number of topics in relation to the final product that we could usefully spend some time on in our chat tomorrow.

If the group decides to go ahead with this [*i.e. his own*] project then, perhaps, we should adopt an experiential approach ... [snip – *goes on to elaborate in some detail on his proposal*]

Betty: ... [snip] ... All the proposals so far sound good. See you tomorrow in chat.

Here Sheena acknowledges Frank's proposal but her concern to ensure everyone has been involved in the discussions and decision-making suggests that she is unsure if this is a proposal that has collective support. Frank acknowledges that his proposal has yet to be agreed on by the group, but continues to provide additional details about it. Betty makes the point that all the suggestions are good, and not just Frank's. Again, I think this suggests a degree of questioning over the emergent accepted status of Frank's proposal.

The chat session takes place the next day. The group discusses some of the various options suggested earlier in the forum, but the weight of the meeting is given over to Frank's proposal. Frank fairly quickly establishes that his proposal is sufficiently generic to allow everyone to be involved, and that it also relates well to the theme of the workshop. He says: 'The intranet proposal concerns the ideas of collaboration and learning community', which are two of the workshop themes. Frank's proposal is finally accepted.

Examination of this short sequence shows that Frank is very quick to make his suggestion, and he presents it in considerable detail and with sufficient eloquence as to make it difficult for the other members not to be drawn into it. The proposals offered by Anne and Betty are made in more conversational language and seem to be inviting others to participate in a discussion about possibilities rather than pushing for one particular proposal.[1]

Frank does take time to ask the others for their comments on his proposal, but by providing a good, solid idea ('something on the table') it can be argued that he is making it quite difficult for others not to accept it. Although, as he says, it can be 'replaced or amended', the tactic of starting with a proposal rather than starting with a discussion about proposals places his proposal in the limelight and affords it a special status. This could have the effect of inhibiting members proposing, even tentatively, other topics for their project. Perhaps – because the group is new to working together – no one feels able to challenge such a strong proposal by suggesting an alternative way forward, although it may be that Michael is trying to do this in Excerpt 6.2 above.

Frank uses the language of persuasion. He is enthusiastic about his topic and wants the group to adopt it. When he takes part in discussions about other possible projects he is quick to bring discussion back to his own proposal and expand on his own ideas in order to persuade others of their relevance and suitability for producing a good final product in keeping with the assessment requirements of the course.[2]

The initial choice of a problem to investigate defines subsequent work of the group and is therefore a central period in the group's life. Once the problem is defined, the group quickly moves into action. They spend time in the asynchronous forum reworking the proposal, sharing ideas about what it might involve and how they might organize themselves to work on it.

The emergence of community

Cooperative and collaborative e-learning involves dialogue between learners, and a high degree of interaction generally (Hodgson and Zenios 2003). This helps to increase the student's grasp of conceptual material. In developmental terms, each learner who works closely with their peers will be exposed to situations where their own conceptual skills are stretched by the interactions with their peers. Their actual developmental level and their potential developmental level are narrowed by the interactions they engage in with their peers. This is called the zone of proximal development (Vygotsky 1978: 86). Making this happen in e-learning environments is quite a challenge.

Working in a learning community involves new learning relationships:

> It is not enough to learn how to direct one's own learning as an individual learner abetted by artefacts such as textbooks. Learning to learn in an expanded sense fundamentally involves learning to learn from others, learning to learn with others, learning to draw the most from cultural artefacts other than books, learning to mediate others' learning not only for their sake but for what that will teach oneself, and learning to contribute to the learning of a collective.
>
> (Salomon and Perkins 1998: 21)

The question of what keeps a DPBL group of this kind working together when there is no physical, face-to-face contact, is an intriguing one. It is a central question of concern about education in distributed learning environments. How, then, does this group sustain itself?

The first point to make is that the level and quality of interaction, discussion and collaboration in this group is very high. Clearly the particular context in which any virtual or distributed learning course is run will contribute to its success. In the present case, students were researching how the Internet and the Web might be used to support learning, especially group learning. They were also using the Internet and the Web as their learning and communication environment and were encouraged to reflect on their experiences as a source of learning. They were therefore positively oriented to participating and working collaboratively.

The design of any learning event, and the way in which the technology supports distributed learning, are important factors. Extrinsic incentives to collaborate and work together – such as assessment procedures that reward collaboration – are also central to keeping the group of students together. But in analysing the work of this very effective and highly productive group, it is immediately clear that much of the driving force behind their work comes from intrinsic sources. They themselves take a great deal of responsibility for managing their focus, processes and production of the final product. They participate fully and prodigiously because they see themselves as something more than a just group carrying out some task. They come to view themselves as a community. Their communications come to focus on themselves as a community:

> My view of collaborative learning is that we all contribute to the efforts of the others in our 'learning community'.

> The purpose of the intranet is to establish ourselves as a learning community.

Concerning the use of the intranet:

> Using an intranet to improve annual monitoring and the development of a learning community amongst tutors.

> I certainly think that we have made tremendous strides in the past few weeks in terms of building a learning community.

When reviewing their DPBL work:

> As I worked through the analysis of the online conversations it certainly highlighted that as a learning community we were determined to succeed.

In coming to see themselves in this way they engage fully in their project because they identify with each other as members of a community, and realize the need to actively participate in order to sustain the community.

How does this work? Several characteristics of this group can be identified that help explain how it sustains itself as a community of learners. Two of them will be considered here. The first is the achievement of milestones throughout their work. The second is the ways in which the members of the group negotiate identity and knowledge as they participate in their work.

Achievement of milestones   A milestone is a point in the work of the group when something pivotal occurs. Various kinds of milestones can be discerned, such as the group making an important decision, members agreeing to adopt it and then the group proceeding to carry out work related to it. Another kind of milestone is an event that helps to focus their work on one particular task and which seems to help them understand where they are with their work, and how to go beyond this point. Milestones are points in the work of the group when energy rises. The group members often become excited and highly communicative, sharing ideas and searching for solutions.

The term 'milestone' is used here as an analytical tool, it is a way that the researcher helps to explain the meaning of events taking place in the work of the group. Students are not aware of these events as 'milestones' themselves, although they are probably aware that something important is taking place. Figure 6.1 indicates at what points in the group's early work some milestones take place. An example of a milestone may help to illustrate their general importance.

The production of the group's intranet site was in itself a milestone. It was the first concrete artefact produced by the group. One of its major purposes was to allow each member the opportunity to explore the tools and facilities of the intranet in order to experientially learn about using intranets. They had agreed they would then write a 'story' about their experience, aimed at 'selling' the idea of intranets to colleagues in their place of work who were unlikely to know about them and their potential educational benefits.

This activity – the intranet stories – was clearly an important event in the life of the group. It was the first time each member had taken time out to produce a piece of work to be shared with the others. In this respect it was therefore challenging as well as potentially risky. It brought a sense of excitement to their work and was highly motivating. Each story was posted on the WebCT forum over a two-week period. Students commented on the activity as they participated in it:

It seems as if this phase of the project will be a real eye opener.

I do believe we are all actually enjoying the work as it is very applicable to our professional working lives.

The stories help in the development of the emerging identity of the group because:

1   They are the ones who have chosen this particular activity for their DPBL project. They have not been told to focus on this issue by any external stakeholder (such as a tutor). It is the members of the group who 'own' it.
2   In addition, each member has negotiated a particular aspect of the work which they wish to research and which is related in some important way to their professional practice. For example, Anne has chosen to work on the potential of intranets for supporting language teaching. Betty is researching the ways in which intranets can be used in nursing education. Michael is interested in the ways in which he can use intranets to support tutors in a virtual management education course, and so on. This helps to keep their work focused on authentic problems that have real relevance to their practice.

The community is thus forged through processes of self-management, sharing, engagement with each other's stories and the insights this affords into each other's practice.

The constant presence and availability of everyone online means that it is possible for them to continue discussing the nature of their work and the different perspectives that can be brought to it. In traditional, face-to-face problem-solving situations, time is limited. Decisions are made and people leave the group to attend to other issues. There can be little discussion after the event. Afterwards, each member has to make sense of what was agreed. In this distributed learning environment, members continue to communicate about the enterprise. As a milestone in the work of the group, the period of story telling

- gives the members access to new ideas and opportunities;
- helps them understand each other's professional practice and the different contexts in which each member works;
- helps them 'see' the diversity of their group and appreciate the importance and richness of this;
- offers members opportunities to discuss and share ideas, Web and other resources and insights into their practice;
- helps them set new goals for their work;
- allows them to redraft their stories on the basis of members' comments and feedback.

The achievement of the work associated with a 'milestone' seems to be integral to the group's development and to the production of the final collective product. The achievement of milestones frees up the group to be creative, challenging and at times risk-taking. With the achievement of a milestone the group often moves into a period of very focused, highly interactive discussion accompanied by a great deal of 'off-stage' research activity by each member. Achieving a milestone helps move the group forward.

From the analysis of the online transcripts of this group's work, several kinds of milestone can be discerned, each having a particular purpose and impact on the group:

- *Decisions in chat sessions leading to agreements*, which in turn lead to increased activity. Synchronous chat sessions provide an opportunity for the group to 'convene', focus on a specific topic that has been agreed in advance in the asynchronous forum, and forge their identity as a group. The importance of chat sessions is often a source of comment by members of the group. Missing a chat session appears to lead to feelings of disconnection with the group: 'It's amazing the impact of missing a session like that had on me ... for me the feeling was ... of being lost and detached from the group.' Another member comments on their importance: 'I suppose it's because it's the nearest we get to meeting for real'. Although not every chat session leads to the group's making decisions, their very existence seems to enable the group in some useful way. Chat sessions often lead to increased activity in the asynchronous forum as the group picks up on points covered in the chat, negotiates new meanings and discusses how to take their decisions forward.
- *The production of artefacts* such as drafts of the product report and the

design of an intranet site. The production of artefacts seems to serve the purpose of letting the group see, in some concrete way, that they are making good progress with their project. The production of each artefact is a milestone towards the production of the final 'product' and a useful concrete reminder of the history of the group's work

- *Sharing input to the production of documents*, such as the sharing of each member's story of how they learned to use an intranet; sharing their experiences about the completion of an online group-dynamics questionnaire that they all agreed to do. These kinds of milestones galvanize the group and bring the members together at one point in their journey. Whereas at other times they are working individually or in dyads, triads and other small group arrangements on specific parts of the project, these events serve to give them a common collective focus that calls for the full and complete participation of each member.

- *The adoption of new forms of working patterns*, such as working in sub-groups in Phase 2 outlined above. Although analysis of the transcripts indicates that communications in the group often naturally take place between twos, or threes or fours, the formal adoption of new sub-groupings signals a different kind of relationship and focus. Here the focus is on sub-groups taking charge of particular tasks which the large group has agreed are necessary in order to meet the requirements of the general, collective task. Adopting new forms of work patterns serves to give sub-groups permission to work separately. They also give permission to these sub-groups to take initiatives such as inviting other members to participate in some activity which they have devised in order to gather data or which is designed to facilitate the sharing of members' experiences on a particular topic or exercise.

Negotiation, identity and knowledge   The second theme that I want to use to illustrate the development of this group of students as a community is the way in which members of the group negotiate identity and knowledge. As was mentioned earlier, the Masters is designed to enable a wide variety of social interactions. It is therefore not surprising that identity and the issues associated with it become a focus of attention.

In looking at negotiation, identity and knowledge, we move from looking at the group as the object of analysis, to looking at the individual within the social environment of the group.

What is identity? Wenger (1998: ch. 6) suggests that we experience identity in practice: it is a lived experience in a specific community. We develop identity by looking at who we are in relation to the community in which we are practising. Practically, this occurs through participation in the work of the community. The process of becoming accountable to the work and purposes of the group has been described by Wenger (1998: 152) as a display of competence involving three dimensions:

- *Mutual engagement*: in which we develop expectations about how to interact, how to treat each other and how to work together.
- *Accountability to the enterprise*: the enterprise helps define how we see the world of the community. We develop a shared understanding of it, its culture and how to participate in its values and activities. We know what we are there for.
- *A process of negotiating a repertoire*: through constant membership of the community we begin to understand its practices, interpret them and develop a repertoire of practice that is recognizable to members of the community. We make use of what has happened in the community as a way of achieving this.

According to Wenger, these three dimensions are necessary components of identity formation within the community of learners and lead to the development of competence. Meaning needs to be negotiated through dialogue and discussion. In communities of practice, 'meaning making' is negotiated through the processes, relations, products and experiences of the community (Wenger 1998).

Throughout the life of this DPBL group, negotiation is a central process and can take many forms. The group negotiates around:

- meaning: for example, the meaning of their enterprise, the meaning of their identity;
- the focus of the problem they wish to examine;
- who should work on what in order to accomplish the task;
- time-scales for producing the final product;
- protocols for communicating and working together.

The identity of the members of the group with the group, and the development of their own individual identity within the group, occurs through these complex forms of negotiation.

Problem-based learning, as it occurs in this particular context, has an effect on, and implications for, the identity of students. The focus of DPBL is the boundary between the student's identity as a member of the learning community and their identity as a practitioner in their own professional field. The action research approach – which is an important underpinning method supporting learning on the course – helps students make links between these two boundaries. They are invited to act within the DPBL group and at the same time act within their practice. The boundary between the two may be distinct on starting the course (Figure 6.2), but becomes blurred and intersects as students move between the two communities (Figure 6.3).

Members of communities of practice are likely to simultaneously belong to multiple communities. As they experience this multi-membership, they have to work at maintaining their identity across the boundaries (Wenger 1998: 158). This can have beneficial effects on their learning. They can be forced to reflect on their identity in those different communities, and if this

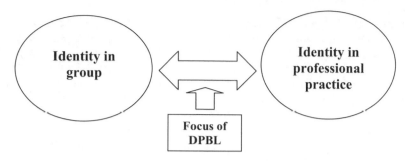

Figure 6.2 Boundary between Identity in Group and Identity in Member's Practice at Beginning of Course

Figure 6.3   Boundaries Intersect as Students Experience DPBL

is used as a source of learning and development, they may use the opportunity to realign their identity formation. This can be a powerful learning experience.

Analysis of the transcripts shows how this works in these DPBL communities. Discussion within the group involves reflection on their practice and critical discussion and analysis of theory and concepts from the literature they are reading. What each student learns from these discussions is taken out of the group into each their place of professional practice, where it is applied and tested. By focusing on this they help to produce 'development' in their professional practice (as teacher, lecturer, librarian, consultant or whatever their current practice is). The action research approach and problem-solving activities that underpin learning in these collaborative groups help to focus on the interplay between what they are learning in the group and what they can examine in their practice.

The insights and knowledge gained from this are then brought back into the ongoing work of the DPBL group, where it is used as content for discussion and where it eventually becomes material to be woven into the various products of the group. This is an important facet of the knowledge-building work that takes place in the group. Sometimes students are aware as they are doing it that they are developing knowledge in this way; often they are not and it is only when they come to collectively review their work later in the workshop that they gain some insight into the process. The weaving together of work around theory and practice becomes almost natural as the members of the group examine the literature, discuss it and relate it to their present group work and to their professional practice 'back home'. It also works in the other direction, where their practice in the group and their practice as professional educators become the catalyst for finding theory to help explain it.

The construction of identity is a central aspect of learning (Lave and Wenger 1991; Packer and Goicoechea 2000). It can be argued that when learning is viewed as social co-participation, the focus is on each individual constructing their identity within the social space of the learning group. This view of identity within learning is one that poses interesting questions about the 'hidden' ontology of socio-cultural theories of learning:

> Whereas much psychological research treats identity simply as self-concept, as knowledge of self, that is, as epistemological, the sociocultural conception of identity addresses the fluid character of human being and the way identity is closely linked to participation and learning in the community.
>
> (Packer and Goicoechea 2000: 229)

This occurs through (among other things) processes of social participation (Packer and Goicoechea 2000; Wenger 1998). More precisely, in this case, it occurs through processes of collaborative learning. The textual entries to the various asynchronous forums and synchronous chat sessions are written in the knowledge of who the community is. They are written by individuals who 'imagine' themselves to be in this virtual community. They are written both as a way of communicating about 'content', processes and other aspects of the group's work, but also as ways of communicating about who they are as individual students in this community. They reveal the identity of the writer within the community.

The negotiation of identity is a very reflexive thing. Students are encouraged to reflect on their DPBL group experiences throughout the course. And as we have seen in an earlier chapter, they are provided with opportunities when they have to formally stand back and review their own and each other's communications and contributions. This can be a very revealing, challenging and risky thing for them to have to do. Identity – of self and of groups – is something to be creatively worked at in order to be sustained: 'The altered self has to be explored and constructed as part of a reflexive process of connecting personal and social change' (Giddens 1991: 33).

How is identity constructed in these settings? Within these DPBL groups, identity is presented, challenged and reshaped with respect to:

1   *Themselves as learners*: as DPBL learners they are challenged to change their identity as learners by:

- taking responsibility for developing skill in judging the quality of their own and each other's work;
- identifying as a member of a new (Masters) community of practice;
- understanding that assessment is a learning process and not a unilateral process of judgement;
- writing for a definite audience, i.e. the community of peers and tutors;
- coming to view each other as an important source of expertise and learning;
- coming to realize that they can produce knowledge.

It also has the effect of changing members' attitudes towards themselves as learners and seems to facilitate the taking of responsibility for their own learning.

2   *Their purpose as learners*: within this community they are asked to participate in a variety of activities and events they do not normally associate with the purpose of learning, such as participating in collaborative assessment processes; tasking some responsibility to help others learn; reflecting on their learning and using that as a source of new learning.

3   *Their relationship with tutors*: they are asked to take on some of the traditional responsibilities that they associate with the role of a 'tutor', such as assessing themselves and each other; developing relationships of a qualitatively different kind with their tutor, more akin to working with them as a peer than as a tutor. They are encouraged to talk with tutors as 'friends', to challenge them and their expertise when necessary and to share the power that tutors hold.

4   *Their place in the academic world*: students often have strong conceptions of what it means to be 'academic' and to participate on university course. They tend to view the academic world as a place where individuals work alone and produce abstract, theoretical writing. Some of them aspire to this. Some think it too detached and unrelated to the 'real' world, and therefore do not aspire to it. Being asked to work as a member of a learning community can produce conflict in their self-identity in a number of ways (this is a phenomenon noted by others, for example Lave and Wenger 1991; Packer and Goicoechea 2000), not least in their view of themselves in the academic world. It can cause them to question their views on the meaning of learning and scholarship. This is a source of discussion in the group as they come to identify with the meaning of 'learning community' and realize that it is possible to study as a community rather than solely as individuals.

5   *Their professional practice*: the boundary between members' work in the group and their professional practice is a major source of change and development, at both a personal and a professional level. Group

members are challenged to consider their existing practice in the context of their work in the group. They are also challenged to consider their practice as learning members of the group.[3] They discuss who they are (implicitly discussing their identity) as professional people (teachers, librarians, lecturers, course designers) and work towards 'developing' their new identity. The work that occurs at the boundary of identity in the two communities can sometimes be highly developmental.

There is a tangible shift during the history of the group from seeing themselves as individual learners to seeing themselves as people learning in a social environment where collaboration and cooperation are expected, rewarded and worthwhile. All of this impinges on each member's identity as they shift from one community to another (the complexity of participation in these groups is discussed in the next chapter). The ways in which they experience themselves through participation helps them define who they are (Wenger 1998).

Discussion and implications for practice

The two themes of this chapter – group development in distributed problem-based learning (DPBL), and the ways in which DPBL groups develop and sustain themselves as communities of learners – have implications for the use of DPBL as a learning and teaching method.

Although I describe the development of the group discussed in this chapter as occurring in phases, each phase is not necessarily completely separate from the others. They are not strict stages where one phase is completed before the group can move on to the next one, as is suggested by group development stages by other authors. For example, Tuckman's model of group development is presented as a unitary sequence involving separate stages of forming, storming, norming, performing and adjourning (Gersick 1988). In this model a group cannot progress to Stage 3 until it has passed through Stages 1 and 2.

In the analysis of the work of this DPBL group it is clear that despite there being a strong sense of movement forward from Phase 1 (which is characterized by negotiation), to Phase 2 (characterized by collaboration and sub-division of work) and on to Phase 3 (characterized by production), the development of the group is not quite that simple or clear-cut. There is movement forward and backwards within the phases, involving members in work around such things as forming themselves as a group and making sense of who they are; carrying out work (performing) throughout the different phases, and producing artefacts and products at different stages for different purposes. The architecture of asynchronous learning environments such as WebCT supports different kinds of work carried out at the same time. The interplay between the technology and the processes and procedures of the group support this kind of multi-dimensional group development.

My analysis also shows that each phase takes place over different periods of time. Models of group development do not address the issue of the time devoted to each stage. It seems that DPBL groups may need to use time in different ways in order to carry out their work. The negotiations in the first phase take a great deal of time, and therefore prolong this phase in relation to the other three phases. The third phase, largely about production, seems to hurry forward as members of the group work towards meeting their deadline.

It would be interesting to know if other distributed problem-based learning groups exhibit similar stages of development to this one. If not, what are the differences in the development of those groups, and how can we account for them? If they are similar what does this suggest about the ways in which tutors might intervene in facilitating the work of any group?

How can teachers use this knowledge about the development of DPBL groups? Can it be used to help guide them in facilitating the work of such groups? I think it can. For example, in the initial phase when the group is formulating the 'problem', the tutor may suggest that each member is given the time and space to suggest a topic if they wish, and that each suggestion is discussed openly and equally until everyone has had a say and a suitable problem has been collectively defined. Additionally, tutors may wish to encourage DPBL groups to use their time effectively in accordance with the findings of this study. They may be encouraged to take time to evaluate their situation at the end of Phase 1 in order to be clear about how they might work in Phase 2. Phase 3 is likely to involve a 'rush' towards producing the product. Tutors may assist them at this point by ensuring they fully understand the course requirements and assessment procedures so that they can put their energy and resources into producing the product according to those requirements.

Knowledge of the ways in which DPBL groups develop into learning communities also has implications for our practice. Looking at the learner's experience of community should help us understand their identity. As the members present themselves in the group and are challenged to reshape their identities through the collaborative problem-solving activities, they are gradually becoming accountable to the work and purposes of the group. The work of this DPBL group as described in this chapter can be seen to exhibit aspects of the three characteristics of accountability to the group that Wenger (1998) describes as being necessary ingredients for success. Tutors may wish to consider the relevance of helping learners focus explicitly on the way the group is negotiating its work, and how this is affecting the identity of members within the group and within their place of professional practice. Indeed, it may be worthwhile in some contexts to deliberately focus on this and use it as 'content' and as a source of learning to help group members in their development. By alerting learners to this, tutors can help them reflect on the choices open to them.

Research of this kind – open-ended, exploratory, descriptive, grounded in real learning situations and contexts, addressing both broad themes and micro-issues – helps us understand the complexity of learning and teaching in DPBL environments and offers insights that can be useful in developing our practice.

This chapter highlights a variety of issues relating to the work of distributed problem-based learning groups. One theme concerns the development of DPBL groups and the ways in which their work changes over time. Another theme is about the ways in which DPBL groups work towards developing and sustaining themselves as learning communities.

Knowledge of this kind is particularly useful at the moment in helping us understand what happens in a DPBL group. This is a new form education, and course designers and tutors will need to understand its implications for learning and teaching.

The contents of this chapter should, however, be taken as tentative. Studies of this kind are useful in helping practitioners vicariously gain insights into their own practice. However, additional research is required across other groups in order to determine how widespread these interpretations are. The next step is to see if there are general common patterns of group development, common typologies of important issues (milestones), and general patterns of negotiation of identity and knowledge. Knowledge about the ways in which DPBL groups work should help us in our practice and stimulate discussion and debate about the purpose of asking learners to participate in this form of learning.

Notes

1 See McConnell for discussion of gendered differences in conversational language in e-learning environments.
2 In focusing on the role of Frank in the group's early negotiations I do not wish to suggest that the efforts of Frank were not of benefit to the group. They undoubtedly were and the group appreciated them. The problem he proposed gave them an excellent vehicle for their work.
3 The work that occurs between these boundaries and the movement between the two communities causes a temporary loss of security as members search for a new sense of self. Giddens (1991: 32) talks of the self becoming a reflexive project and I think this concept can be applied to the situation of these learners. They are involved in a developmental process which is somewhere between education and therapy (Pedler 1981).

7

Group dynamics: a view from the inside

Introduction

Learning through group work in higher education has a long and important history. The principles involved in using groups as a vehicle for learning in face-to-face contexts are well established (Exley and Dennick 2004; Jaques 1991; Reynolds 1994). Central to these principles is a belief that cooperation in learning can help students in a variety of important ways:

> Although the label 'cooperative learning' is used to describe a variety of seemingly diverse activities, and has perhaps different meanings and purposes in different contexts and cultures, there is a common belief that it is a highly beneficial form of learning ... Cooperative learning:
>
> * helps clarify ideas and concepts through discussion
> * develops critical thinking
> * provides opportunities for learners to share information and ideas
> * develops communication skills
> * provides a context where the learners can take control of their own learning in a social context
> * provides validation of individuals' ideas and ways of thinking through conversation (verbalizing); multiple perspectives (cognitive restructuring); and argument (conceptual conflict resolution).
>
> (McConnell 2000: 26)

The shift to a new generation of learning that involves course delivery via the Web and the Internet, and which involves collaborative group work as the main pedagogical method, is slowly but steadily emerging. As we have seen, the literature is growing and there is a particular emphasis on community-building and group work in networked e-learning environments (see for example: Brown 2001; McConnell 2000; Palloff and Pratt 1999; Renninger and Shumar 2002; Rogers 2000; Stacey 1999). However, teachers are still novices in this new arena and require support and opportunities to develop their practice in order to understand the potential of e-learning: 'Technology is leading change at a fast pace, with the result that *there is too little attention to exploring the new forms of pedagogy made possible by e-learning* – teachers and researchers need more time and support if they are to keep pace' (Department for Education and Science 2003).

In this context, research into the ways in which learners work in these new environments is needed. The media of the Web and virtual learning environments provide novel contexts for exploring new forms of pedagogy involving group work. Our understanding of the dynamics of groups in face-to-face contexts may not apply in these settings. We may have to reconsider what we know about learning in groups, and ask ourselves if it applies in 'virtual' contexts.

We saw in Chapter 3 that students said they often take risks in the work and discussions carried out in the learning sets and that many of them felt empowered to be open and expose themselves and their ideas in the sets. I suggested that this indicated that the collaborative learning processes that underpin learning in the sets are highly effective from the perspective of those taking part in them. The questionnaire survey showed that students were, on the whole, very satisfied with the learning processes.

But what actually happens in these e-learning groups? This chapter examines the dynamics of these groups by looking at some of the paradoxes that exist in them. A paradox is a particular relationship between opposites, a contradiction, enigma or puzzle. I want to show that collaborative e-learning groups and communities often exhibit paradoxes around their identity, around the way they work and around the way they strive to exist as groups. I want to illustrate that there are significant differences in the dynamics of e-learning groups, in the way they negotiate and carry out their collaborative work, and in the way they produce their final products. Finally, I will show how an understanding of the dynamics of networked e-learning groups and communities may be of benefit to teachers and students working in these new environments.

The patterns of group work

In Chapter 3 I discussed how we can analyse the work of e-learning groups and communities from various perspectives. In that chapter I drew on a conceptual framework that emphasized the analysis of groups from three perspectives, namely the process of group work, social presence in groups, and the outcomes and products of group work. Students' experiences of group work in relation to these three characteristics were examined and discussed, using data from a questionnaire distributed to them after they had completed their studies.

In this chapter I follow the ethnographic tradition outlined earlier and look at what happens when groups of e-learners work collaboratively in cyberspace on a joint project. My intention here is to draw on the tools and methods of ethnography in order to interpret the groups' social discourse through close examination of their activities (Geertz 1973). The purpose throughout is to remain close to the natural world being researched, and immerse myself in the life of the groups through analysis of the transcripts of their work and communications.

The study looks at the activities of three e-learning groups working at the same time in the WebCT environment. In the analysis of the transcripts, it was clear that members of the groups take time to reflect on the ways in which they communicate and collaborate online. The language they use in these reflections indicates their concerns about the complexity of working in an online learning environment. For example, some of the issues they focus on include their ability to work 'harmoniously' and to take account of 'diversity' in the groups. They are concerned to 'produce' 'good' assignments and to ensure members 'collaborate' in their work. At times they talk of being 'happy', 'anxious' and 'guilty', all of which suggest a deep concern for their personal identity and ontological security. This also suggests a concern by them to understand how members of the groups exert 'control' over the work of the groups (and implicitly, exert control over each other).

A set of analytical frames was developed from the analysis of the transcripts that attempts to recognize this and uses the words, terms and constructs that members of the groups themselves use to describe their activities. In doing this, I do not wish to imply any value judgement on my interpretation of the work of each group, but rather wish to draw attention to the ways in which the groups 'saw' themselves and talked about their work.

Two of the groups (Groups 1 and 3) worked in ways that might typically be termed 'harmonious', and successfully produced a collective end-product or course assignment with which they were happy. The other group (Group 2) exhibited extreme anxiety and division, and required extra resources from its members in order to sustain itself and produce its collective end-product. Anxiety became a major inward-looking focus for this group, and this had the effect of diverting them from effective collective production. The group did produce a collaborative assignment, but one that they were not entirely happy with.

The patterns of work and communication of the three groups are summarized in Table 7.1.

Patterns of Group 2

I want to start by discussing the work of Group 2 before considering the differences between the three groups. Group 2 exhibited extreme forms of

Table 7.1   Patterns of Work in the Three Groups

Group 1: Patterns of work
Negotiation
Discussion
Agreement
Work and research
Collaboration
Production

Group 2: Patterns of work
Struggle – over leadership; over project focus and group processes
Argument
Changing minds and direction
Personality and identity
Anxiety
Learning conflict
Closed-ness: use faxes, chats, telephone, email as well as open forums. But this has
    not been agreed by members, but brought about by division and struggle to be
    productive
High introspection that 'becomes' a major component of their project

Group 3: Patterns of work
Negotiation
Support for each other
Openness
Discussion
Agreement
Work and research
Collaboration
Production

communication and group dynamics, and an analysis of this helps in
understanding the dynamics of the two other groups. I want to show what
happened in this group, and why the members of the group worked in the
way they did. A variety of communication and group dynamic patterns
can be discerned from analysis of their work that illustrates some of the
issues they faced.

1   Members not replying to requests or questions from other members   Throughout
the life of this group it was evident that members often did not reply to
requests and questions about the work of the group from other members.
For example, sub-groups often met in the chat rooms to discuss their work,
and an analysis of this shows members posting summaries of decisions
made by the sub-groups in the asynchronous forums, and inviting (by
name) those not present to comment on them, with no response from them.
Another example involved a member who took time to reflect on the
dynamics of the group and post her thoughts on why there were no replies,

but she received no response. Another member tried to get the large group to discuss how they were working together at one particular point, but received no response.

At other times, some members posted sets of possible communication guidelines that had been devised by sub-groups for improving the work of the group as a whole – but received no response from others. A member tried to summarize where they had got to in their group work, with no response (she was not asked to provide the summary, but in other groups when this happened members were always grateful and acknowledged such help). Another member invited others to brainstorm ideas about group effectiveness, but nobody participated. Finally, a member posted the final plan for the group's collaborative work after negotiations in a chat session. Nobody responded other than one person, who disagreed with its contents.

2 Anxiety   Members refer to themselves as being anxious, or to the group itself being in a state of anxiety over its work. For example, this included the perception that some members were deliberately contriving to produce division in order to examine its effects on the group. There was considerable questioning about, and reflection on, their own group processes and their 'struggle' (a term often used by some participants) to collaborate in effective ways. One member said to the group that they felt excluded, while analysis of the transcripts shows other members trying hard to ensure everyone was indeed included, especially in the decision-making processes of the group.

3 Strong personalities   Some individuals took very strong views on issues and were not willing to negotiate around them. There was disagreement among individual members, sometimes extreme. There were differences in perceived levels of previous experience and expertise, leading to perceptions that some members were better equipped than others to fulfil certain tasks, or that some had greater experience and knowledge.

4 Decisions only being made by some members   In the early stages of the group's work, it proved impossible to find appropriate times when everyone could meet in the synchronous chat sessions to discuss their work and make decisions. Sub-groups therefore met in the chat rooms and later posted in the asynchronous forum the outcomes of their discussions and any decisions made so that those not present could read them and have their say. This proved unworkable as those not present began to question the focus and outcomes of the chat sessions, which often led to feelings of frustration by those who had attended. Decisions made had to be renegotiated, which took time and also caused members to feel that little progress was being made.

5 Changing ground rules and focus of project   In addition, the interpretation of decisions made in chat sessions was often questioned afterwards in the asynchronous forums by some of those who had taken part in them. It seemed that the ground rules were being changed. This sometimes led to ill feeling and a degree of mistrust. Agreement on the focus of the group project was a major example of this. Considerable time and effort was put into negotiating the focus in several chat sessions, and on several occasions it seemed that the group had successfully negotiated what they should work on, only for the interpretation of that decision to be challenged afterwards in the asynchronous forum. The group never satisfactorily resolved this (and it emerged frequently throughout their period together as a point of argument and disagreement). They finally agreed that each member of the group should work on their own professional interests (according to how they individually interpreted that), and report back to the group on progress and findings in two or three weeks' time. This is when the sub-groups were formed. At the end of this period the group opened a new thread to discuss their findings, and at this point they did begin to work successfully as a whole group.

6   The role of the tutor   The tutor's role and participation in the group was for some a source of anxiety. Members made reference to how tutors in other groups were participating in their groups by way of pointing out how their tutor 'should' be working with them. However, there was division over this group's view of the role of their tutor. Some members were critical and looked for 'stronger' tutor guidance. Others took the opportunity to thank the tutor publicly for his support, signalling that they thought he was doing a good job.

The lack of effective group functioning in the early stages of the group's work caused some members to seek 'outside' intervention from the tutor to tell them what to do. The tutor agreed to do this, but it had the effect of forcing the tutor to make some important decisions on behalf of the group, which were not therefore owned by the group. For example, at one point the tutor suggested the group should have a manager, chosen from its members, to help steer the group through its work. At another point the tutor suggested that, because they had spent quite a bit of time negotiating their differences, they should 'just get on with it' and work towards producing their product. Both these decisions were perhaps understandable given the circumstances, yet they had the effect of unwittingly dividing the group even further. Someone did take on the role of group manager, but was largely ignored by most members. The group members did 'get on with it', but did so in their sub-groups, perhaps using the tutor's directive as a way of avoiding having to face up to the divisions in the group.

7   The role of 'closed' chat sessions   Compared with the other two groups, this group made extensive use of the synchronous chat facility. Chat sessions were very important in the life of this group, and a great deal of the work of the group was conducted in them compared with their use of the asynchronous forums. As we have already seen, not everyone could attend the chat sessions. On some days one sub-group would meet in the morning in a chat room and make certain decisions about their work, which they would post in the asynchronous forum for everyone else to read. Those who could not attend would often meet later in the day and try to 'catch up' on the work of the first group. This often had the effect of making those who attended the second chat session feel they were working 'at the tail end', having to address and essentially agree to an agenda devised by the other group. These sub-groups also used other 'closed' forms of communication such as faxes, telephone calls and emails.

By contrast, the other two groups carried out the vast majority of their communications in the open asynchronous forums where everyone could participate and follow what was happening.

Comparison of the groups

In this section I draw on the differences between what might be termed the cohesive groups and the 'anxious' (or less cohesive) group. The ethnographic approach used to analyse the work of the groups helps to show the ways in which the groups 'saw' themselves in relation to issues of identity, control, ontological security and guilt in their collaborative e-learning groups.

Harmony, communication and conflict

The analysis of the group interactions shows that the members of Groups 1 and 3 have a high need to collaborate harmoniously. Their starting point is to make each group a really 'good' (their language) collaborative group that works harmoniously. They put considerable time and effort into ensuring this happens. For example, they deliberately address the need to support members' differences and to ensure mutual recognition. They actively involve everyone in decision-making, group processes and production. The members work in ways that are open and accessible to everyone and make reference to this being an important requirement for success. They talk of 'really wanting the collaborative project to work'. These groups could perhaps be described as 'dutiful'.

Group 2 supports difference but also uses it as a source of conflict. The members of the group bring 'differences' to the forefront and refer to them constantly in negotiations and discussions. However, as a group they cannot seem to reconcile some important differences in a way that helps them work together to be productive. They therefore sub-divide to achieve their tasks. They also bring a high degree of closure to their group processes by the sub-groups' using faxes, telephone and email rather than conducting their work in the open discussion forums, therefore making it impossible for others to participate and know what is going on. Members never talk of 'really wanting their collaborative project to work' in the way the other two groups do. They seem to be less concerned with 'duty' and therefore less likely perhaps to collaborate as a group and more likely to diverge, confront and question. Their high introspection causes them to constantly refer inwardly to themselves in a struggle to understand why they are working in the way they are. As a consequence, experiential learning is high and the opportunity to investigate group dynamics is high, and in a sense, this becomes the focus of this group's project. In producing their final assignment product, some members say the group 'contrived' to produce it, rather than collaborated in its production.

All three groups at some point divide their work so that sub-groups can focus on accomplishing particular parts of the final product. This works in different ways, and Groups 1 and 3 formally and openly divide and come to an agreement about how the sub-tasks relate to the task of producing the final product. They support each other in their sub-group work, which is open and accessible to all members of the group. Group 2 works in sub-groups by default – perhaps as a mechanism for avoiding conflict in the large group. They cannot easily find a way of working as a community. It seems members form liaisons in order to deal with the lack of agreement over the focus of their project. Collaboration in the sub-groups is carried out in closed circles, with little communication between sub-groups or, at times, within the large group. There is some evidence of the sub-groups deliberately keeping their work closed from others.

Having said this, it is clear from the analysis of the online transcripts that Group 2 does see itself as a group. For example, there is evidence of their collectively comparing themselves to the other two groups, and using them and their work as a reference point for themselves.

Reflexivity within groups

Each group is highly reflective about its work and learning processes, but in Group 2 reflection becomes something of an obsession, and actually becomes a major focus for the work of the group without their collectively agreeing to its being so. It could be argued that in the absence of an agreed focus, this group 'naturally' (because of its particular circumstances and dynamics) chooses its focus to be itself.

Considerable time, thought and energy are devoted to this by:

1   The group struggling to understand itself. Members take time to discuss the group's dynamics as a way of explaining what is happening to the group. They appear to do this in order to show how the group goes about justifying its actions, how it controls the actions of individual members, how it compares itself to the other groups, how members are

taken to task about various aspects of their project work. The members generally ruminate on the sense of distrust within the group.

2 Sub-groups (sometimes dyads) devoting time in their chat sessions to trying to understand the group as a whole. The high level of distrust and anxiety seems to force some members of the group to seek greater intimacy, which leads to increased levels of self-disclosure and what might be termed 'intense connections' (a phenomenon observed by Gillette 1990).

3 Individuals choosing to focus their project work on finding out about group processes and dynamics by searching appropriate websites and collecting literature on the topic.

Contemporary psychological thinking about distrust in collaborative groups suggests that rumination and reflection are not always valuable in producing clarity in difficult situations or in producing insights into how to cope with them:

> it seems reasonable to hypothesize that rumination about others' motives and intentions in situations where concerns about trust already loom large will increase individuals' distrust and suspicion of others' behavior. In particular, one might argue that the more individuals ruminate about the intentions and motives underlying the behavior of other actors with whom they are interdependent in a trust dilemma situation, the greater their tendency to make more sinister attributions regarding their behavior.
>
> (Kramer 1999: 172)

Finding the balance between taking time to ruminate and reflect, and leaving aside their differences and 'moving on' cannot be easy when a collaborative learning group is in the middle of a difficult situation. This group could have chosen not to spend time ruminating and reflecting. They could just have got on with the 'task' of producing a final product. But by focusing on themselves and their struggle to collaborate I think they show a real and genuine concern for each other. To ignore the issues they are facing would be tantamount to saying that they did not care. But there is evidence throughout their discussions that, at the individual level, they do care. They are trying to look after themselves. This is evidenced in part by their continuing to communicate and not give up. They even remark on this themselves, showing that they have a high degree of self-awareness. They do share and discuss, they produce work, and they never talk of splitting up or giving up.

Group identity and self-identity

In his analysis of the self and society, Giddens suggests that 'self-identity . . . is not something that is just given, as a result of the continuities of the individual's action-system, but something that has to be routinely created and sustained in the reflexive activities of the individual' (Giddens 1991: 52). Drawing on the work of the psychoanalyst R. D. Laing, Giddens suggests that one way of analysing self-identity is to consider those whose identity is fractured or disabled. From such a viewpoint, the ontologically insecure individual may display one or more of the following characteristics.

- They may lack a consistent feeling of biographical continuity; they cannot sustain a continuous narrative about themselves.
- They may be in a constant state of anxiety, which prevents them from carrying out practical actions.
- They may fail to develop trust in themselves and their identity, and often subject themselves to constant self-scrutiny.

Can the concept of self-identity and the analytical framework provided by Giddens be applied at the group level? For example, can a group be described as being 'anxious'? The analysis of the work of the three groups in this study shows that they are all highly reflexive: they are aware of themselves as groups and address their histories, development and their future. The anxiety among the members of Group 2 may work towards producing a sense of the group that is fractured or disabled. Participants subject their behaviour and thoughts to constant scrutiny, which at times becomes obsessive. This group is obsessed about questioning itself in a way that the other groups are not. The other groups do reflect on their processes and procedures and use the reflections as a source of learning. But, at times, Group 2 is very single-minded about its reflections, and it pervades the life of the group. The group never seems to get over its anxiety about itself, and the members constantly discuss and scrutinize themselves and their actions.

What lies behind this? Is the group afraid it will not achieve its objectives? Are the members afraid they are not 'working' as a group? Do they perhaps feel they are not 'fitting' into the required model of an effective group (whatever that is)? Do they feel they are being judged (for example, by those in other groups or by the tutor)?

The group doesn't seem to know itself – a condition that Giddens (1991) suggests is necessary for ontological security. It seems to be struggling to find some kind of collective identity: some kind of ongoing narrative (Giddens 1991: 54) of itself. In a real sense it does not know who it is or where it is going. This seems to be a major source of anxiety. The transcripts show members of the sub-groups trying to work out how they came to be where they are, and how they can bring about change and development so that they can influence where the group is going. But this is perhaps inevitably doomed to failure as long as it is the work of the sub-groups and not the work of the group as a whole. Factions, no matter how well intentioned and how insightful they are, cannot mend the fractured group. As long as some individual members are not involved in the project of making the group 'better', it is probably the case that the group will not function well as a collective. If some members of the group are withholding their engagement, then the other members of the group will either

- carry on the group's work without those people, or
- spend time and energy trying to understand why those people are engaging in the way they are. They can function as sub-groups and get some of their work done, but the division will make it impossible for them to achieve a collective group product.

Analysis of the transcripts indicates that in the other two groups there is a high sense of self-identity as a group. They have a strong ongoing narrative, which they keep active throughout the collaborative project. These groups are inclusive and mainly work in harmony. Subgroups evolve from collective work and discussion and their work feeds into the main group task of producing the final product. Divisions, differences of opinion and the like do exist, but the groups want to achieve and be successful, so they are handled with considerable understanding and show the members' willingness to be inclusive and supportive. The focus on the well-being of the members of the groups and their need to succeed seems to ensure this. These two groups work at establishing their identity, constantly creating and sustaining it through reflexive processes.

Control and ontological security

Implicit in the actions of Groups 1 and 3 is a high degree of 'routinized control' (Giddens 1991: 56) that helps protect the members of these two groups against themselves. Their high need to collaborate and be productive within the agreed parameters of the course requirements may mean that each member monitors themself so as to prevent schism and division within the group. Competition and disagreement do exist, but are supported in subtle ways by processes of negotiation, give-and-take and reciprocity. Members are willing to 'give' so long as that is taken as a criterion for existence in the group and for successful production.

Self-control can be a powerful mechanism in these two cohesive groups. The language used in these two groups is perhaps an indicator of this: it is always positive and the group members tell themselves that they are working well. They say they are collaborating and succeeding in their work. They sustain an ongoing narrative about collaboration and success, the likes of which are largely absent in Group 2. They believe what they say, and it has the effect of sustaining that belief. They trust each other in these circumstances. This helps produce a sense of ease within the group about who they are and about how they are working. The effort needed to sustain the group is therefore greatly reduced, and with it any anxiety about the group is reduced. All of this helps the performance of the group.

On the other hand, the members of Group 2 tell themselves they are not doing any of this, and in doing so seem to reduce the chances of its happening. They come to believe that they cannot collaborate successfully. They seem unable to begin to develop a positive, ongoing narrative about themselves, let alone sustain it throughout their time together. This keeps the level of anxiety high within the group, which in turn has the effect of requiring extra resources from the members in their efforts to sustain the group. Their anxiety is a source of constant examination and questioning that diverts them from effective collective production.

This raises the question: do members of groups need to control each other in order to produce harmony and effectiveness? An analysis of the work patterns of these three groups may indicate the ways in which control is established and maintained. The conventionally 'successful' or cohesive groups discuss and support each other. Members do not go off and do their own thing. Members do, however, work in sub-groups, but only after the whole group has given them 'permission' to do so. At other times the enthusiasm to achieve and be productive and the interest inherent in their collective work make it possible for individuals to legitimately go off and work separately and not be punished or ignored for doing so. This is possible because trust has been established in this group through the repetition of cooperative exchanges (Burt 1999). By contrast, Group 2 does not easily perform and is less cohesive and has not developed routines conducive to sustaining the group and its work. At the end of the collaborative work, this group is still trying to develop its routines. It is still negotiating with itself.

The way Group 2 functions helps throw light on how the other two groups function, and vice versa. I do not wish to suggest that any one group is 'typical', 'correct' or 'normal'. Groups 1 and 3 may achieve collaborative and collective products which they are pleased with and that meet the requirements of the course, but Group 2 learns in different ways: it learns about itself, and it learns about the dynamics of groups working in difficult circumstances. Members may choose not to view this as learning or may see it as not being worthwhile, though several of them do in fact see its learning potential, and say so. The members of this group may in fact experientially learn so much about collaborative group work that they are better equipped to participate and survive in future groups. Disharmony and division open up the group processes and make them available to the members for scrutiny in ways that do not occur in more harmonious and less divided groups. The experience may be difficult and challenging, but the potential to learn from it (if taken) can be high.

Guilt, trust, dependence and the community

Clearly, emotions of the members of these groups play an important part in shaping the work of the groups. Anxiety is present in all the groups to some extent, but is pervasive in Group 2. The members of this group talk of their 'struggle' to collaborate, and at some time or other they all indicate a certain degree of guilt about the way they are interacting and behaving. Their identity does not match up to the implicit contract of collaborative learning, which is to work together through processes of negotiation and participation. The existence of feelings of guilt pre-supposes people going against norms sanctioned by the group or community (Giddens 1991). The very presence of guilt therefore suggests the existence of some kind of community.

At times, trust is lost in Group 2 between certain individuals. This has the effect of unsettling the group by raising questions about trust generally. Although it is never actually mentioned openly, a reading of the communication transcripts indicates an implicit lack of trust between one particularly strong-minded, and therefore significant, member and the others. Trust is present in the sub-groups, but not always between all individuals. Their language and actions are indices of this. In the other two groups, trust does seem to exist between individuals. Members are loyal to each other. They do not abandon decisions made collectively after the event. We have seen that in Group 2 there is a pattern of decisions being made only to be questioned afterwards, or abandoned altogether. To some members of the group, this feels like being 'betrayed'. Groups 1 and 3 work hard at developing a sense of trust, and at individuals winning the trust of others in the groups. They are very open about themselves, their interests, worries and concerns. They actively support each other by making every effort to 'listen' and respond quickly in the asynchronous forums. They offer to share the workload. They show commitment to the members of the group and to ensuring that the group sustains itself and carries out its work. These are characteristics of people with a well-developed sense of identity (Giddens 1991). These groups could be characterized as being highly sociable.

In Group 2 being sociable is openly questioned by the significant member. They say they are not interested in socializing or in getting to know the others. They are concerned only with getting on with the job of producing a collaborative product. This admission has profound effects on the other members of the group, and as we have seen, acts to stop their being productive. At the same time this person says they feel like an outsider, and talks of the group being made up of 'cliques' and of being 'apart' from them. This position in itself unwittingly leads to cliques forming whose purpose is to have conversations about the social structure of the learning set. It might be argued that the 'significant' other had an awareness of the distrust in the group and that they may have helped create that distrust. They may have had a heightened feeling of being under scrutiny, and have experienced this as a 'conspiracy'. This may have led to a spiralling pattern of distrust and suspicion for all involved: 'self consciousness about one's predicament leads to a form of vigilance and scrutiny of others' (Kramer 1999). This could have been the case for the significant 'other' in their relationship with the group, and for the other members of the group in their relationship with the 'significant' other.

Although liking others, socializing and getting on with them are not always necessary criteria for successful cooperation (Axelrod 1990), it does seem that in the context of a learning environment such as this, there is a real need for a sense of trust and community. Trust is created by people taking time to listen to each other and to nurture an atmosphere of caring (Giddens 1991). In the arena of discussion groups in cyberspace, trust in the identity of those you are communicating with is central to the development of a sense of shared community: 'Trust in the shared motivations and beliefs of the other participants – in other words, their social identity – is essential to the sense of community' (Donath 1999). This helps produce feelings of security within the members of the groups and encourages participation. In trustful learning situations people are more likely to take risks with their learning and to push themselves and others beyond their present boundaries. This can be highly developmental, as well as more likely to produce useful insights into the groups' learning processes.

From another perspective, trust is related to dependence. A group cannot function without mutual dependence. An individual in a group cannot experience independence if they are not willing to express their dependence on others (Berg and Smith 1990). In examining the paradox of dependence in groups, Berg and Smith suggest that by showing your dependence in a group you come to feel able to be independent too because the group members have proved to be dependable:

> For only as reliable dependencies are established is interdependence possible, and it is the creation of collective interdependence that provides the foundation upon which the notion of independence has its meaning. At a group level there is no way for a group to develop a fabric of reliable, interdependent relationships unless its individual members give expression to their dependency even when this may mean depending on (trusting) that which has yet to be proved to be dependable. Only as individuals allow themselves to depend upon others in the group does the group become a dependable entity. This network of interdependencies frees individuals from the kind of independence that is based upon fear and allows them to express an independence of thought and action that is rooted in the underlying stability of the relationships in the group.
>
> (Berg and Smith 1990)

This I think is the situation with members in the two 'cohesive' groups. We can see individuals in those groups working in independent ways that have developed as a consequence of their dependence on others in the group. The group has proven to be dependable. It might be argued that the 'significant' other in the 'less cohesive' group is unable or unwilling to show dependence on the other members of their group, and the group as a whole is still striving to prove that it can be dependable. As we have seen, a paradox can be described as a particular relationship between opposites. In this group, the paradoxes continue to hold their grip on the members.

Conclusion

From a grounded theory analysis of the transcripts of the work of three networked e-learning groups, I have attempted to examine issues of self-identity and group identity, drawing on concepts and frameworks derived from the examination of individuals in modern society. This has, I hope, offered some interesting and potentially useful insights for teachers and students into the ways in which e-learning groups function. Two of the groups examined here worked cohesively, and successfully produced a collective end-product. They developed routines conducive to sustaining the groups and their work. The other group exhibited extreme anxiety and division, and required extra resources from its members in order to sustain itself and produce its collective end-product. Anxiety became a major focus for this group, which had the effect of diverting it from effective collective production. I draw on these differences and paradoxes as a point of departure in order to consider the place of identity, control, ontological security and guilt in collaborative e-learning groups.

When students are willing to give time to cooperative learning processes and negotiations, the outcomes are often favourable and the time involved seems to provide them with a real sense of engagement and collective identity. Their work together forges a sense of community. Although time-consuming, the potential benefits to them in developing trustful relationships which in turn will support and foster their collaborative work are enormous. This, I think, is not always explicitly anticipated by the groups, but on examining their work it is apparent to any outsider. When this does not happen, whether that is by deliberate choice or the circumstances of the social processes of these virtual learning environments, it is apparent that the members of the groups are less likely to feel engaged with each other or to feel they have been involved in a truly collaborative learning experience.

Collaborative e-learning groups exhibit complex dynamics and diverse learning processes and outcomes. Pedagogical designers who ask learners to work in such groups need to be aware of this. It is all too easy for teachers to include group work in a collaborative learning design on the assumption that the technology itself will support the work of the group. This is unlikely to be the case (Mantovani 1994).

Comments on an early draft of this chapter suggested I should conclude by suggesting ways in which to 'better coordinate' the 'problematic' group to bring it on the 'right path'. I am grateful for this person's comments: they made me think hard about the issue. I am, however, reluctant to end the chapter with a list of conclusions, or a set of procedures for the better coordination of the 'problematic' group. To do so would be to suggest that as an observer I can easily translate my examination of the work of these groups into some general, pedagogical formula which will ensure that all such future groups work harmoniously and on the 'right path'. I am not entirely sure what the 'right path' is, or should be, in such networked e-learning groups. Nor am I sure that working 'harmoniously' is always educationally beneficial or that 'good' equates with being 'happy' and productive.

As I stated in Chapters 1 and 2 of this book, the collaborative issues and problems on which members of these groups work are complex and are not defined in advance, but are defined by the groups themselves as they proceed with their work. There is of course an expectation that each group should produce a collaborative end-product, or assignment, of some kind, no matter how ill defined that is, and that they should enter into collaborative assessment of their work. It seems to me that the particular context of each group, the people involved, their different purposes and expectations, and their personal and professional backgrounds and concerns are all likely to be influential in how the groups work. To suggest that we might be able to define in advance how each group should work, and provide a set of procedures that make that happen, is surely to ask the impossible. We are not here involved in a form of instructional design that is linear, deterministic, predictable and closed (You 1993). It is in the nature of experiential group work that there will be diversity and unpredictability in the dynamics of e-learning. Each e-learning group exhibits a high degree of reflexivity and it might be in these processes that their own individual understanding of what it means for them, in their particular context, to be on the 'right path' will emerge.

The role of the tutor in all of this is of course worthy of further examination too. As we have seen, tutor intervention has its own consequences and the outcomes of any intervention cannot be fully anticipated. Once again, to suggest that tutor intervention will always put the group on the 'right path' is to put too much hope in the skill, perception and facilitative ability of tutors. Certainly, tutors can learn from their experience of facilitating e-groups, and they can learn from reading about the ways in which such groups work. From this, the likelihood of their being able to facilitate online group work more generally and become more able to help groups in trouble, or less cohesive groups, will no doubt emerge. But they can never be sure of the outcome of any particular intervention. The outcome of each intervention is likely to depend on the context and circumstances in which the group is working at any one time. We need to understand more about the nature of tutor interventions in collaborative e-learning groups.

The issues discussed in this chapter – the 'reflexive organization of self' as Giddens puts it – are perhaps characteristic of the period in which we live. Reflexive self-control and moral imperatives appear to be guiding principles for the members of these collaborative e-learning groups. However, as we have seen, their application has different effects in each group. Seen from this viewpoint, networked e-learning courses are highly moral, both in their implicit and explicit educational philosophy and in their learning processes. Courses of this kind can perhaps be seen in this light: as examples of the need to be self-referential in a postmodern society. Identity – of self and of groups – is something to be creatively worked at in order to be sustained: 'The altered self has to be explored and constructed as part of a reflexive process of connecting personal and social change' (Giddens 1991: 33). In the context of these e-learning groups, it would seem that this applies as much to individuals within the groups as to the groups themselves.

8

Understanding groups, communities and learning technologies

The issues concerning e-learning groups and communities discussed in this book are wide ranging and complex. The experience of students has been analysed and explored and we have seen that the vast majority of students view learning in e-groups and communities extremely positively. Their experience of learning in this way tells them that it is worthwhile, that it 'works' and that the quality of learning that takes place is very high. Their experience tells them that learning in the company of others in these social course designs and environments is not only enjoyable and rewarding but also challenging and demanding. They are compelled to engage with the course design and make it their own, as far as possible.

Compared with many 'conventional' e-learning courses, courses of this kind provide a new kind of learning experience. The question arises: how can we judge the quality of e-learning groups and communities?

Judging the quality of e-learning groups and communities

When judging learning and teaching, conventional criteria are likely to focus on the effectiveness of teachers in their *teaching*, and the relationship between curriculum aims and objectives and learning outcomes. But, as we have seen, learning in collaborative groups and communities of the kind discussed in this book is qualitatively different from this. Teachers do very little direct teaching of a conventional kind: their role changes to facilitator, resource provider, course designer, co-participant, adviser and peer assessor. Students do not follow a predetermined curriculum: in conjunction with their tutor and peers, they define a curriculum based on the problems and issues they are interested in, or which they face in their everyday lives or professional practice. Aims and objectives are negotiated, collaborative projects are set up, research is carried out and presented, and students and tutors participate in self-peer-tutor assessment.

Validating new forms of teaching and learning should take place in real-life situations, and should be based on examinations of the usefulness, meaningfulness and appropriateness from the perspective of the alternative model. Guidelines and procedures for the validation of teaching and learning models need to be devised to fit the functions and purposes of the model in question (You 1993).

It is likely that in judging the validity of learning in these new contexts we will have to define what we mean by learning as it occurs in these contexts. The kinds of learning that take place here, and the learning outcomes, are different in some ways, and perhaps more wide-ranging, than might ordinarily be expected. In e-learning groups and communities, a great deal of emphasis is given to learning processes, and to the ways in which students are encouraged to participate, share, explore, collaborate, negotiate, present, critically reflect and co-assess, in addition to the more conventional emphasis on production of learning artefacts, such as essays and reports.

An important aspect of what counts as learning in these e-learning groups and communities is the kind of relationship that takes place among the members. In Chapter 1 I asked the question: what social engagements and processes provide the 'proper' context for learning?, and I suggested that learning is a way of being in the social world. I also indicated that the cornerstone of online learning communities lies in the presence of 'socially close, strong, intimate ties', the development of trust, and shared values and social organization. The *quality* of people's relations is an important characteristic in an online community. I have shown at various stages in this book that these characteristics can be developed in e-learning groups and communities. Members of these communities do form strong intimate ties, trust is developed, values are developed and the quality of their relations is important to them. But we have also seen that these things are not played out artificially but take on an existence that is strikingly real and complex and that produces ups and downs for all involved. The experience of these online communities reminds us that 'community' is never arrived at – it is something that we strive to develop. And although its dynamics may ebb and flow, we have seen that those involved continue to care about each other and about what is happening in the community. When we see this happen it is surely a true sign of the existence of a community.

For some teachers, the ideas presented in this book may appear quite radical. I don't know if they are, but they do question some existing forms of teaching in e-learning contexts.

The ways in which we assess and evaluate student learning in e-groups and communities are also different, and involve processes that support and sustain the kinds of learning that I am making claims for here. I have suggested that self-peer-tutor reviews and assessment processes are the most appropriate ways of assessing students in e-learning groups and communities. In the minds of many students, there is a direct link between the ways in which they learn and how they are to be assessed. If we ask them to learn collaboratively in groups and communities, we need to match learning of that kind with assessment processes that support and reward it, otherwise we risk undermining the collaborative effort. These forms of assessment have much in common with the ways that communities of academics assess each other's work, that is, by peer review within the community.

The contents of this book indicate that not only are students capable of doing all of this, but most of them actually want to be involved in learning of this kind. It is seen as more authentic, more related to real-life situations, more likely to have an impact on their personal and professional lives, and the outcomes are more likely to be used in real-world situations. It is meaningful, useful and appropriate.

Earlier in the book I said that we implicitly think that existing forms of learning 'work' and are 'perfect', when in fact we know they are not. So when e-learning is sometimes criticized we have to remind ourselves that face-to-face learning is not 'perfect'. It has many imperfections, and learners and teachers face considerable problems in its practice. And even if face-to-face is considered better, it is not always an option, even when courses are run on campus.

The impact of technology on pedagogy and community: a personal note

In looking back at the evolution of our practice in designing e-learning groups and communities, it seems clear to me that every time we run the masters course we are in fact running a new course.

Each iteration of the course is different, and in many ways unique. What we learn about the design in one cohort shapes our practice in the next one. Each tutor engages with the same design in different ways, and with each cohort differently too. Each student has a unique relationship to the design: students on each cohort approach the design from their own individual perspective. We tutors are constantly amazed at how different each presentation turns out to be. We attribute this partly to the ways in which each cohort of students makes the course their own, and how the design of the course calls for their engagement and ownership. Students do not enter an already existing community, they enter a new one that has yet to define itself, develop its rules and norms and ways of working. Tutors act as 'old timers' and bring their shared mental models in a knowledge transmission process, and work with the new students in the development of new shared models that will come to define the nature of this new community. Each cohort produces its own particular dynamic and rhythm, and develops its own issues and concerns, and these are carried out in ways that have particular and specific consequences for those involved.

So learning of this kind, in these contexts, is complex and multi-faceted. It is 'emergent' and there are shifting relationships to the values underpinning the design. The micro-political context of each cohort brings about negotiations around its meaning.

Many teachers are concerned about the potential negative effects of introducing technology into their practice. They often ask if technology will impose itself on the teaching and learning process. They ask if their practice will become technologically determined, and not pedagogically determined. I have great sympathy with their questions and concerns.

Looking back on our history of designing for virtual learning communities I can see a gradual move away from highly open, relatively unstructured course designs where collaboration and cooperation in the learning process occurred informally, to newer, more recent ones where we have deliberately designed for structured collaborative and cooperative learning as a requirement for participating in the course.

In the early years of our practice we deliberately tried to emulate those community-building and -sustaining processes that we had been using in face-to-face meetings. These were very open, unstructured processes that attempted to offer opportunities for all members to participate and engage in the development of the community and in making decisions about the content and design of the course. In these large communities it was possible to 'hear' each member's interests and concerns, and attempt to come to an understanding of the personal and collective needs of the community. We felt this was an important aspect of developing community, where time was given to knowing who the members of the community were. Some of this was carried out in face-to-face sessions and then continued online in the learning sets. Initially we had face-to-face meetings at the beginning of each workshop, followed by the online component, which was the major part of the workshop. As we attempted to make the course more widely available across the globe, we moved to face-to-face sessions only at the beginning of Year 1 and Year 2 of the programme. This allowed our overseas participants to attend the meetings prior to each year's online work, without too much financial travel expense.

To make the course completely accessible to anyone anywhere in the world eventually forced us to abandon all face-to-face meetings and to redesign the entire course as a completely virtual one. At this point we attempted to design learning events and processes which could support as many of our values and beliefs about openness, negotiation, self-management, personal and collective decision-making and so on as was possible.

With the move to a completely virtual course other issues emerged. The community in the learning sets develops through discussion and negotiation. With numbers greater than about 12 participants and a tutor, this becomes difficult, and at times impossible, to achieve. Discussion and negotiation in large virtual community groups (for example of 20–30, which is often now the course intake each year) is cumbersome. The amount of information produced in such communities when everyone is actively participating is extremely large and burdensome. The possibility for diversity of views is great, but the effort required to follow discussions and negotiate from the many different viewpoints is high.

For example, in one of the workshop reviews where we focused on our experiences of the previous workshop and then moved on to forming new learning sets for the next workshop, we attempted to have a very open process in which participants and tutors could start discussion threads on any review topic they wished. The focus was on encouraging diversity of view and opinion. There was a high degree of negotiation leading to an extended period of discussion. We attempted not to be driven by reaching consensus. But for some participants this caused a high degree of frustration. Not everyone participated, and tutors felt obliged to work 'behind the scene', analysing what was happening and trying to make sense of it. The production of views and interesting and innovative ideas about the design of the next workshop was a great strength of this approach, but the asynchronous communicative process took longer than we had anticipated. At some point we had to attempt to reach a collective view of where we were going and why. The discussions could have gone on for many additional weeks as participants 'listened' to each other, considered each other's views and then added their viewpoints. It was clear that as an open-ended community-discussion process it was working very well, but as a method for coming to some collective view on where we were going, it proved difficult to handle. As a community we had to make the decision to close down the discussions in order to move on to the next workshop.

The tutors finally intervened by offering their collective analysis of the emerging issues and concerns. Students seized on this. To the tutors this felt like being forced to have to bring closure too early. It was a solution to an increasingly complex and diverging process, yet seemed inappropriate for what we were trying to achieve as it made the tutors, rather than the community, the final arbiter.

We have seen in Chapters 6 and 7 how early closure is sometimes also seen in the smaller learning set groups where, after extensive asynchronous and synchronous discussion and negotiation on the focus of their collaborative work, members sometimes accept the first 'good' proposal offered by one of them in order to get them started on their work. It seems their willingness to negotiate and discuss is tempered by their concerns to forge ahead and get the work done. Reaching consensus through negotiation is sometimes difficult and protracted. Balancing this with their feelings about 'doing' the collaborative project sometimes leads them to accept the first 'good' proposal offered, which relieves them of the continued need for negotiation.

The question arises: does computer-mediated communication (CMC) close down the possibility for negotiation and diversity of opinion in learning communities? Synchronous CMC offers opportunities for the community to come together in small groups to focus on decision-making. But even here, on reading some of the transcripts of the chat sessions, decision-making does not seem to be easy. That is partly because the technology of chat rooms is clumsy and discussion processes can be very time-consuming when carried out synchronously and when 'hearing' everyone is a major value. Closure is sometimes forced by people having to leave the event. To overcome this, students often place the transcript in the asynchronous forum so that they can reflect on the content of the chat session. They often summarize the chat outcomes in these forums. They then continue the discussions in the forum itself. They sometimes take part in another chat session where they develop their ideas and reach agreement. All of this is, however, very time-consuming.

When participants are willing to give time to these processes and negotiations, the outcomes are extremely favourable and the time involved usually provides them with a real sense of engagement and collective identity. Their work together forges a sense of community. Although time-consuming, the potential benefits for them in developing trustful relationships which in turn support and foster their collaborative work are enormous. This I think is not always explicitly understood by the groups, but in looking at their collective work it is apparent to any outsider. When it does not happen, whether by deliberate choice or because of the circumstances of the social processes of these learning environments, it is apparent that the members of the groups are less likely to feel engaged with each other or feel that they have been involved in a truly collaborative learning experience.

Does this suggest a trend towards consensus-making and closure? In the early days of the Masters, the course could be characterized as very open. It facilitated wide-ranging diversity among those involved, was highly engaging and had a high level of negotiation. The price to pay for this was, at times, a huge overload of information.

Now, with the deliberate, formal introduction of collaborative and cooperative processes, strategic scaffolding and clear work phases, discussion and negotiation are more focused. Discussion is still very high but occurs within well-defined time periods after which everyone involved moves on to the next phase of their work. Decisions are sometimes made by tutors on their own. This is sometimes due to the fast pace of work in the learning sets, where so much happens at the same time. Some tutors intervene to 'help' the members of the set. There is perhaps more strategic learning taking place than in the earlier days. Sometimes learning set members choose to address the course requirement to produce an end-product as a priority over community development and 'true' collaborative learning.

These changes in our use of the technology, or perhaps in the way we allow the technology to direct us, and in the changes to our practice have several consequences:

Consequences for the tutor   It does seem that the move towards providing more structure and scaffolding, and to course designs that formally require collaborative and cooperative participation, provides both positive and negative effects. These changes may be causing tutors to become slightly more distant and less participatory in the community. Some tutors are more likely to have a presence as an interventionist than as a participant. They are more likely to 'step in' and offer solutions for the students in the learning sets, rather than be part of the set and involved in understanding the set and its project and purpose from the perspective of an active member. This shift in power relations may signal to participants that the tutor is there to intervene and present direction and closure, and they may come to expect that from the tutor. We have seen some evidence of this in Chapter 7 where some members of a learning set asked the tutor to intervene and manage the group's dynamics when they themselves were finding it difficult to do so. The outcomes of this were not what they and the tutor had anticipated.

From the perspective of a community of practice, these changes in the tutor's relationship with the members are bound to have consequences for the community. If tutors are moving towards a relationship that is peripheral, purely diagnostic and outside the actual productive work of the community, then they are likely to be seen by members as outsiders who exert control and unilateral power.

Consequences for community   We have seen that communities of practice require considerable time to develop and sustain themselves. They are in a constant process of change and flux. They do not, however, deliberately set out to focus on their learning. Learning communities (Pedler 1981), on the other hand, do focus on learning as a community issue. We have seen in Chapters 3 to 7 that they are deliberately reflective in their practices, looking at themselves and their learning processes. They are therefore often knowledgeable about themselves and about what they are trying to achieve. They are largely self-organizing through their formal learning processes. In developing communities in e-learning environments, both of these concepts – communities of practice and learning communities – offer strong conceptual models which help us in the design of spaces, events and courses that focus on the social practice of working together.

Negotiation in e-learning communities poses certain problems and issues for students and tutors. In the groups, members are faced with at least two practical issues relating to their work:

- production versus community processes
- structure versus negotiation and openness

If too much time is taken up with the act of production in the community, less time will be available for negotiating shared repertoires, collective responsibility and collaborative learning generally. Early models of our Masters degree had a major focus on community development and collective responsibility. The move to completely virtual learning that takes place within the confines of a virtual learning environment where there is greater reliance on the technology, has led to a design that is more structured, more product-related with less emphasis on the whole community negotiating the course design. The whole (or large) community still exists, but there is less time for negotiating collective meaning and identity.

This is, of course, all relative. Many students taking the course today experience it as highly community centred, with many of opportunities to develop their ideas and negotiate meaning and identity. Some tutors also experience it in this way, and welcome the imposition of more structure and more emphasis on students 'getting the work done'. Those tutors new to e-learning, and to this form of e-learning in groups and communities in particular, often find the course demanding and seem to need these structures to help them make sense of their role in the course. So, in many important ways, the change from what I perceive as a more open learning model, to one that is more structured by tutors, seems to meet the needs of many students and tutors.

In conclusion, the following question can be asked: is there a contradiction in our wish to share the course design with students, and our employment of more technology in our practice? Does the use of more technology in a virtual context inevitably lead to a reduction in openness? Or does openness still occur, but in ways that are not always as obvious or readily observable to us tutors? Does the technology allow for more activity and participation, but in smaller groupings of students and tutors rather than at the whole community level? There is some evidence to support this view. We have seen in Chapter 3 that students express a preference for working in the small learning sets rather than in the large community. When this happens, there may be greater opportunity to feel engaged and to participate more, and this may support greater difference and diversity across the community. But there will be less engagement with the community at large, and less involvement in those community-building activities that were so prevalent in the early model. The shift is away from the large community to the smaller, more focused and more engaging communities of the learning sets. This is possibly no bad thing as it allows students to focus on their personal and professional interests and collectively share understandings in depth, with greater urgency.

The project of designing courses to support collaborative e-learning groups and communities is a demanding one. It is likely to challenge both teachers and students alike. Education is largely based on a logic of individuality: teachers teach on their own, and students learn and are assessed on their own. Collaborative e-learning groups and communities have a different kind of logic based on social processes and solidarity. There are always 'tensions between the logic of individual competition and the logic of social solidarity' (Castells 2001: 278), and in the world of education we will have to negotiate new forms of social contracts with and between our students in order to develop and sustain these new forms of collaborative learning and assessment.

Bibliography

Asensio, M., Hodgson, V. and Trehan, K. (2000) Is there a difference? Contrasting experiences of face to face and online learning, in Asensio, M., Foster, J., Hodgson, V. and McConnell, D. (eds) *Networked Learning 2000: Innovative Approaches to Lifelong Learning and Higher Education Through the Internet*. Sheffield: University of Sheffield, UK.

Ash, C. and Bacsich, P. (2002) The costs of networked learning, in Steeples, C. and Jones, C. (eds) *Networked Learning: Perspectives and Issues*. London: Springer Verlag.

Axelrod, R. (1990) *The Evolution of Cooperation*. London: Penguin Books.

Banks, S., Goodyear, P., Hodgson, V. and McConnell D. (2002) (eds) *Networked Learning 2002: A Research-Based Conference on E-Learning in Higher Education and Lifelong Learning*. Sheffield: University of Sheffield, p. 685.

Banks, S., Goodyear, P., Hodgson, V. and McConnell, D. (2003) Introduction to the Special Edition of Instructional Science on 'Advances in Research on Networked Learning', *Instructional Science*, 31 (1–2).

Banks, S., Lally, V. and McConnell, D. (2003) *Networked E-Learning in Higher Education: Issues and Strategies*. Sheffield: University of Sheffield, School of Education.

Barajas, M. and Owen, M. (2000) Implementing Virtual Learning Environments: looking for a holistic approach, *Educational Technology and Society*, 3(3): 39–53.

Bateson, G. (1973) *Steps to an Ecology of the Mind*. St Albans: Paladin.

Beaty, E. Cousin, G. and Deepwell F. (2002) Introducing networked learning via a community network: a teaching and learning strategy in action, in Banks, S., Goodyear, P., Hodgson, V. and McConnell D. (eds) *Networked Learning 2002: A Research-Based Conference on E-learning in Higher Education and Lifelong Learning*. Sheffield: University of Sheffield, p. 685.

Becker, H. S., Geer, B. and Hughes E. C. (1968) *Making the Grade: The Academic Side of Academic Life*. New York: John Wiley.

Berg, D. N. and Smith., K. K. (1990) Paradox of groups, in Gillette, J. and McCollom, M. (eds) *Groups in Context: A New Perspective on Group Dynamics*. Reading, Mass.: Addison Wesley.

Bird, L. (undated) *Action Learning Sets: The Case for Running Them Online*. Coventry: Work-Based Learning Unit, Coventry Business School.

Bonamy, J. and Haugusliane-Charlier, B. (1995) Supporting professional learning: beyond technological support, *Journal of Computer Assisted Learning*, 11 (4): 196–202.

Boot, R. and V. Hodgson (1987) Open Learning: Meaning and Experience, in Beyond Distance Teaching – Towards Open Learning. Hodgson, V., Mann, S. and Snell, R. (eds) Milton Keynes: SRHE/Open University Press.

Booth, S. and M. Hulten (2003) Opening dimensions of variation: an empirical study of learning in a web based discussion, *Instructional Science* 31 (1–2): 65–86.

Boud, D. (1995) *Enhancing Learning Through Self Assessment*. London: Kogan Page.

Boud, D. (2000) Sustainable assessment: rethinking assessment for a learning society, *Studies in Continuing Education*, 22 (2): 151–67.

Boud, D. and Feletti, G. (eds) (1997) *The Challenge of Problem-based Learning*. London: Kogan Page.

Boud, D. and Walker, D. (1998) Promoting reflection in professional courses: the challenge of context, *Studies in Higher Education*, 23 (2): 191–206.

Bowen, B., Bereiter, C. and Scardamalia, M. (1992) Computer-supported intentional learning environments, in Philips, F. Y. (ed.) Thinkwork: Working, Learning and Managing in a Computer Interactive Society. Westport, Conn: Praeger.

Boyd, H. and Cowan, J. (1985) A case for self-assessment based on recent studies of student learning, *Assessment and Evaluation in Higher Education*, 10 (3): 225–35.

Bringelson, L. S. and Carey, T. (2000) Different keystrokes for different folks: designing online venues for professional communities, *Educational Technology and Society*, 3 (3): 58–64.

Broadfoot, P. M. (1996) *Education, Assessment and Society: A Sociological Analysis*. Buckingham: Open University Press.

Brown, R. E. (2001) The process of community-building in distance learning classes, *Journal of Asynchronous Learning Networks*, 5 (2): 18–35.

Burt, R. S. (1999) Entrepreneurs, distrust, and third parties: a strategic look at the dark side of dense networks, in Thompson, L. L., Levine, J. M. and Medddick, D.M. (eds) *Shared Cognition in Organizations: The Management of Knowledge*. Mahwah, NJ: Lawrence Erlbaum Associates.

Carr, W. and Kemmis, S. (1986) *Becoming Critical: Education, Knowledge and Action Research*. Brighton: Falmer Press.

Castells, M. (2001) *The Internet Galaxy: Reflections on the Internet, Business and Society*. Oxford: Oxford University Press.

Choy, C. K. (2003) An Exploratory Study on E-Learning: How Students in the Polytechnic use E-Learning Approach to Learning a Computer Programming Language. Unpublished Masters Dissertation, Educational Studies Department. Sheffield: University of Sheffield, p. 143.

Clarke, A. E. (1997) A social worlds research adventure: the case of the reproductive science, in Strauss, A. and Corbin, J. (eds) *Grounded Theory in Practice*. Thousand Oaks: Sage.

Collis, B. (1998) *Implementing Innovative Teaching Across the Faculty via the WWW*. http://www.coe.uh.edu/insite/elec_pub/HTML1998/keynote.htm (accessed 7 August 2005).

Colliver, J. A. (2000) Effectiveness of problem-based learning curricula: research and theory, *Academic Medicine*, 75 (3): 259–66.

Crock, M. and Andrews, T. (1997) *Providing Staff and Student Support for Alternative*

Learning Environments. http://ultibase.rmit.edu.au/Archives/articles.htm# dec97 (accessed 7 August 2005).

Cunningham, I. (1987) Openness and learning to learn, in Hodgson, V., Mann, S. and Snell, R. (eds) *Beyond Distance Teaching, Towards Open Learning.* Milton Keynes: SRHE/Open University Press.

Davies, C. A. (1999) *Reflexive Ethnography: A Guide to Researching Selves and Others.* London: Routledge.

Davis, D., Thomson O'Brien, M. A., Freemantle, N., Wolf, F. M., Mazmanian, P. and Taylor-Vaisey, A. (1999) Impact of formal continuing medical education, *JAMA*, 282 (9): 867–74.

Davis, M. and Denning, K. (2000) Online learning: frontiers in the creation of learning communities, in Proceedings of the Conference: Banks *et al. Networked Learning 2000: Innovative Approaches to Lifelong Learning and Higher Education Through the Internet,* University of Sheffield, Sheffield, UK.

Dearnley, C. and Gatecliff, L. (1999) Supporting supporters in open and distance learning, *European Journal of Open and Distance Learning.* http://www1.nks.no/eurodl/shoen/Bradford/Bradford6.html (accessed 7 August 2005).

Department for Education and Science (DfES) (2003) *Towards a Unified E-Learning Strategy. Consultation Document,* DfES reference number: DfES/0424/2003, UK.

Dey, I. (1993). *Qualitative Data Analysis: A User-Friendly Guide for Social Scientists.* London: Routledge.

Dillenbourg, P. (1999) Introduction: What do you mean by 'collaborative learning'? in Dillenbourg, P. (ed.) *Collaborative Learning: Cognitive and Computational Approaches.* Oxford: Pergamon/Elsevier Science Ltd.

Dirckinck-Holmfeld, L. and Fibiger, B. (2002) *Learning in Virtual Environments.* Copenhagen: Samfundslitteratur Press.

Dirckinck-Holmfeld, L., McConnell, D., Kolbæk, D., Sorensen, E. K., Tolsby, H., Banks, S. and Lally, V. (2003) Researching and evaluating collaborative e-learning groups and communities, in Wasson, B., Baggetun, R. and Hoppe, U. (eds) *International Conference on Computer Support for Collaborative Learning (CSCL2003),* 14–18 June, Bergen, Norway, pp. 206–7

Donath, J. S. (1999) Identity and Deception in the Virtual Community, in Smith, M. A. and Kollock, P. (eds) *Communities in Cyberspace.* London and New York: Routledge.

Elden, M. and Chisholm, R. F. (1993) Emerging varieties of action research, *Human Relations*, 46 (2): 121–42.

Emms, J. and McConnell, D. (1988) An evaluation of tutorial support provided by electronic mail and computer conferencing, *Aspects of Educational Technology*, XXI: 263–70.

EQUEL (2004) Equality in e-learning. www.equel.net (accessed 7 August 2005).

Exley, K. and Dennick, R. (2004) *Small Group Teaching.* London: Routledge.

Falchikov, N. and Boud, D. (1989) Student self-assessment in higher education: a meta-analysis, *Review of Educational Research*, 59 (4): 395–430.

Falchikov, N. and Goldfinch J., (2000) Student peer assessment in higher education: a meta-analysis comparing peer and teacher marks, *Review of Educational Research*, 70 (3): 287–322.

Fox, S. (2005) An actor-network critique of community in higher education: implications for networked learning, *Studies in Higher Education*, 30 (1): 95–110.

Garrison, D. R., and Anderson, T. (2003) *E-Learning in the 21st Century: A Framework for Research and Practice.* London: RoutledgeFalmer.

Geertz, C. (1973) *The Interpretation of Cultures.* New York: Basic Books.

Gersick, C. J. G. (1988) Time and transition in work teams: toward a new model of group development, *Academy of Management Journal*, 31 (1): 9–41.

Giddens, A. (1991) *Modernity and Self-identity: Self and Society in the Late Modern Age.* Cambridge: Polity Press.

Gillette, J. (1990) Intimacy in work groups: looking from the inside out, in Gillette, J. and McCollom, M. (eds) *Groups in Context: A New Perspective on Group Dynamics.* Reading, Mass.: Addison-Wesley.

Glaser, B. and Strauss, A. (1968) *The Discovery of Grounded Theory.* London: Weidenfeld and Nicolson.

Goodyear, P., Banks, S., Hodgson, V. and McConnell, D. (eds) (2004) *Advances in Research on Networked Learning.* Boston: Kluwer Academic Publishers.

Goodyear, P., Jones, C., Asensio, M., Hodgson, V., and Steeples, C. (2004). Undergraduate students' experiences of networked learning in UK higher education: a survey-based study, in Goodyear, P., Banks, S., Hodgson, V. and McConnell, D. (eds) *Advances in Research on Networked Learning.* Boston: Kluwer Academic Publishers:, pp. 91–122.

Greener, I. and Perriton, L. (2005) The political economy of networked learning communities in higher education, *Studies in Higher Education*, 30 (1), 68–80.

Gros, B. (2001) Instructional design for computer-supported collaborative learning in primary and secondary school, *Computers in Human Behaviour*, 17: 439–51.

Hara, N. and Kling, R. (1999) Students' frustration with a Web-based distance education course: a taboo topic in the discourse. CSI Working Paper, Indiana University, Bloomington, USA. http://www.slis.indiana.edu/CSI/wp99 01.html (accessed 7 August 2005).

Harris, D. (1987) *Openness and Closure in Distance Education.* Brighton: Falmer Press.

Harris, R. and Muirhead, A. (2004) Online learning community research: some influences of theory on methods, in Banks, S., Goodyear, P., Hodgson, V., Jones, C., Lally, V., McConnell, D. and Steeples, C. (eds) *Networked Learning 2004: A Research Based Conference in Higher Education and Lifelong Learning.* Networked Learning, Lancaster University and University of Sheffield.

Haythornthwaite, C. (2002) Building social networks via computer networks, in Renninger, K. A. and Shumar, W. (eds) *Building Virtual Communities: Learning and Change in Cyberspace.* Cambridge: Cambridge University Press.

Haythornwaite, C., Kazmer, M. M., Robins, J. and Shoemaker, S. (2000) Community development amongst distance learners: temporal and technological dimensions, *Journal of Computer-Mediated Communications*, 6 (1).

Henri, F. (1992) Computer conferencing and content analysis, in Kaye, A. R. (ed.) *Collaborative Learning Through Computer Conferencing: Tha Najaden Papers.* London: Springer-Verlag, pp. 117–36.

Heron, J. (1981) Self and peer assessment, in Boydell, T. and Pedler, M. (eds) *Management Self-development.* London: Gower.

Hiltz, S. R. (1984) *Online Communities: A Case Study of the Office of the Future.* Norwood, NJ: Ablex Publishers.

Hiltz, S. R. (1986) The virtual classroom: using computer mediated communication for university teaching, *Journal of Communication*, 36 (2): 95–104.

Hine, C. (2000) *Virtual Ethnography.* London: Sage.

Hodgson, V. and McConnell, D. (1992) Information technology-based open learning: a case study in management learning, *Journal of Computer Assisted Learning*, 8 (3): 136–150.

Hodgson, V. and Reynolds, M. (2005) Consensus, difference and 'multiple communities' in networked learning, *Studies in Higher Education*, 30 (1): 11–24.

Hodgson, V. and Watland, P. (2003) Researching networked management learning, *Management Learning*, 35 (2): 99–116.

Hodgson, V. and Zenios, M. (2003) Designing networked environments to support dialogical learning, in Wasson, B., Ludvigsen, S. and Hoppe, U. (eds) *Designing for Change in Networked Learning Environments*. Dordrecht: Kluwer Academic Publishers, pp. 405–9.

Isaacs, G. (1997) Developing the developers: some ethical dilemmas in changing times, *International Journal for Academic Development*, 2 (1).

Jaques, D. (1991) *Learning in Groups*. London: Kogan Page.

Johnson, D. W. and Johnson, R. T. (1990) Social skills for successful group work, *Educational Leadership*, 47 (4): 29–33.

Johnson, D. W. and Johnson, R. T. (2003) *Learning Together and Alone: Cooperative, Competitive, and Individualistic Learning* (8th edn). London: Allyn and Bacon.

Jones, C. R. (1998) Context, content and cooperation: an ethnographic study of collaborative learning online, PhD Dissertation, Manchester: Manchester Metropolitan University.

Jones, C. R. (2000) Understanding students' experiences of collaborative networked learning, in Asensio, M., Foster, J., Hodgson, V. and McConnell, D. (eds) *Networked Learning 2000: Innovative Approaches to Lifelong Learning and Higher Education Through the Internet*. Sheffield: University of Sheffield.

Jones, C. and Steeples, C. (2002) Perspectives and issues in networked learning, in Steeples, C. and Jones, C. (eds) *Networked Learning: Perspectives and Issues*. London: Springer Verlag, pp. 1–14.

Jones, S. (1995) *Cybersociety*. Thousand Oaks, California: Sage.

Keisler, S. (1992) Talking, teaching and learning in network groups, in Kaye, A. R. (ed.) *Collaborative Learning through Computer Conferencing*, Berlin, Springer Verlag, NATO ASI Series.

Koschmann, T. (ed.) (1996) *CSCL: Theory and Practice of an Emerging Paradigm*. Mahwah, NJ: Lawrence Erlbaum Assoc.

Kramer, R. M. (1999) Social uncertainty and collective paranoia in knowledge communities: thinking and acting in the shadow of doubt, in Thompson, L. L., Levine, J. M. and Medddick, D. M. (eds) *Shared Cognition in Organizations: The Management of Knowledge*. Mahwah, NJ: Lawrence Erlbaum Associates.

Laurillard, D. (2002) *Rethinking University Teaching: A Framework for the Effective Use of Learning Technologies* (2nd edn). London: RoutledgeFalmer.

Lave, J., and Wenger, E. (1991) *Situated Learning: Legitimate Peripheral Participation*. Cambridge: Cambridge University Press.

Lincoln, Y. and Guba, E. (1985) *Naturalistic Inquiry*. London: Sage.

Lynch, L. and Corry, M. (1998) *Faculty Recruitment, Training and Compensation for Distance Education*. http://www.coe.uh.edu/insite/elec_pub/HTML1998/de_lync.htm (accessed 7 August 2005).

Mantovani, G. (1994) Is computer-mediated communication intrinsically apt to enhance democracy in organizations? *Human Relations*, 47 (1): 45–62.

McConnell, D. (1986) The impact of Cyclops shared-screen teleconferencing in distance tutoring, *British Journal of Educational Technology*, 17 (1): 37–70.

McConnell, D. (1988) Computer conferencing in teacher inservice education: a case study, in Harris, D. *World Yearbook of Education 1988: Education for the New Technologies*. London: Kogan Page.

McConnell, D. (1997) Interaction patterns of mixed-sex groups in educational computer conferences: Part 1– Empirical findings, *Gender and Education*, 9 (3): 345–64.

McConnell, D. (1998) Developing self-assessment in networked lifelong learning environments, in Banks, S., Graebner, C. and McConnell, D. (eds) *Networked Lifelong Learning: Innovative Approaches to Education and Training Through the Internet*. Proceedings of the First International Conference, University of Sheffield.

McConnell, D. (1999) Examining a collaborative assessment process in networked lifelong learning, *Journal of Computer Assisted Learning*, 15 (September).

McConnell, D. (2000) *Implementing Computer Supported Cooperative Learning*. (2nd edn). London: Kogan Page.

McConnell, D. and Sharples, M. (1983) Distance teaching by Cyclops: an educational evaluation of the Open University's telewriting system, *British Journal of Educational Technology*, 14 (2): 109–26.

McDowell, L., and Sambell, K. (1999) *Students experience of self evaluation in higher education: preparation for lifelong learning?* Paper presented at the bi-annual conference of the European Association for Research on Learning and Instruction (EARLI), Gothenburg, 24–28 August 1999.

McGrath, J. (1990) Time matters in groups, in Galegher, J., Kraut, R. and Egido, C. (eds) *Intellectual Teamwork: Social and Technological Foundations of Cooperative Work*. Hillsdale, NJ: Lawrence Erlbaum Assoc.

McKendree, J., Stenning, K., Mayes, T., Lee, J. and Cox, R. (1998) Why observing a dialogue may benefit learning, *Journal of Computer Assisted Learning*, 14 (2): 110–19.

Middlehurst, R. (2000) The business of borderless education. Paper presented at the Conference on the Business of Borderless Education, QEII Conference Centre, London.

Miller, C. M. L. and Parlett, M. (1974) *Up to the Mark: A Study of the Examination Game*. London: Society for Research into Higher Education.

Moon, J. A. (1999) *Reflection in Learning and Professional Development*. London: Kogan Page.

Moustakis, C. (1994) *Phenomenological Research Methods*. London: Sage.

Packer, M. J. and Goicoechea, J. (2000) Sociocultural and constructivist theories of learning: ontology, not just epistemology, *Educational Psychologist*, 35 (4): 227–41.

Paloff, R. M. and Pratt, K. (1999) *Building Learning Communities in Cyberspace: Effective Strategies for the Online Classroom*. San Francisco: Jossey Bass.

Parlett, M. R. (1981) Illuminative evaluation, in Reason, P. and Rowan, J. (eds) *Human Inquiry: A Sourcebook of New Paradigm Research*. Chichester: J. Wiley & Sons.

Patton, M. Q. (1990) *Qualitative Evaluation and Research Methods* (2nd edn). Newbury Park: Sage.

Pedler, M. (1981) Developing the learning community, in Boydell, T. and Pedler, M. (eds), *Management Self-development: Concepts and Practices*. Aldershot: Gower.

Perriton, L. and Reedy, P. (2002) Walk on by: anarchist possibilities for the reconceptualization of the virtual community, in Banks, S., Goodyear, P., Hodgson, V. and McConnell, D. (2002) (eds) *Networked Learning 2002: A Research Based Conference on E-Learning in Higher Education and Lifelong Learning*. Sheffield: University of Sheffield.

QAA (2001) Subject Review Report, University of Sheffield, Education (Q391,2001), Quality Assurance Agency for Higher Education (UK). www.qaa.ac.uk.

Ragoonaden, K. and Bordeleau, P. (2000) Collaborative learning via the Internet, *Educational Technology & Society*, 3 (3).

Ramsden, P. (1988) Context and strategy: situational influences on learning, in Schmeck, R. R. (ed.), *Learning Strategies and Learning Styles*. New York: Plenum Press.

Renninger, K. A. and Shumar, W. (eds) (2002) *Building Virtual Communities: Learning and Change in Cyberspace*. Cambridge: Cambridge University Press.

Reynolds, M. (1994) *Groupwork in Education and Training: Ideas in Practice*. London: Kogan Page.

Reynolds, M., Sclater, M. and Tickner, S. (2004) A critique of participative discourses adopted in networked learning, in Banks, S., Goodyear, P., Hodgson, V., Jones, C., Lally, V., McConnell, D. and Steeples, C. (eds) *Networked Learning 2004: A Research Based Conference in Higher Education and Lifelong Learning*. Sheffield: University of Sheffield.

Rheingold, H. (1993) *The Virtual Community*. Reading Mass.: Addison-Wesley.

Richardson, J. E. T. (1999) The concepts and methods of phenomenographic research, *Review of Educational Research*, 69 (1): 53–82.

Rogers, J. (2000). Communities of practice: a framework for fostering coherence in virtual learning communities, *Educational Technology & Society*, 3 (3): 384–92.

Ryan, Y. (2000) The business of borderless education: US case studies and HE response. Paper presented at the Conference on the Business of Borderless Education, QEII Conference Centre, London, March 2000.

Salmon, G. (2000) *E-Moderating: The Key to Teaching and Learning Online*. London: Kogan Page.

Salomon, G., and Perkins, D. N. (1998) Individual and social aspects of learning, *Review of Educational Research*, 23: 1–24.

Saunders, M. and Machall, J. (1994) *Report on the Evaluation of the User-Trials*. DELTA Deliverable, JITOL Project D2015. Lancaster: CSET, Lancaster University.

Savin-Baden, M. (2000). *Problem-Based Learning in Higher Education: Untold Stories*. Buckingham, SRHE/Open University Press.

Scardamalia, M. (2003) Collective cognitive responsibility, in Jones, B. (ed.) *Liberal Education in the Knowledge Age*. Chicago: Open Court.

Scardamalia, M. and Bereiter, C. (2003) Knowledge building, in *Encyclopaedia of Education* (2nd edn). New York: Macmillan Reference.

Schon, D. A. (1983) *The Reflective Practitioner: How Professionals Think in Action*. New York: Basic Books.

Searby, M. and Ewers, T. (1997) An evaluation of the use of peer assessment in higher education: a case study in the School of Music, Kingston University, *Assessment and Evaluation in Higher Education*, 22 (4): 371–83.

Seufert, S. (2000) The Net Academy as a medium for learning communities, *Educational Technology and Society*, 3 (3): 122–36.

Shafriri, N. (1999) Learning as a reflective activity: linkage between the concept of learning and the concept of alternative assessment. Paper presented at the bi-annual conference of the European Association for Research on Learning and Instruction (EARLI), Gothenburg, 24–28 August 1999.

Sharan, S. (ed.) (1990) *Cooperative Learning*. London: Praeger.

Short, J., Williams, E. and Christie, B. (1976) *The Social Psychology of Telecommunications*. London: Wiley & Sons.

Sklar, E. and Pollack, J. (2000) A framework for enabling an Internet learning community, *Educational Technology and Society*, 3 (3), 393–408.

Slavin, R. E. (1995) *Cooperative Learning: Theory, Research, and Practice* (2nd edn). London: Allyn and Boccon.

Slavin, R., Sharan, S., Kagan, S., Lazarowitz, R. H., Webb, C. and Schmuck, R. (1985) *Learning to Cooperate, Cooperating to Learn*. New York: Plenum Publishing Corporation.

Smith, M. and Kollock, P. (1999). *Communities in Cyberspace*. London: Routledge.

Snell, R. (1989) Learning to work in a peer learning community, *Group Relations Training Association Bulletin*, 1 (1): 6–9.

Somerville, H. (1993) Issues in assessment, enterprise and higher education: the case for self-, peer and collaborative assessment, *Assessment and Evaluation in Higher Education*, 18 (3): 221–33.

Spector, J. M. (2000) Towards a philosophy of instruction, *Educational Technology and Society*, 3 (3): 522–5.

Stacey, E. (1999) Collaborative learning in an online environment, *Journal of Distance Education*, 14 (2): 14–33.

Stahl, G. (2002) Contribution to a theoretical framework for CSCL, in Stahl, G. (ed.), *Computer Supported for Collaborative Learning: Foundations for a CSCL Community. Proceedings of CSCL 2002*, Boulder, Colorado, USA, Jan 7–11. Hillsdale, NJ: Lawrence Erlbaum Associates, Inc., pp. 265–74.

Stefani, L. (1994) Peer, self and tutor assessment: relative reliabilities, *Studies in Higher Education*, 19 (1): 69–75.

Stefani, L. (1998) Assessment in partnership with students, *Assessment and Evaluation in Higher Education*, 23: 339–50.

Stephenson, J. and Weil, S. (eds) (1992) *Quality in Learning: A Capability Approach to Higher Education*. London: Kogan Page.

Strauss, A. and Corbin, J. (1990) *Basics of Qualitative Research: Grounded Theory Procedures and Techniques*. London: Sage.

Strauss, A. and Corbin, J. (1998) *Basics of Qualitative Research: Techniques and Procedures for Developing Grounded Theory*. London: Sage.

Tansley, C., and Bryson, C. (2000) Virtual seminars – a viable substitute for traditional approaches? *Innovations in Education and Training International*, 37 (4): 335–45.

Thomas, B., Jones, P., Packham, G. and Miller, C. (2004) Student perceptions of effective e-moderation: a quantitative investigation of e-college Wales, in Banks, S., Goodyear, P., Hodgson, V., Jones, C., Lally, V., McConnell, D. and Steeples, C. (eds) *Networked Learning 2004: A Research Based Conference in Higher Education and Lifelong Learning*. Networked Learning, Lancaster University and University of Sheffield.

Thompson, L. (1997) *Professional Development for Online Learning*. http://www.nw97.edu.au/public/papers/thompson.html (accessed 7 August 2005).

Thousand, J. S., Villa, R. A. and Nevin, A. (1994) *Creativity and Collaborative*

Learning: A Practical Guide to Empowering Students and Teachers. Baltimore, Maryland: Paul H. Brookes Publishing Co.

Veen, W., Lam, I. and Taconis, R. (1998) A virtual workshop as a tool for collaboration: towards a model of telematics learning environments, *Computers and Education*, 30 (1–2): 31–9.

Vygotsky, L. S. (1962) *Thought and Language* (trans. E. H. Vakar). Cambridge, Mass.: MIT Press.

Vygotsky, L. S. (1978) *Mind in Society: The Development of Higher Psychological Processes* (trans. V. J.-S. M. Cole, S. Scribner and E. Souberman). Cambridge, Mass.: Harvard University Press.

Wegerif, R. (1998) The social dimension of asynchronous learning networks, *Journal of Asynchronous Learning Networks*, 2 (1): 34–49.

Wellman, B. and Gulia, M. (1999) Virtual communities as communities: Net surfers don't ride alone, in Smith, M., and Kollock, P. (eds) *Communities in Cyberspace*. London: Routledge.

Wenger, E. (1998) *Communities of Practice: Learning, Meaning and Identity.* Cambridge: Cambridge University Press.

Wenger, E., McDermott, W. and Snyder, W. M. (2002) *Cultivating Communities of Practice*. Boston, Mass.: Harvard Business School Press.

Whitehead, J. (1989) How do we improve research-based professionalism in education ? A question that includes action research, educational theory and the politics of educational knowledge, *British Educational Research Journal*, 15 (1): 3–17.

Wills, S. (1998) *Teaching Academics About Flexible Delivery. Invited Panel Speech for RIBIE98 Conference.* http://cedir.uow.edu.au/CEDIR/ (accessed 7 August 2005).

Winter, R. (1989) *Learning from Experience: Principles and Practice in Action-Research.* London: Falmer Press.

Wood, M. R. and Zurcher, L. A. (1988) *The Development of Postmodern Self*. New York: Greenwood Press.

You, Y. (1993) What can we learn from chaos theory? An alternative approach to instructional systems design, *Educational Technology Research and Development*, 41 (3): 17–32.

Zammit, M. (2004) The advent of the e-world: learning together across boundaries and beyond: virtual or real? Unpublished Masters in Education Dissertation, University of Sheffield.

Zhao, J (2006) Group knowledge building in a blended e-learning environment in Chinese higher education: modelling, implementation and evaluation. Unpublished PhD thesis, University of Sheffield.

Index

The Society for Research into Higher Education

The Society for Research into Higher Education (SRHE), an international body, exists to stimulate and coordinate research into all aspects of higher education. It aims to improve the quality of higher education through the encouragement of debate and publication on issues of policy, on the organization and management of higher education institutions, and on the curriculum, teaching and learning methods.

The Society is entirely independent and receives no subsidies, although individual events often receive sponsorship from business or industry. The Society is financed through corporate and individual subscriptions and has members from many parts of the world. It is an NGO of UNESCO.

Under the imprint *SRHE & Open University Press*, the Society is a specialist publisher of research, having over 80 titles in print. In addition to *SRHE News*, the Society's newsletter, the Society publishes three journals: *Studies in Higher Education* (three issues a year), *Higher Education Quarterly* and *Research into Higher Education Abstracts* (three issues a year).

The Society runs frequent conferences, consultations, seminars and other events. The annual conference in December is organized at and with a higher education institution. There are a growing number of networks which focus on particular areas of interest, including:

Access	FE/HE
Assessment	Graduate Employment
Consultants	New Technology for Learning
Curriculum Development	Postgraduate Issues
Eastern European	Quantitative Studies
Educational Development Research	Student Development

Benefits to members

Individual

- The opportunity to participate in the Society's networks
- Reduced rates for the annual conferences

- Free copies of *Research into Higher Education Abstracts*
- Reduced rates for *Studies in Higher Education*
- Reduced rates for *Higher Education Quarterly*
- Free online access to *Register of Members' Research Interests* – includes valuable reference material on research being pursued by the Society's members
- Free copy of occasional in-house publications, e.g. *The Thirtieth Anniversary Seminars Presented by the Vice-Presidents*
- Free copies of *SRHE News* and *International News* which inform members of the Society's activities and provides a calendar of events, with additional material provided in regular mailings
- A 35 per cent discount on all SRHE/Open University Press books
- The opportunity for you to apply for the annual research grants
- Inclusion of your research in the *Register of Members' Research Interests*

Corporate

- Reduced rates for the annual conference
- The opportunity for members of the Institution to attend SRHE's network events at reduced rates
- Free copies of *Research into Higher Education Abstracts*
- Free copies of *Studies in Higher Education*
- Free online access to *Register of Members' Research Interests* – includes valuable reference material on research being pursued by the Society's members
- Free copy of occasional in-house publications
- Free copies of *SRHE News* and *International News*
- A 35 per cent discount on all SRHE/Open University Press books
- The opportunity for members of the Institution to submit applications for the Society's research grants
- The opportunity to work with the Society and co-host conferences
- The opportunity to include in the *Register of Members' Research Interests* your Institution's research into aspects of higher education

 Membership details: SRHE, 76 Portland Place, London W1B 1NT, UK Tel: 020 7637 2766. Fax: 020 7637 2781. email: srheoffice@srhe.ac.uk world wide web: http://www.srhe.ac.uk./srhe/ *Catalogue*: SRHE & Open University Press, McGraw-Hill Education, McGraw-Hill House, Shoppenhangers Road, Maidenhead, Berkshire SL6 2QL. Tel: 01628 502500. Fax: 01628 770224. email: enquiries@openup.co.uk web: www.openup.co.uk

BEYOND MASS HIGHER EDUCATION
Building on Experience

Ian McNay (ed)

- What are the key elements of mass higher education?
- How does mass higher education affect students and staff?
- What are the policy, pedagogic and management issues that need to be addressed?

More is now expected of higher education provision. It has to meet demands for expansion, excellence, diversity and equity in access and assessment, teaching and research, as well as entrepreneurial engagement with the world outside. Thirty years ago, Martin Trow wrote of higher education systems moving from elite provision through a mass system to universal levels of access. The UK is now approaching such universal levels; Scotland has already reached them. It is nearly fifteen years since Trow's mass threshold was reached. Despite being on the brink of universal provision, there is still no clear picture of what a mass system should look like. This collection looks forward to the next decade of higher education, and identifies strategic issues that need to be tackled at institutional and management levels. It considers how far the higher education system has adapted to respond to the requirements of a mass and universal system, rather than struggling to sustain an elite system with mass participation.

Beyond Mass Higher Education is key reading for those leading and managing universities and colleges, as well as higher education researchers and policy makers.

Contributors: Grainne Conole, Stephen Court, Jim Gallacher, Peter T. Knight, Carole Leathwood, Brenda Little, Lisa Lucas, Ian McNay, Bob Osborne, Richard Pearson, Wendy Saunderson, Michael Shattock, Marilyn Wedgewood, Celia Whitchurch and Mantz Yorke.

Contents: Acknowledgements – Contributors – **Part one: Introduction** – Delivering mass higher education the reality of policy in practice – **Part two**: Student Issues – Accessing higher education: policy, practice and equity in widening participation in England – Differentiation and stratification in Scottish higher education – Participation and access in higher education in Northern Ireland – The student experience and the impact of social capital – The demise of the graduate labour market – **Part three: Academic policies and processes** – What impact are technologies having and how are they changing practice? – Assessing complex achievement – Formative assessment and employability: some implications for higher education practices – 'To them that have shall be given, but …': the future of funding and evaluating research in UK universities – Mainstreaming the third stream – **Part four: Staff and system issues** – Managing institutions in a mass HE system – Academic staff in a mass HE system: the state we're in – Gender [in]equality in mass HE: the need for change – Administrators or managers? The shifting roles and identities of professional administrators and managers in UK higher education – University governance and the role of the state – **Part five: Looking forward, moving on** – The agenda ahead: building on experience – Index.

2005   256pp   0 335 21857 1 Paperback   0 335 21858 X Hardback

HIGHER EDUCATION PEDAGOGIES

Melanie Walker

- What does higher education learning and teaching enable students to do and to become?
- Which human capabilities are valued in higher education, and how do we identify them?
- How might the human capability approach lead to improved student learning, as well as to accomplished and ethical university teaching?

This book sets out to generate new ways of reflecting ethically about the purposes and values of contemporary higher education in relation to agency, learning, public values and democratic life, and the pedagogies which support these. It offers an alternative to human capital theory and emphasises the intrinsic as well as the economic value of higher learning. Based upon the human capability approach, developed by economist Amartya Sen and philosopher Martha Nussbaum, the book shows the importance of justice as a value in higher education. It places freedom, human flourishing, and students' educational development at its centre. Furthermore, it takes up the value Sen attributes to education in the capability approach, and demonstrates its relevance for higher education.

Higher Education Pedagogies offers illustrative narratives of capability, learning and pedagogy, drawing on student and lecturer voices to demonstrate how this multi-dimensional approach can be developed and applied in higher education. It suggests an ethical approach to higher education practice, and to teaching and learning policy development and evaluation. As such, the book is essential reading for students and scholars of higher education, as well as university lecturers, managers and policy-makers concerned with teaching and learning.

Contents: Acknowledgements – **Part one: Context** – The context of higher education – **Part two: The capability approach and higher education** – Core ideas from the capability approach – What are we distributing? – **Part three: Pedagogies and capabilities** – Learning and capabilities – Widening participation capabilities – Selecting capabilities – **Part four: Change in higher education** – Pedagogy, capabilities and a criterion of justice – Bibliography – Index.

2005   176pp   0 335 21321 9 Paperback   0 335 21322 7 Hardback

VIRTUAL LEARNING COMMUNITIES
A Guide for Practitioners

Dina Lewis and Barbara Allan

- What are the characteristics of a successful learning community?
- How are successful communities facilitated and maintained?
- What lessons can be learnt from existing learning communities?
- What type of learning community will suit your organisation or situation?

This user-friendly guide is written to help managers, professionals and learners, planning, facilitating or participating in online learning communities, as part of a structured learning programme, as an approach to continuous professional development, as a means of improving performance at work or as a dynamic approach to innovation and collaborative working.

The book is relevant to senior mangers with a responsibility for strategic planning and change management. This can include new work practices involving working in multi-professional teams across traditional boundaries. It aims to engage readers in identifying key issues in relation to their own work situation and prompts readers to find their own solutions

Virtual Learning Communities provides practical guidance and includes extensive examples, case studies and activities. It is key reading for those involved in e-learning courses, professional trainers and staff developers with a responsibility for CPD, and professionals involved in facilitating new approaches to group work.

Contents: *List of tables – List of figures – Acknowledgements – Introduction to learning communities – Learning communities in the workplace – Using information and communications technology – The community lifecycle: Foundation and induction – The community lifecycle: Incubation – Community lifecycle: Improvement, implementation, closure or change – Participation in learning communities – Social learning – Time – Working in partnership – Community evaluation – References – Index.*

224pp   0 335 21282 4 (Paperback)   0 335 21283 2 (Hardback)

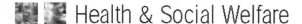